RESEARCH IN THE HISTORY OF ECONOMIC THOUGHT AND METHODOLOGY

Archival Supplement 5 • 1996

RESEARCH IN
THE HISTORY OF
ECONOMIC THOUGHT
AND METHODOLOGY

Editor: WARREN J. SAMUELS
Department of Economics
Michigan State University

ARCHIVAL SUPPLEMENT 5 • 1996

 JAI PRESS INC.

Greenwich, Connecticut   *London, England*

CONTENTS

READER'S GUIDE TO JOHN R. COMMONS *LEGAL FOUNDATIONS OF CAPITALISM*

Warren J. Samuels

INTRODUCTION

John R. Commons was one of this country's, indeed the world's, most original thinkers. Among other things, he was a major historian and interpreter of the U.S. labor movement, a historian and theoretician of the evolution of the economic system in general and of capitalism in particular, and a leading theoretician of institutional economics—and other things as well, including a major draftsman of the modern regulatory and welfare state. All of these things were of a piece, for Commons understood that the economic system as a whole is complex and the evolutionary—which certainly included both the market and the institutions/power structure which formed and operated through real-world markets.

Commons undertook an extraordinary intellectual task, namely, to construct and present the major elements of the whole complex and evolving economic system. He did this in the first third of the twentieth century, after

Reasearch in the History of Economic Thought and Methodology,
Archival Supplement 5, pages 1-61.
Copyright © 1996 by JAI Press Inc.
All rights of reproduction in any form reserved.
ISBN: 1-55938-094-2

such architectonic, synthetic, and synoptic writers as Adam Smith and Karl Marx and more or less contemporaneous with Max Weber and Vilfredo Pareto. But Commons had his own conception of what was required and it was, in comparison to much other literature, strange.

Alas, the enormous comprehensiveness and complexity of his chosen task meant that Commons's major writings, especially his *Legal Foundations of Capitalism* (first published in 1924 and subsequently reprinted by A.M. Kelley, University of Wisconsin Press, Verlagsgruppe Handelsblatt GmbH. [Klassiker der Nationalokonimie series], and Transaction Books—all with the same pagination) and *Institutional Economics* (1934), were anything but transparent and readily comprehensible. Both those who have been sympathetic and those who have been antagonistic to Commons's efforts have agreed that these books are difficult to fathom and that one must work unusually hard to reap serious results. Commons strived to make sense of vast and complicated areas of economic and legal-political life, in part through unusual models, for example, of property and of power.

In order to facilitate the reading and comprehension of Commons's *Legal Foundations of Capitalism*, the following is a reader's guide to the work, one which provides more summary and annotation, and greater use of the author's own words, than is perhaps usual in such materials. Another unusual feature is occasional commentary by me, in which I attempt to speak in an interpretive mode directly to the reader. The principal focus of the guide as a whole is on major themes and on the ways in which Commons both grounded those themes and applied them to his central concern, the legal foundations of the economy and specifically of capitalism. Most complexities and many details are omitted; only a relative few are presented, typically to provide greater focus and/or precision. Special attention is given to both how Commons constructs his discussion to support his main themes and to the question of the ontological status of developments.

Reading this guide is no substitute for reading the original book. But if only the guide is read, at least the reader will have a far better comprehension of what Commons was trying to do than without reading either the book or the guide.

It will be obvious to anyone with hermeneutic insights that any reader's guide/summary will reflect the interests of the person who constructs it. Nonetheless, I have endeavored to carefully reflect the major themes, and so forth which clearly were Commons's intent, with due recognition of the inevitable interpretive element. I also present the guide chapter by chapter, so the reader can readily follow along in his or her own reading. I am indebted to Jeff Biddle and Steven Medema for suggestions responding to the original manuscript of the Reader's Guide.

It is very important for the reader to appreciate the major facets of Commons's approach to the legal foundations of capitalism. These facets include, with some overlap and with enormous interconnections, the following:

1. theories of social control and social change, including a theory of language
2. a theory of behavior
3. theories of systemic and institutional organization
4. a theory of the evolution of capitalism, encompassing in part a theory of power struggle and of conflict resolution processes
5. a theory of markets, especially of the institutions which form and operate through them
6. a theory of the legal-economic nexus as the venue in which all of the foregoing meet—hence, a theory of the legal foundations of capitalism which is at once also a theory of the economic foundations of law, but not strictly in the neoclassical conception of "economic"
7. the use of English and American legal-economic history to illustrate the working out of a particular legal-economic model

The reader should be alert to the various verbal conceptual models that Commons constructs pertaining to these facets, for example, models of property, liberty, inter-agent interrelations, and so on. Indeed, one of his central points is that the linguistic and normative models we use in these matters structure both our understanding of what is going on and the decisions that are reached (or at least the terminology in which they are expressed and rationalized).

At the heart of Commons's analysis is an understanding of public purpose inevitably effectuated through collective action (of various types) and itself subject to revision on the basis of new, or newly powerful, conceptions of public purpose.

JOHN R. COMMONS *LEGAL FOUNDATIONS OF CAPITALISM (NEW YORK: MACMILLAN, 1924)*

PREFACE

Commons says that "the aim of this volume is to work out an evolutionary and behavioristic, or rather volitional, theory of value" (p. vii). The emphasis on evolution and volition will be made clear in the first chapter. It is important to appreciate that by "theory of value" Commons does not mean the explanation of the prices at which goods are bought and sold, which in some sense has been the centerpiece of mainstream economics for over three centuries. Commons is interested in, rather, the values ensconced in the *working rules* that govern who can act as an economic agent and on what basis or condition.

The reader will sympathize with Commons's lament that in his earlier *Distribution of Wealth* (1893) he "tried to mix things that will not mix—the hedonic psychology of Bohm-Bawerk, and the legal rights and social relations which he had himself analyzed and then excluded from his great work on the psychological theory of value" (p. vii). But the reader will also see that the present book combines (1) the socialized, predominantly self-interested behavior of economic actors, (2) a negotiational psychology, and (3) the combination of legal rights and processes and larger social relations.

Commons thus tells us that his focus is on "the central question, What do the courts mean by reasonable value?" and that "Somehow the answer...[is] tied up with reasonable conduct" (p. vii). By *reasonable value* Commons means the values as to the working rules that are deemed to be reasonable as they emerge through the total societal decision-making process, but especially the courts and the Supreme Court in particular. Commons relates his work to that of Thorstein Veblen, especially his suggestion that "an evolutionary theory of value must be constructed out of the habits and customs of social life." For Commons, this meant the "decisions of the courts which are based on these customs" and "the behavioristic theory of value on which...[the courts] were working" (p. vii). Commons's total model thus includes both nondeliberative custom and habit and the exercise of deliberative legal choice. Commons concludes that he and his students "found eventually that what we were really working upon was not merely a theory of Reasonable Value but the Legal Foundations of Capitalism itself" (pp. vii-viii). The point is that as concepts of what conduct was reasonable changed, the working rules changed, and as the working rules changed thereby capitalism both emerged and evolved—both as a general system and in the particular institutionalized forms that evolved in various countries of Europe and North America, especially the United States.

CHAPTER I. MECHANISM, SCARCITY, WORKING RULES

Commons advances the concept of *proportioning* and the processes through which it takes place. Commons intends thereby to refer to the proportioning of resources (allocation), of commodities (as supply and demand), of inducements and inhibitions, and of activities—within both the economy as a whole and individual firms. The economy is a matter of proportioning—anticipatory perhaps of Lionel Robbins's definition of economics (the allocation of scarce resources which have alternate uses among a variety of ends) but much more extensively inclusive.

Commons argues that the concept of good or bad economy, meaning good or bad proportioning, is so self-evident and so continually present that it "has often been either taken for granted or erected as an entity existing outside or above the parts" (p. 2). Rejecting the erection of the habitual, and so on into something transcendental, metaphysical, and mythical, Commons stresses, as did (for example) secularism, utilitarianism, and pragmatism before him, that:

> a mark of the progress that has occurred in economic theory, from the time of Quesnay and Adam Smith, has been the emergence of the concept of good or bad political economy out of mythical entities such as nature's harmony, natural law, natural order, natural rights, divine providence, over-soul, invisible hand, social will, social-labor power, social value, tendency towards equilibrium of forces, and the like, into its proper place as the good or bad, right or wrong, wise or unwise proportioning by man himself of those human faculties and natural resources which are limited in supply and complementary to each other (p. 2).

Whereas early theories avoided human will, developing theories centering on either commodities or mechanisms, "a larger knowledge of the human will" leads to a focus on behavior, which "begins to be formulated into natural laws of its own" (p. 3).

Commons next combines futurity and human will to identify an expectancy theory of value. For Commons, human action and will, not abstract laws, is the material of economic life and this action is oriented toward the future, however much it is influenced by perceptions of the past and present. His theory locates value "in the hopes, fears, probabilities and lapse of time of the future, depending on the will of persons existing in the present." For it, causation originates "in the purposes and plans for the future and... [guides] the behavior of the present." He juxtaposes the expectancy theory to both the labor theory of value ("the stored-up energy of the past") and the hedonic, or utility, theory, which finds "value in the pains and pleasures of the present" (p. 2).

The economy, as the domain of human will, encompasses two relations: a relation of man to nature, and a relation of man to man. Thus, psychology, ethics, jurisprudence, property, and politics are all said to be operative in what amounts to the social construction of economy, ultimately governing the relations of man to man.

In this system, hedonistic theories take a methodologically individualist point of view. But that perspective either takes for granted, ignores, or erects into absolutes positions on psychology, ethics, and so on—factors which are both important and changing in form and content. Commons seeks a theory that incorporates both acting individuals and the system in which they operate in a processs of mutual, cumulative causation.

Commons therefore adopts a volitional theory of psychology that merges a futurist orientation, the role of working rules, and the transaction as the unit of analysis. Transactions, he writes "have become the meeting place of economics, physics, psychology, ethics, jurisprudence and politics" (p. 5). Transactions are the result, always looking to the future, of individual wills-in-action within the collectively established working rules. Attention to commodities and individual feelings must be supplemented with attention to the working rules of going concerns and therefore, within both the individual firm and the national economy, the role of collective control of transactions. "In short, the working rules of associations and governments, when looked at from the private standpoint of the individual, are the sources of his rights, duties and liberties, as well as his exposures to the protected liberties of other individuals" (p. 6).

Commons emphasizes the changing nature of property as recognized by the courts. The physical conception of property has become transformed into a concept of intangible and incorporeal property, with a clearer recognition that such property arises "solely out of rules of law controlling transactions" (p. 7). The rules of property are like other working rules in that they "apportion the conduct of individuals" (p. 8), both limiting and enlarging fields of individual action. For Commons, the role of the courts, notably the Supreme Court of the United States, and their *theories* of property, liberty, and value, are critical. They are critical because it is on the basis of these theories that rights—the apportionment of opportunity for action—are formulated and reformulated, including the rules that govern the "taking" of value (p. 7). The Supreme Court thus "occupies the unique position of the first authoritative faculty of political economy in the world's history" (p. 7). That is a questionable exaggeration but it underscores his point that individual economic activity requires working rules that must be adopted and continually revised and that the courts are, in the U.S. system, a critical (he would say, the ultimate) arbiter of what theories of property, liberty, and value are to govern the adoption and change of the working rules. Commons is operating at the deepest levels of social analysis, identifying processes and phenomena which historically and conventionally are treated as mythic absolutes, as above.

The rest of the chapter consists, first, of further explorations into the nature of transactions and how they take place within social processes and are participated in by going concerns. In this context Commons also discusses the idea of "reasonable value" as it arises in the decisions of courts as they adopt and revise working rules. (Commons seems to contradict his basic analysis at this point, arguing that courts try to make nominal prices represent, as nearly as practicable, the psychological value and the real value, or quantity, of commodities [p. 9]. This is an aberration.) The chapter concludes with a dual emphasis on individual wills and the social psychology which conditions them and on the mutual relation thereof to the ethical, juristic, and political grounds for the working rules.

Two matters are worth noting in passing. First, throughout this chapter Commons employs the energy metaphor, presumably, but not conclusively, from nineteenth-century physics. Second, Commons recognizes words as signs, as nominal and not necessarily real phenomena. "Words, prices and numbers," he writes, "are nominal and not real. They are signs and symbols needed for the operation of the working rules. Yet each is the only effective means by which human beings can deal with each other securely and accurately with regard to the things that are real. But each may be insecure and inaccurate" (p. 9). Commons, and also Veblen, had a social constructivist (or rhetorical), and not a representational, conception of language.

CHAPTER II. PROPERTY, LIBERTY, AND VALUE

Commons first examines part of the late nineteenth-century legal history of the concept of property in order to demonstrates two things: the change in the legal definition of property that transpired and the role of what amounts to judicial theories of liberty and property as the basis for the change. The change that Commons identifies is from a use-value to an exchange-value definition. The change was from a conception or theory of property focusing on physical things having only use-value to the exchange-value of anything. The former centers on the title and possession of the physical tangible thing owned and its use for one's own enjoyment, and thereby freedom from physical restraint. The latter centers on freedom in enjoyment of faculties and opportunities, especially the enjoyment of marketable assets, including rights of access to markets, and thereby freedom from economic restraint.

Commons explores a number of legal dichotomies or conflicts: substantive versus procedural due process and the scope of judicial review in the federal system; police power- versus eminent domain-based theories of regulation and of the substance and scope of "taking"; and the protection of goodwill transformed into the protection of property.

Commons identifies in passing the fundamental problem of the relativity of one's liberty to both law and the rights of others. He first notes that "while liberty of access to markets on the part of an owner is essential to the exchange-value of property, too much liberty of access on the part of would-be competitors is destructive of that exchange-value" (p. 17). And he cites judicial opinions (here and on other matters) acknowledging that one's freedom in the market is only in "all lawful ways" and to "any lawful calling" (p. 17), recognizing the important role of law in determining which and whose opportunities are legal. This effectively sets the stage for his subsequent discussions of how power-play within the legal-economic nexus is directed to the structure of markets and thereby the distribution and conditions of opportunity to participate.

At first glance, it might seem strange for Commons to write that the changed definition of property "was inevitable and proper if the thing itself was thus changing" (p. 14). What is that "thing" which was "itself" changing? Commons is fundamentally saying that property is what the law says it is; in any litigation, in any court decision, what property is, actually what property henceforth is to be, is the object of controversy, that which is to be determined. The court determines property within the confines of the litigation coming before it and on the basis of its *theories* of liberty and property. This is, after all, the gravamen of the discussion in Chapter I of human-centeredness and of how courts determine the working rules which delimit property and eventually generate market values.

All that is true. What Commons has in mind is an additional point, relating the practices of people to the dockets, decisions, and theories of courts. Under feudalism exchange was for the most part limited and property predominantly meant use-value. Under capitalism, production for market and exchange became a way of life and property meant the value of what one could acquire in market exchange. Commons says, first, that "when property began to yield exchange-value as well as use-value, the term 'uses' was simply enlarged by the courts to include it" (p. 20) and second, that the change from the use-value to the exchange-value meaning of property was "more than a transition—it is a reversal. The reversal was not at first important when business was small and weak—it became important when Capitalism rules the world" (p. 21).

The point is that when capitalism displaced feudalism or colonialism, "the meaning of property and liberty spreads out from the expected uses of production and consumption to expected transactions on the markets where one's assets and liabilities are determined by the ups and downs of prices" (p. 21). As for the courts, they have enormous latitude of discretion as to whose interests are to count in particular cases, but they came to operate under a new economic system, and its practices gradually became accepted by the courts. In a world of business, property was in fact different because life and practice were different. It is upon the court's theories of property, liberty, and value, says Commons, "that modern business is conducted and that American legislatures, executives and inferior courts are held in conformity to the Constitution of the United States... as latterly interpreted by the Supreme Court... " (p. 7).

Capitalism is what it is, and takes the form and structure that it does, in part because of the Supreme Court's theories of liberty, property, and value; but the Court must recognize the general capitalist scheme of property, even when it decides between different claims of (property and other) right. It must do so not only because the members of the Court are conservative in their identification with the business system but because the issues that come before the Court are derivative of the system of business. As Commons puts it, "the new meanings of property and liberty were found in Adam Smith and the customs of business, and not in the Constitution of the United States" (p. 14) itself. The Court's ultimate activity had been to reconstruct, through reinterpretation, the Constitution in the light of the transformation from a landed-property agrarian society to a nonlanded-property urban capitalist society. Commons is thus a social constructivist with regard to jurisprudence as well as language—that is, the language and meanings of law.

One further point, apropos of Commons's use of the phrase "lawful": It has to be understood that for Commons a central task of the legal system, indeed of the legal-economic nexus as a whole, is to determine what is and what is not lawful. In simple models of legal-economic analysis, what is lawful/unlawful can be taken for granted. In more sophisticated and deeper models, what is lawful and unlawful constitutes precisely that which is to be determined. The reader will also appreciate that such determination encompasses a fundamental role of the state.

Finally, Commons comes next to a distinction between two relatively new types of property in the modern business system: *incorporeal* property, essentially debt instruments, which are encumbrances; and *intangible* property, assets which are functional as opportunities in the acquisition of income (p. 19). It also brings him to a further distinction between producing power and bargaining power: *producing power* increases the supply of goods in order to increase the quantity of use-values; *bargaining power* restricts the supply of goods in proportion to demand in order to increase or maintain their exchange-value. The former enlarges the wealth of nations; the latter enlarges the value of business assets (pp. 20-21). Although Commons does not say so, the basic orthodox theory of capitalism has it both that the former is functional to the latter and that pursuit of the latter is functional to the achievement of the former (Adam Smith's invisible hand metaphor is used to affirm this dualism). Commons, and other institutionalists, maintained that problems could arise from a disjunction between the two.

In the second part of this chapter, Commons explores aspects of the varieties of interpersonal economic relations represented by different types of property, in terms of rights/opportunities and duties/encumbrances, intangible and incorporeal property, and, to some extent, the various types of transactions in which they figure. For Commons, property is a matter of expected behavior, involving both the expected restraint or compulsion placed on others on one's behalf and the opportunities afforded by them and open to the protected individual. The institution of property (as distinguished from but constituted by the particular rights of property) is therefore a structuring of relations involving liberty, or the absence of duty, and duty.

Property thus has to do with both restriction and liberation of behavior and with the future. Property has to do with behavior and especially with future behavior. It has to do with expectations, with legitimate expectations and with conflicts of expectations. Property is also a matter of legal sanctions, comprising both compulsion and protection. The economic significance of property in these regards always and most fundamentally has to do with expectancies of the future. "All value," writes Commons, "is expectancy" (p. 25).

Commons asserts that "the terms Property, Value, Capital, Assets, Liberty, and The Will have come to mean the same thing from different points of view" (p. 28). The meaning has to do with rights and expectations with regard to the future and the behavior (encumbrances and opportunities) of various parties. "Capital," for example, "is the present value of expected beneficial behavior of other people" (p. 28).

The third section of this chapter treats power. Using the concepts liberty and opportunity, power is explored in terms which effectively may be understood as participation in the economy, the exercise of choice within individual opportunity sets, and the impact of one's economic power— understood in part as the capacity to withhold what others want except on terms satisfactory to oneself. The context is largely that of several famous court cases in one of which private property is understood as capable of economic coercion potentially warranting legal control under the police power and in another in which the legislative enactments in pursuit of that control were subjected to judicial review. At bottom are conflicting theories of property and of judicial control and conflicting perceptions of the economic role of the state, especially when it comes to legal change of law and the changing metaphysics of legal theory. Commons also finds that in these cases the meaning of power changed from physical control to economic control, and the meaning of property passed from use and enjoyment to value in exchange. Liberty increasingly became comprehended not solely in terms of choice of opportunity but of economic power and its consequences for others—for others' economic power.

Part of the significance of these discussions is the gradual transformation of the meaning by the courts of the police power. In this connection it is worth noting that in a footnote (pp. 35-36) Commons quotes an Oregon case in which the Supreme Court of that state says that "we no longer say that we will expand the police power to reach and remedy the evil. Instead we say that a new evil has arisen which an old principle of government—the police power—will correct." Thus does the change in legal semantics incorporate a change in legal theory and the role of law in the social construction of the political economy.

Commons also indicates the privileging of certain specifications of private property as natural and therefore antecedent to and independent of government—in contrast to the actual process of the human social construction of property. Everything that Commons discusses is to be seen as part of the complex linguistic, philosophical, and institutional process of working out the structure of participation in decision making in the political economy, and therefore the organization and control structure of the economic system, through the legal-economic nexus, a process laden with selective perception and marked by ubiquitous contingencies.

The final section is burdened by several esoteric distinctions and analogies. But Commons's overall argument is clear. He is exploring volitional interpersonal economic relations in terms of the will-in-action. People choose and may thereby enlarge their economic power relation to other persons. An important aspect of this to Commons is forbearance, the exercise of a lesser rather than a greater degree of power by an individual. People can pursue the enlargement (called Expansion) of their economic power. They can also choose to proportion their powers and opportunities to obtain the maximum self-realization (called Economy). Commons writes that "The economic aspect is the proportioning of all the external factors according to their *instrumental* value in realizing this scheme of human values" (pp. 38-39).

Here enters the concept of a limiting factor, applied to the available input of complementary factors and the supply of other commodities as well as the degree of bargaining power. The point is that the production of any wealth and of the total amount of wealth generated is a function not of individual-input productivity but of all inputs together, the totality of "limiting and complementary factors. Each is productive simply because it is a necessary part of the whole" (p. 43). Furthermore,

> It is this good proportioning that gives rise to the phenomena of value. None of the factors of production produce *value* unless they produce things in limited quantities. Restriction of physical production is as necessary as expansion of physical production. The important purpose of each of the economic factors is, not the production of things, but the production of values (p. 43).

In his own way Commons is indicating that production is a joint affair among the factors of production, that individual proportioning of factors relates to the larger social proportioning, that production must be undertaken, and that in the capitalistic economic system it is, however, production of value, rather than physical output alone, that matters, and that value accordingly is a function of scarcity.

The foregoing discussion in this section is in aid of his general point that liberty has four facets: opportunity, power, forbearance, and economy. It is because of the foregoing discussion that Commons maintains that in the modern economic system it is not use-value, or use and enjoyment, of property that is distinctive, but exchange-value. The opportunity and power of one individual is relative to that of another/all others, and exchange-value is central to this process of mutual constraint.

CHAPTER III. PHYSICAL, ECONOMIC, AND MORAL POWER

This chapter surveys parts of the complex English legal history of liberty and property in the seventeenth century, in part as historical prelude to the discussion of U.S. law presented in Chapter IV and in part elaborative of the argument of Chapter II. Commons identifies the transformations and inversions of legal concepts as legal privileges for the aristocracy under Magna Carta were later interpreted, selectively, into common rights, and as the prerogatives of the monarch became constrained during the rise of republican, or representative, government. Commons points to a double meaning of liberty: liberty as the privileges of landlords and monopolists granted by the monarch, and liberty to buy and sell. The freedom to buy and sell in the market grew out of this complex legal history and thereby constituted part of the legal foundations of capitalism. But it also represented one stage both in the dualism of private rights and government action discussed in Chapter II and in the tension between maintenance of existing law and rights and legal change of law and rights.

The conceptual structure is exceedingly complex. Physical power is juxtaposed to economic power. The old prerogative power of the monarch is juxtaposed to the police power of the legislature. "In the one case competition is physically prevented; in the other case competition is economically prevented. In the one case the monopolist is favored by the sovereign against the equal competitive liberty of others; in the other case the owner is favored by his economic situation while the sovereign treats his property and liberty equally with all others"—and in which the legislative police power may be used to protect others from privately held economic power, the "power to withhold from others what they need" under conditions of recognized economic inequality. Thus property changes "from a concept of *holding* things for one's own use to *withholding* things from others' use, protected, in either case by the physical power of the sovereign" (p. 52). The market is a process of potential mutual coercion structured by the actions of government in protecting property from the exercise of power by both government itself and other property owners. Rights are the interests to which government gives its protection when in conflict with other interests. When the courts transformed the meaning of property into exchange-value, in order to protect property against legislative control of private coercive power, they were willy nilly protecting certain interests and not others; in each case the interested recognized as property over against what was not so recognized, the language and legal theory of the courts notwithstanding. All this is further complicated by the situation that the economic system was transformed from one characterized by exclusive holding for one's own use to one in which the power to withhold from others became an "economic attribute of property"—a "power to extract things in exchange from other persons" (pp. 53, 53-54). In the former system, holding and use meant "a merely passive choice between social opportunities" (Economy); in the new, the exercise of power in search of enlargement (Expansion) (p. 55).

Commons discusses other topics, such as "waiting-power," the separation of management from ownership, and the slowness of economic change inhibiting recognition by the courts (and others) of the transformed meanings of property and liberty. He also explores the legal concepts of "undue influence," "duress," "coercion," and "inadequacy of compensation." Apropos of *coercion* he establishes the distinction between that economic coercion which is unlawful and that which is lawful, the substantive content of each category being determined through the combination of the legislative and judicial processes of governance, each with its own modes of procedures, language, and theorizing.

Commons also points out that although the Constitution prohibits *ex post facto* legislation, by their very nature courts necessarily reach decisions *ex post facto,* the litigating parties not knowing in advance whose claims the court will recognize and which interests will be protected, as property or otherwise. "When, then, in such cases, the court adheres to the old definition and vetoes the statute, it prevents the legislature from advancing the definition of property to fit the new facts of power, although the court itself, in other cases, had advanced the definition to fit the new facts of liberty" (p. 60). Thus the conflict between substantive and procedural due process of law is essentially the question of legislative versus judicial determination of policy—although the court does not use such revealing language, preferring to speak of rights as if they had been in existence from time immemorial, and Commons does not use the terminology, which became prominent later. But, as Commons makes clear, the story is also one of the gradual recognition by the courts of the increased economic power of property under "modern economic conditions" (p. 62). But even here, the courts must adopt some theory of property (and liberty) and of the basis of restraining it under modern conditions and therefore of whose private economic interest is to be protected and whose left exposed thereto.

The chapter concludes with reiterated recognition of physical and economic power and the identification of a third, moral power, the power of personal influence. "It is the relative predominance of these three types of power that distinguishes the three great types of going concern" to be discussed subsequently, namely, the state, the business, and "the great variety of modern cultural, religious, or moral concerns, based only on the fear of opinion unsupported by fear of violence or poverty" (p. 64; poverty relates to withholding). Thus does Commons, in identifying the three types of power, also establish the principal modes of social control.

CHAPTER IV. TRANSACTIONS

The concept of the transaction, disaggregated into several types not all of which were clear to Commons when he wrote the *Legal Foundations*, is an analytical tool by which he is able to examine the interrelationships between individual economic actors. This chapter, almost 80 pages long, therefore covers somewhat the same ground as the preceding discussions of property, as one basis of economic power, and liberty, as well as the critical role of government in sorting out and choosing between conflicting theories and rights' claimants. Commons wants here to develop a complex model centering on the transaction, a microcosmic level of the task of the book as a whole.

In the opening section, Commons distinguishes between actual, potential, possible, and impossible transactions. He argues that an actor's choice is between the two best accessible options, so that there is a minimum of four parties to a transaction, two active and two passive but present, providing alternatives to the two contracting parties. The four parties constitute the field of persuasion and coercion and their limits, that is, their combinations of opportunity and power. But the likelihood of disputes between the parties implies what is historically evident, the presence of a fifth party, the conflict resolver. This party operates within and is itself limited by the working rules of the relevant social group. While of historical origin, these working rules of going concerns have

> been ascribed to many different sources, such as gods, ancestors, conquerors, "nature," "will of the people," etc., the general idea being to clothe them with a certain sanctity or authority above that of the particular [conflict resolver, e.g., priest, chieftain, judge] (p. 68).

The working rules thus legitimized both limit and enlarge choice and power for individuals, albeit differently for each individual. Commons identifies four "volitional verbs" that point to the effects of the rules on individual opportunity sets: may, must, can, and cannot; which amount to permissions, compulsions, capacities, and incapacities. When organized into formal ethical or juristic systems, they are distinguished as liberty or immunity, duty or liability, right or power, and disability or exposure;—all of which demarcate who can do what to whom in a system of transactions in which it is five individuals doing something to each other within the limits of working rules laid down by those who determine how disputes shall be decided. It should be noted that Commons has thus differentiated the elements or terms of his analytical model from the concepts in terms of which people, including courts, spell out and legitimize what they are doing.

The basic nature of the transaction, therefore, is spelled out by Commons in a manner emphasizing the same general points made in the previous chapters. In now quite famous words, Commons writes that

> there is a fifth party to every transaction, namely, the government, or rather, the judge who lays down the working rules of the concern under the name of rights, duties, liberties, etc., involving the further social relation of command by a superior representing the power of the group, and obedience by inferiors, who are members of the group.

> A transaction, then, involving a minimum of five persons, and not an isolated individual, not even only two individuals, is the ultimate unit of economics, ethics and law (p. 68).

The remainder of the chapter elaborates and goes beyond these ideas.

Two preliminary points: First, Commons emphasized the role of the courts, rather than government in general, because of the activist role of judicial review then practiced in economic affairs, a situation now somewhat altered. Second, when Commons writes, in the last statement quoted, of superior and inferior persons, he is not reverting to the hierarchical structure of more or less absolute monarchs, but to the role of elections and other processes of republican government, in the adoption of some of which Commons figured, by which authoritative conflict resolvers must generally comport with commonly held views of justice, and so forth.

The second section examines performance, avoidance, and forbearance as aspects of the exercise or non-exercise of will. The reader will observe that Commons does not create most of these distinctions himself; for the most part, he distills them from the works of past writers, including John Locke. These distinctions embody both implicit theorizing and when used by judges to determine or express or rationalize a decision they are made to bear normative weight. Commons uses them in an essentially positive, analytical way.

Commons begins with several further distinctions: between power as potency of will (faculties) and power in action; between an act and a non-act; between behavior and intentions; and between dimensions of the equality and inequality of wills. Apropos of the last, Commons further distinguishes between equality of formal rights regarding the faculty of acting or non-acting, and equality of economic and/or physical power. The latter "is a question of valuation and the proper proportioning of relative degrees of power of persons over persons" (p. 73); a question, that is, not of logic but of public policy. In this connection, Commons quotes Justice Holmes regarding the result of combining the quests for certainty and for legitimation:

> Perhaps one of the reasons why judges do not like to discuss questions of policy, or to put a decision in terms upon their views as law-makers, is that the moment you leave the path of merely logical deduction you lose the illusion of certainty which makes legal reasoning seem like mathematics. But the certainty is only an illusion, nevertheless. Views of policy are taught by experience of the interests of life. Those interests are the field of battle. Whatever decisions are made must be against the wishes and opinions of one party, and the distinctions on which they go will be distinctions of degree (p. 73).

Commons distinguishes between an individual transaction and process as a flow of transactions over time. He then analyzes the core distinctions of this section, regarding aspects of the will in action or not in action. *Performance* is power put forth in acting. A right of one person carries a correlative duty of performance by another person. *Avoidance* involves the right of one person and the correlative duty of another to avoid certain behavior. *Forbearance* "is the limit which...[an actor] or a superior authority places on the degree of power in acting" (p. 77); it is an intentional omission, a limit placed on performance by the actor himself or by others. It includes the right to be left alone beyond a certain degree of power in acting; it is the difference between economic persuasion and coercion, that is, the other party having the duty of forbearance.

Returning to the subject of transactions, Commons says, first, that behavior in transactions has a three-fold dimension: physical, economic, and psychological; and second, that "every transaction is a double-ended performance, avoidance, forbearance" (p. 77), each party acting/not acting in all three aspects, two wills acting on each other. Again, there is both intention and the exercised degree of power, growing out of faculties as the total possible power and power as the actual exercise of power. "Power is actual performance, and the amount of difference between faculty and power is forbearance" (p. 78). Applicable to these concepts are judgments as to right and wrong, legal and illegal.

Throughout these pages Commons acknowledges two kinds of individual decision making. One is conscious and deliberate; the other is instinctive, habitual, unconscious. Acts are shaped by both kinds together. The will itself—including what economists often refer to as self-interest and what psychologists refer to as identity—is continually redefined in terms of purpose reacting to experience (pp. 69, 71, 72, 73; see also 79, 80 and passim).

In the third section, Commons distinguishes actual, potential, and possible transactions from the infinite, impossible, or inaccessible, and examines various relevant nuances thereof. Most important to Commons is the futurist nature of the potential and the possible. He notes first that what is important is "what the person *believes* is potential or possible, probable or improbable" (p. 80), a function of mental processes. But his principal focus is this:

> It is in view of the potential and possible that the act of transaction has its value. And, if we say that each actual transaction is the physical dimensions of the will-in-action at a moving point of time, then all of the potential and possible transactions are the economic, ethical and juristic dimensions of the future, the great field of Desire or Purpose, the field of mental anticipation, that gives value to the part which is in the present, and determines how far the act or transaction shall go in its actual performance, avoidance and forbearance.... playing its little part towards realizing the whole that lies in the future (pp. 80-81).

—that is, the complex modes through which the social construction of the future is accomplished.

The reader will appreciate that these discussions are, first, important in themselves in facilitating understanding of the complex economy; and second, materially in aid of appreciating the operation of legal processes (the legal foundations of markets and therefore, in part, of capitalism) in determining (or being used to determine) rights and duties and therefore who can do, and cannot do, what to whom, that is, the substantive content of performance, avoidance, forbearance. Much more on this anon, but Commons concludes this section with the statements that:

> the will acts in a world of limited resources and...these resources are tied up or loosened up by means of working rules that vouchsafe to the individual certain rights, duties, and liberties of performance, avoidance or forbearance.... Freedom is a social product whereby society opens up for the individual an enlarging world of the potential and possible within which he may construct his own future as well (p. 82).

Thus each transaction has a multiplicity of dimensions, including "its ethical and legal dimensions of rights, duties, liberties, and exposures, and its political or governmental dimensions of authority and authorization in the use of physical power, economic or moral power, according to common rules or working rules that set the limits and directions of conduct" (p. 83). The remaining three sections of this chapter therefore deal with authorized transactions, authoritative transactions, and working rules.

With regard to *authorized* transactions Commons explores the relative nature of rights and duties; the nature of rights; the role of hopes, fears, expectations, and obedience; the significance of conflicts of desires and expectations; an initial model of rights and duties, and no-rights and no-duties; and the role of conflict-resolving authority (the fifth party to a transaction). Authorized transactions involve "the will of a superior party or parties...[imposing] limits on their transactions by imposing or interpreting a rule of conduct applicable to the dispute"—involving "[a] government of some kind...[setting up] its working rules" (p. 87). Apropos of the formation of conflict resolution, government and working rules, Commons indulges in conjectural history, in a manner reminiscent of Adam Smith—on the same and similar subjects.

Commons notices the role of ethical ideals and also the role of sympathy (somewhat like Smith). But his principal focus is on the combination of legal and nonlegal social control in the form of legal and nonlegal relations; "Each is economic and each is ethical, but the one is official ethics and political economy, the other is private ethics and business economy or cultural economy" (pp. 90-91).

Next Commons considers the system of jural opposites (or limits) and correlatives constituting the fundamental nature of legal concepts advanced by Wesley N. Hohfeld. Commons summarizes, critiques, interprets, and renames Hohfeld's terminology. He also identifies three points of view which can be taken about legal relations: the legal practitioner, the logician, and the court, legislature, or economist. One of his points, regarding the semantics of law, is that "These three points of view will be found to occasion decided differences in the meanings and use of words" (p. 92). It is, after all, one of Commons's objectives to indicate how ordinary discourse about legal policy is profoundly influenced by the terms that are used. At any rate, it is Commons's immediate objective to elucidate the dimensions of authorized and nonauthorized behavior and transactions constituting an important part of the network of interpersonal relationships. He displays a model using such terms as right, no-right, privilege (or liberty), disability, exposure, immunity, liability, and so on, in the production of which the legal process is critically, if often inconspicuously, operative willy nilly.

With regard to *authoritative* transactions, Commons begins by summarizing English political and legal history with regard to the formation over several centuries of the modern state from an autocratic monarchy. Property is separated from sovereignty for both king and all citizens (formerly subjects). The essential features of the new state, "constituting a compromise set of working rules" (p. 104), include government as a collective bargaining process (a concept very important to Commons; see also p. 107), a representative rather than participatory parliament, the delegation of power to officials of government, and the imposition of official responsibility.

Commons emphasizes that the same model of relations applies to government as well as to nominally private relations.

> Officials have reciprocal powers, liabilities, disabilities and immunities in their relations to each other, and, most important, the will of the citizen can take advantage of these reciprocal relations in order to assert for himself a share in sovereignty and thus be able to bring the collective power in support of what he deems to be his own rights and liberties and the corresponding duties and exposures of others.... In this way the citizens themselves become sovereign and lawgivers to a limited extent, and a reciprocal relation is set up between them and officials, partly their own subjection to officials, partly the responsibility of officials to them (pp. 105, 106).

These relations include the dimensions of performance, avoidance, and forbearance as well as the exercise of remedial and substantive powers (p. 107). Before examining the latter, it is of the upmost importance to take note of the sentence in the book which follows the last indented quote. This sentence refers to the Act of Settlement which significantly revised the relationship of king to all other citizens (see pp. 50, 104). It reads:

> This situation, consummated by the Act of Settlement in 1700, is the culmination of the business revolution and the origin of modern capitalism (p. 106).

The reason for this is that "property was finally separated from sovereignty; not only for the King, but also for all other citizens" (p. 104).

Remedial powers are those which "may be employed on occasion of *wrongful* acts of other persons, substantive powers on occasion of *rightful* acts of self" (p. 107). Commons says that the "substantive power creates legal relations, the remedial power enforces them" (p. 115): "A substantive power arises out of lawful acts of the principal party creating legal relations for the future. A remedial power arises out of an unlawful act of an opposite party infringing on legal relations created in the past" (p. 115). Thus, for example, the "limit of power to impose compulsion on the others is... [an actor's] exposure to their liberty through his legal disability which is the disability of officials to aid him" (p. 117).

All this deals with what Commons calls, in the first subsection under Authoritative Transactions, "collective power," which incorporates the role of the state, especially the modern state, into his general model. The second subsection treats remedial power over wrongful acts. Here Commons makes a number of points, in addition to distinguishing between substance and form (p. 112). One is that "[w]hen there is no remedy there is no right. The ethical [not used in an honorific sense] remedy is a fight. The legal remedy is lawful compulsion, either with or without a proceeding in court" (p. 110).

The second is that "private law is inseparable from public law, which is the procedure designed to enforce responsibility upon officials" (p. 111). In a later statement regarding the "two sets of relationships—those between private citizens and those between private citizens and the state," Commons says, therefore, that "The two are [functionally] equivalent for, when the relations between citizens and officials are determined this determines also the relations between citizens themselves" (pp. 123-124).

Third, he says that legal "capacity is none other than the extent to which... [the actor] is clothed with power of participation in government. It might be designated simply as 'citizenship.' Historically it is Freedom as distinguished from Liberty. Liberty is absence of restraint. Freedom is participation in government" (p. 111).

Fourth, inasmuch as there must be *some* basis for adopting one working rule or another, Commons writes of "the public purpose that justifies the rules governing official and private transactions" (p. 114).

Fifth and most importantly, Commons says that:

> It is to these substantive powers and remedial powers that modern capitalism owes its powers of expansion, for it is they that enable the business man who is citizen of a great enduring nation to extend his sway...; that endow him with power to breathe into his going business the immortality of a corporation (p. 121).

The third subsection treats substantive powers and lawful acts. Included here, in addition to elucidation of the general topic itself, is a further discussion of freedom and liberty, in part using the example of slavery and the position of the former slave after emancipation. Commons writes, *inter alia,* that "While he gained his liberty he did not gain the freedom of choice needed to complete his liberty, nor the power of the state to back him up in exercise of liberty" (pp. 119-120). Throughout these discussions the reader will see that one's power involves one's participation in economic decision making, and the legal and other bases thereof, in relation to other persons, as well as the opportunity to influence those legal and other bases.

The fourth subsection, aptly entitled "Determining Powers," examines the work of officials and of legal processes in forming the substance of all of the categories of rights, immunities, and so on. Hitherto, he says, he has considered only "the rational or logical relations existing between legal and economic ideas," but not "the behavior to which the reasoning applies. These rational relations are simply abstract concepts emptied of all content and then correlated mathematically [in the form of matrices] in such a way as to be true no matter what happens" (p. 121). But, he says, "the actual relations between them, which determine how much immunity, liability or liberty there actually is [and for whom], depends on what is done; and what is done is determined by that choice of alternatives which we name 'discretion'" (p. 122).

Here we come to one of Commons's central points regarding the legal foundations of capitalism and their on-going revision. He rejects the "illusion of certainty"— given, for example, by natural law and natural rights doctrines— which "gives rise to metaphysical 'entities' and 'substances' conceived as existing apart from and independent of the behavior of officials and citizens.... These illusions naturally arise," he says, "from the hopes and fears of mankind which substitute wishes for behavior. We conceive that what we wish is the reality, the real thing. Thus rights and duties also, like the state, are given the illusion of a reality existing apart from the conduct of officials" (pp. 124, 125).

As Commons expresses it, his point is that "The state is what its officials do. And what they do is proportion the behavior of citizens by offering inducements in the directions which they consider important and away from the direction which they reprobate" (pp. 122-123). Stated differently, Commons is arguing that there is a legal, or legal-economic, decision-making process into which enters the preferences of citizens, which are somehow weighted, and from which issues (more or less revised) rights, duties, immunities, exposures, and so on, that is, the ones that count in this world insofar as economic transactions depend on inter-agent relations which in turn depend on their respective powers, and so on, which in turn depend on what the state, in its discretion, or in the discretion of its officials, does, which in turn is influenced by those in a position to influence those officials. "Legal rights and duties are none other than the probability that officials will act in a certain way respecting the claims that citizens make against each other" (p. 125). This is all empirical rather than metaphysical or mythic, though Commons is obviously aware of the use of such ideas for legitimation and psychic balm.

Three related points: First, Commons again stresses the critical role of the Supreme Court in the system of the proportioning of opportunities and inducements:

> Over all is the Supreme Court, enjoying the immunity of determining its own immunity within which it proceeds and with its definitions, feelings, valuations, weighing of facts, and then determining the limits beyond which legislatures, executives, minor judges and itself may not go...(p. 123).

Contrary to another popular mythology, such powers of discretion "are legislative in character, but are exercised also by courts, executives and administrative officials..." (p. 123).

Second, the illusion of certainty is "concealed in double and even treble means of words." Concepts are selectively reified and given substantive content not existing prior to, transcendental to, and independent of the total legal-economic decision-making process which does in fact determine and revise their substantive content. Thus "right" is said to have one meaning in contrast with "wrong" and another when contrasted with "duty" and the latter has both an ethical and a legal meaning. What they mean in practice is a matter of selective social construction. The same is true of the economic system.

Third, Commons stresses that the overwhelming majority of all transactions in the modern economy are conducted directly independent of formal law. They are conducted in the domain of ethics rather than law, though there is a mutual interdependence between ethics and law. In other words, the typical transaction does not directly depend upon the sanction of state violence. (p. 126). Law, ethics, and economics are said by Commons in this regard to be matters of different probabilities of human behavior (p. 127).

In a further subsection, having already emphasized human determination of the contents of his relational categories, Commons identifies the role of human purpose that willy nilly is ensconced in and expressed by those determinations. Behavioral definitions, he says, are classificatory; volitional definitions have to do with the choice of probabilities. Without the concept of purpose, "the social scientist falls into either physics or metaphysics" (p. 127). What purpose?: "The purpose in imposing duties of avoidance on some persons is that of creating liberty in other persons" (p. 127), such that the determination both enhances and restricts the opportunity sets of the different parties, and such determination gives effect to purpose, the purpose to structure power, and so forth, in one way rather than another.

This brings Commons to the concept of *reciprocity* by which he means that "Opposite parties are clothed each with a similar outfit of rights, exposures, duties and liberties" (p. 129). The law embodies *public policy* in providing either equal or different reciprocal advantages and disadvantages for opposite persons. It does this—in a manner "usually concealed by the court under an intellectual process of changing the definitions of words as used in the Constitution" (p. 129)—by changing the meanings of terms such as property, liberty, and equality itself. Government can place limits on "astounding inequalities...such that a more reasonable degree of equality may be maintained," or it can be satisfied with formal equality of right and ignore substantive inequalities of liberty and power. In every case, some private purpose becomes raised to the level of public purpose, and "[h]ow far this preference shall go is a matter, not of equality or logic, but of opinion and valuations.... Those who exercise the determining powers of the nation make a choice between classes of human beings and resolve to employ the sovereign powers on behalf of one class by placing disabilities and responsibilities on the other class. Thus reciprocity is the official valuation of the virtues and vices of human beings" (pp. 130-131).

Commons model is very broad: He says that all this applies to both the working rules of political government and to the working rules of industrial governments; the former with the sanctions of physical coercion, the latter with the sanctions of economic coercion; as well as to the working rules of cultural governments, with "their sanctions of favorable and unfavorable opinions of those whose opinions are deemed worth while" (p. 134).

We come to the sixth and final section of Chapter IV, "Working Rules." In the complex totality of Commons's system of specifying the interrelations between nominally legal and economic processes, the role of the working rules can be singled out as critical. The evolution of the economic system, its structure of power, the operation of power players, its process of working out the allocation of resources, and so on, are all what they are, according to Commons, because of the working rules. The working rules are both dependent and independent variables. As dependent variables they emerge from the complex total decisional process; as independent variables they systematize and channel the total decisional process. As Commons has already been seen to understand, it is illusory to think or to pretend that the working rules are transcendent to human purpose and choice, or that the economy and the polity are independent and self-subsistent processes—or for that matter that the working rules uniquely resolve the problems and conflicts to which they are addressed, and from which situations they in fact emerge.

This section is both important and easy to read; what is more, it represents the structural meeting ground of many of the foregoing lines of reasoning and must be read with care.

The working rules "simply say what individuals, must, must not, may, can and cannot do, if the authoritative agency that decides disputes bring[s] the collective power of the community to bear upon the said individuals" (p. 138).

Commons first contrasts the working rules which emanated from arbitrary monarchical authority with those which "originated from the principles of custom and habit, and, in Anglo-American jurisprudence, were known as the common law" (p. 136). These latter were also given mythical names and considered metaphysically, but those of a "more modern and sophisticated bent (p. 137) think of them simply as the working rules, that is, as secular and human." Eighteenth-century writers, such as Adam Smith, says Commons, thus referred to "that 'invisible hand' or divine providence which was none other than the working rules of an orderly society..." (p. 137). (Commons's obvious secular/empirical analysis of the formation of the working rules parallels one major interpretation of Smith's theory of the formation of moral rules in his *Theory of Moral Sentiments*.)

Commons next juxtaposes social analysis predicated upon the individual *qua* individual and that postulating the individual as a product of the working rules:

> Starting, as they [the eighteenth-century jurists and economists] did, with individuals rather than the working rules of going concerns, both the historical and causal sequence were reversed. For to the individual the important thing is his rights and liberties protected against infringement by others. Hence the inference is that the working rules were designed by a rational being for the protection of preexisting rights and liberties of individuals. But, as a matter of fact, the notion of individual rights is historically many thousands of years subsequent to the full development of working rules, and as a matter of causal sequence the working rules are designed primarily to keep the peace and promote collective action and only secondarily to protect rights and duties (p. 137).

The working rules "actually do regulate behavior" in a manner to which the "name of rights, liberties and so on" is given. The working rules proportion opportunities and inhibitions (limitations), acting typically in cases of conflict to achieve public, that is, collective, purpose, as that purpose emerges from the total decisional process, ultimately in the Supreme Court.

Commons next addresses the question of the on-going process of the selection of working rules. He writes of "the selection of good habits and practices of individuals as against bad habits and practices that weaken the group as a whole" (p. 138). This, of course, has to be understood as a formal statement, for what constitutes good and bad and what weakens the group are matters which must be worked out. No independent test of these exists. The process is not to apply these concepts but somehow to reach determinations which will then be called good and bad with regard to strengthening/ weakening. It is the meaning given to these concepts, and not their mechanical application, which characterizes the process. (Part of the process, Commons notes, is the work of lawyers [p. 138].)

Commons then identifies the proliferation of types of working rules and their different venues: church, state, business, and labor organization. The multiplicity of these different sources of rules coupled with socioeconomic change means that there will be new conflicts to which perhaps new working rules will apply. Thus the working rules consequent to the courts taking over the customs of feudal agriculture and modern business increasingly confront the claims of the working rules of labor organizations (p. 140).

Further as to the nature of the working rules, Commons writes that:

> It must not be thought that working rules are something external, fixed or compelling, existing apart from the actual behavior. They reveal themselves only as acts, transactions and attitudes—the attitude being a readiness to act in a certain direction rather than other directions.... No working rule can be stated in such form that it can be said always to be exactly observed or accurately interpreted (p. 140).

This latter is because each working rule is variegated in its interpretation and observation, a situation

> which makes possible the gradual change in the working rules with the incoming of changing conditions that tend to shift the behavior in one direction or another, away from the earlier formulation of the rule (pp. 140-141).

Commons then states the nub of the matter:

> A working rule, in other words, is a social process and not a metaphysical entity, a more or less flexible process of acts, transactions and attitudes; yet with a discernible trend; and it is this trend that may be abstracted in thought and formulated in words as a statement of the rule in question (p. 141).

Finally, Commons considers the tendency of those who know and administer the working rules to prefer secrecy, as instrumental to the maintenance of their power. He argues that the principal ways to make the ruling authorities responsible for their acts are, first, publicity, and second, an independent judiciary (which is to say, an impartial arbiter). This leads him to consider what he calls the "constitutional development of working rules" or what might be called their political sociology and psychology. Commons writes,

> ...we can see that the evolution of working rules in almost any concern or type of concern, passes through four stages. First the stage of ignorance and confidence, wherein faith, loyalty of submission accepts without protest the working rules as concealed and interpreted by those having authority. Second, the stage of skepticism and protest which is satisfied with the mere publicity of the rules. Third, the stage of resistance, revolt and insistence on a participating voice in amending and recasting the rules. Fourth, a stage of an independent judiciary interpreting the rules as disputes arise (p. 142).

Commons concludes with pointing out that serious revolutions involve the overthrow and supplanting of old working rules by a different set "without the stages of publicity, participation, or independent judiciary" (p. 142).

CHAPTER V. GOING CONCERNS

For Commons, if the transaction is the unit of activity and therefore analysis, the going concern is the combination of legal entity (entity with legal rights, etc.) and decisional process that organizes activity. Going concerns are collections of working rules that both give effect to and engender faculties and opportunities, that comprise and produce assets and liabilities, that are engaged in valuation and apportionment, and so on. Going concerns and their ramifications are the subject of Chapter V, as transactions and their ramifications were the subject of Chapter IV.

Commons starts with the working rules of political, industrial, and cultural concerns. Both natural individuals and organizations such as the corporation (artificial individuals) are given identity by the state "by granting and imposing rights, duties, liberties, exposures" and so forth (p. 143) which "determine the scope within which the will may operate" (p. 144). There are the working rules "indicating how the officials of the state shall act in the future" (p. 144), the rules which both empower and restrain natural and artificial actors, and "the intended behavior of a going concern set forth in the working rules for its employees, agents and functionaries" (p. 143).

"The going concern," for Commons, "is animated by a common purpose, governed by common rules of its own making, and the collective behavior in attaining that purpose" he distinguishes "as a 'going business'" (p. 145). The going concern possesses rights, and so on due to the law, but in practice "it exists prior to the law in the intentions and transactions of its members, and thus exists in the very nature of the human will as well as 'in contemplation of law'" (p. 145). Many of the same characteristics of relationships in the economy as a whole also apply within the corporation: The corporation per se has exposures and immunities and so on, relative to others, and so do the various parties within it, to each other as well as to outsiders. The internal working rules apportion power, liberty, and so on, within the organization.

For Commons the objective function of the going concern, while "guided by acts of participants in the past" (p. 147), is not a given. It is always being worked out by all those with discretion in their acts. The will of the going concern is a composite will, "the organized symposium of all the discretionary acts of all participants as they go along from day to day, according to the rules of the organization" (pp. 146-147) which themselves are subject to change. All of this working out of the internal working rules (referring to both the evolution of the rules themselves and the influence on the formation of the collective will and practice in the form of transactions) takes place within the working rules imposed by the state. Individuals operate on the basis of the discretion allowed them by the working rules and "limited by the alternatives actually open" to them (p. 148). As in the larger economy, discretion is exercised both within and over the working rules which always condition the exercise of discretion, even in the matter of changing the rules.

The going concern is an interaction of individual wills that form its collective will. The working rules of the state structure relationships but cannot thereby combine wills (p. 149).

Moreover, the state itself is but one of many going concerns. It is "the working rules of the discretionary officials of the past and the present" who put their will into effect within the limits of the working rules in the present and the future (p. 149). The principles of relationships that apply to the economy as a whole and to the corporation and other nominally private organizations also apply to government (pp. 150-151 and passim). Government "is the series of transactions going on between officials and the citizens, and between officials and other officials of the same or other states," so that "[t]he government is not a thing, it is a process according to definite rules" which are subject to change; it is a "going business" (p. 150). (The concept of "going concern" is more clearly defined and more elaborately discussed in Commons's *Institutional Economics* [1934]).

Organizations, such as the state, are more than the sum total of individuals; they are also the working rules that hold them together. As a going concern, moreover, each "is more than an entity, it is collective action; it is mass movement and mass psychology; it is the working rules that decide disputes and keep the mass together in support of the rules" (p. 152).

The second section treats faculties and opportunities in terms of the generalized concept of property. Property continues to be defined in terms of reciprocal rights, duties, liberties, and exposures. Commons argues that property involves "human faculties in preparation for, in occupation of, opportunities" (p. 156). Labor, therefore, is property; "That which is owned is one's own physical, engineering and managerial faculties" (p. 155). Assets are the capitalized value of expected opportunities to received net incomes (p. 153). The implication, of course, is that the formation of both opportunities and values (prices or values in exchange, net incomes, etc.) is a function in part of the reciprocal rights and so forth, constructed through law, as well as of the activities of individual agents or organizations in competition with others.

The third section continues the foregoing with a discussion of assets and liabilities. The distinction is clarified by Commons thus: "Liabilities are assets belonging to other people" (p. 158). The important points are time and the formation of intangible property in a manner corresponding to the formation of capitalism, such that here too the law enabling intangible property to have legal and therefore market status constitutes the legal foundations of capitalism. Time enters through property as present expectations of a future stream of transactions: property is "the present right to a future ratio-of-exchange" (p. 157); "assets are, in substance, the present value of the expected purchasing power of things now owned or used" (p. 163). Among the things now owned are intangible property, such as patents, trade name, goodwill, good credit, and so forth. This enables Commons to distinguish between the value of the separate assets of an owner and "the value of the going business as a unit" (p. 160), which includes expectations of future income and so on. The "going concern thus owns two types of assets, its physical, incorporeal and intangible assets which are the parts of the whole, and its going business which is nothing else than all of the expected transactions" (p. 162). All of this is treated in the context of the transformation of liberty and of property as use-value regarding things to property as exchange-value, centering on access to markets, as developed over the centuries in legal cases. Commons concludes this section with efforts to identify and relate to one another the several different concepts and elements involved in the transition in the meanings of property and liberty. The crux of the meaning of property remains the capitalization of expectancies as assets and liabilities.

The fourth section continues the discussion with the topics of valuation, apportionment, and imputation. Firms continually engage in transactions which continually proportion and re-proportion its many limiting and complementary factors of production. Out of this comes an income perhaps "expected to continue indefinitely into the future" which is then "capitalized for the purpose of sale and purchase of the going business" (pp. 166-167). *Valuation* is thus the capitalization, or present value, of the total expected net operating income, giving the value of the going business as a whole. *Apportionment* is the assigning of the expected operating net income among bondholders and stockholders. *Imputation* is the identification of the sources of the net income (p. 171).

Central to Commons's discussion is his theory of capital. He rejects the physical notion of capital and property which conceives of "capital to be something fixed, predetermined as it were, and as solidly established as...buildings and land," a "predetermined substantial entity" (p. 167). He rejects it in the form of J.B. Clark's "fund of value" theory. He applauds Irving Fisher's theory which considers capital as the present value of expected net income but rejects his ascribing its source to physical things. For Commons, "modern capital is not capital in the physical sense, but is capital in the behavioristic sense. The behavior is the expected transactions on commodity markets and money markets" (p. 168). Commons therefore distinguishes between the title of ownership and the substance of ownership in regard to the corporation; stocks and bonds represent the latter, not the former: What is crucial is not the ownership of the physical property but of "residual shares in the expected net income" (p. 169).

In the next section Commons considers the implication—notably for purposes of taxation—of the transition "in the meaning of property from that of tangible property owned by individuals to that of a going business owned by a going concern" (p. 173) which grows out of the transition from property as use-value regarding physical things to exchange-value regarding expectations of future net income-generating transactions. The "unit rule" involves valuation of property for tax purposes not as the sum of the individual physical units but as the value of a going concern, including intangible property. Commons traces the legal history of the transition, a history which resembles his earlier accounts but with this difference: whereas the earlier decisions tended to protect the exchange-value of property from government regulation, these expose that value to taxation in the form of "the expected gross income as a unit" (p. 181).

Apropos of the tax cases and the development of the unit rule, Commons notes that

> the concept of a going concern with its going business was developed as a by-product of the effort to secure equality of burdens in support of government.... The value of property to be ascertained in tax cases is not merely the value of a thing to its owner, but is a value *as between taxpayers*. A certain sum of money is required in order to operate the government, and it must be shared by taxpayers. If one pays less than his proportionate share, the others are compelled to pay more than their share. A taxation case is therefore a litigation between all other taxpayers and a certain taxpayer or class of taxpayers, in order to apportion the expenses of government among them (p. 180).

Such an insight, or formulation, is characteristic of the mode of Commons's thinking.

One point of all this is, of course, that neither property nor capital nor value (price) are absolute, preexistent, and transcendental. Each is always a matter of social construction, one facet of which is entrepreneurial and other activity by economic actors and another, the role of law. The latter includes the law of taxation, for if the unit rule were not used, corporate tax liabilities would be different (presumably lower) than when it was used, and the capitalized net income flows, or capital asset prices, would be different.

In the sixth section of Chapter V, Commons starts by critiquing several late nineteenth- and early twentieth-century Supreme Court cases. For Commons these cases represent several things: "recognition by the court that the value of a business goes beyond the sum of its physical plant to its value as a going plant and going concern; transformation of the meaning of property from physical to exchange value; the protection of a privately owned legal privilege as property, enabling the capitalization of the value of a publicly granted franchise, including that which results from customer physical connections to the company's plant; recognition by the courts that ordinary usefulness is itself valuable" (p. 190); and that "it was only the common law that took the ordinary practices of unprivileged persons and erected them into a system of legal rights, duties and liberties" (p. 185). The distinction between early autocratic and modern democratic states continues to be relevant. Commons has his own conceptions as to how the law should have developed but these are secondary to the main purpose of the overall discussion: how court decisions regarding the legal meaning, and protection, of going concerns constituted the legal foundations of the capitalism he had come to know.

Apropos of the theme that ordinary usefulness itself is valuable, Commons notes that this applies only to government action acquiring a going concern formerly private and erected on the basis of a franchise. The value consequent to the lawfulness of a going concern has compensable value. Contrariwise, Commons notes that "It does not follow, *as against other lawful* property, that lawfulness has a value. Competing property is also lawful there, and this competing property lawfully keeps down the price of other lawful property. Lawfulness is worth having but does not have additional value in competition with others who have equal lawfulness" (p. 190). This latter is significant in two respects: first, that the protection is against government; and second, that competition is a lawful means of eroding, that is, taking, the value of property, even after the transformation of the meaning of property from physical to exchange value.

The legal history is complicated. Courts are taking positions, not always consistently, on several questions: Against whom is the franchise a protected value and thus subject, or not, to compensation in the event of a cessation or taking? Against whom is goodwill a protected value and thus subject to compensation from customers and in the event of a taking? What interests Commons are the abstruse conceptions of property which are manifest in legal reasoning and therefore the form which capitalist property, or property under capitalism, is given. It is easy to get caught in, or lost, in the tangle of cases (actually there are relatively few compared to what might have been covered and what would be covered in such a book written in the 1990s), but the arguments in aid of which the cases are discussed are those identified just above.

Commons treats the value of a franchise as that due to a privilege, and the value of goodwill as unprivileged; the former due to a government grant, the latter due to a going concern having built up a series of dealings recognized to be fair but facing customers who are free to go elsewhere as they see fit without obligation (pp. 194-195). The former includes "[*p*]*olitical value*, the value added by advantageous treatment from politicians, whether legislators, judges, executives, or administrative boards, in the exercise of the several powers of sovereignty, in so far as this value exceeds that of the ordinary lawfulness and exposure to competition out of which the value of going plant or goodwill emerges" (pp. 199-200). In this connection, the reader will note that Commons recognizes the several different values that a particular property may have in different contexts (pp. 199-200).

In the final section of Chapter VI, Commons initially returns to the grand theme distinguishing mechanical transcendental explanations from those involving the exercise of human choice.

We have noticed the interesting contrast [he says] that while the economists, since the latter half of the eighteenth century, have been constructing theories of value out of man's relation to nature in the form of commodities and feelings, the courts have been constructing theories of value out of the approved and disapproved transactions of man with man in the form of goodwill and privilege. These processes of valuation are inseparable, but they belong to different orders of thought (p. 203).

Part of the burden on the courts was due to the perception that the pursuit of private interest did not always also conduce to the achievement of social interest. Commons refers to Adam Smith (whose own formulation of the problem was not as absolute as has sometimes been made out to be), writing that:

Adam Smith had to assume that man is guided by an 'invisible hand,' a 'law of nature'— his name for divine providence,—which leads man, while seeking his own self-interest to satisfy the wants of others without intending to do so. But experience has discovered that it was exactly the invisible hand that produced adulterations and the 'cheap and nasty' goods which consumers had to put up with...(p. 204).

The main concern, however, of the final section is not so much with "the visible hand of the court" as with the "invisible utility of confidence" (p. 204) and how the courts treated it as goodwill. The going business is a flow of transactions in a process of investment and returns which is tied up with, indeed is dependent on, market forces as confidence and alternatives change. He returns to the theory of capital, reiterating the three notions of capital and their corresponding notions of property, emphasizing that capital is the present value of accrued yet uncompensated service (p. 211). He also reiterates the point that since value arises in a process of valuation, different values can arise for different purposes (p. 211). Implicit in all this is the reiterated point that the values protected by courts are the ones given effect by courts as they follow one or another theory of property.

CHAPTER VI. THE RENT
BARGAIN—FEUDALISM AND USE-VALUE

The next three chapters illustrate the same basic themes as do the first five, but in the context of the legal foundations of the markets and prices for land, commodities, and labor, respectively, rather than from the angle of transactions and going concerns. It is Commons's argument that these modern markets, and the prices which emerge in them, exist in the form they do because of the form given them by human action, in part through the actions of courts giving effect to particular legal theories of property and so forth; and that such action by the courts effectuated over the centuries major transformations of legal thinking. Adam Smith maintained that different systems of government, law and property existed in the different stages of society. Although Commons likely was not aware of it (few economists, it seems, have been), he, Commons, in this book was spelling out the details of the transformation to the modern commercial/capitalist economy in the first century or so after Smith (building, of course, on earlier foundational changes). Center stage for Commons is the elevation of the decisions of common law courts over royal prerogatives and the absorption into common law of the practices and general world view of an increasingly commercial, and subsequently, capitalist, economy. An age of republican, judicial, and bourgeois law followed the age of monarchical and feudal law.

Early in Chapter VI Commons surveys the relevant early institutional history, going back to the period of feudalism and the early years of the second millennium. He recounts the combination of property and sovereignty that constituted feudalism, so that dominion was over both things and persons ("a part or the whole of human behavior" [p. 215]); the presence of more or less absolute monarchs with their royal prerogatives; the emergence of royal courts and courts at the levels of the lower aristocracy; conflicts between monarch and lesser nobility, between monarch and courts, and between monarchical and other courts; and the growth of the common law of freemen arising from the use of their customs and beliefs in the resolution of local interparty conflicts. "Tenancy," writes Commons, "was inseparable from government...But the feudal estate differed from the slave plantation in that the free tenants had certain customary rights, often inherited from pre-Conquest times, but more often they had contract rights of service on the one side and of protection on the other, which became custom in post-Conquest times. And the determination of these rights came from the private courts of the lords of various degree, from the King downward, each governing his immediate tenants" (p. 218; the use of "private" here is somewhat anachronistic, since in the feudal world property and sovereignty were united and there were no private and public sectors in the sense understood today; Commons, of course, is aware of this, since his point is that of evolution of law, government, and property).

This brings Commons to the early "rent bargain" in which "no distinction was made between ownership and government. The king was both landlord and sovereign. So with the barons and sub-barons. Each was both landlord and a combined legislature, executive, and chief justice of his baronial estate." The rent-bargain, therefore, "was two-fold, economic and governmental. One was rent, the other was taxes" (p. 219; again the use of the term "taxes" in somewhat anachronistic—he notes that the two were "[a]s yet undifferentiated"—but it clearly points to the umbilical relation between private, in contrast with feudal, property).

Commons traces a 450-year evolution of private property in land. This evolution involves several strands, together constitutive of the complex transformation from feudalism to capitalism: changing the foundations of society "from bargains in terms of use-values to bargains in terms of exchange values" (p. 224); the elimination of private baronial courts and armies; the monetization of feudal obligations; escape from unilateral monarchical setting of rents and related obligations in various forms; and the creation of "an agricultural commonwealth" in replacement of baronial fiefdoms (p. 224). The details of the story vary as between different hitherto subordinate groups.

The monetization of feudal obligations was deeply significant, a critical part of the formation of modern private property. Taxes became relatively definite, established collectively by the monarch and representatives of the tax payers, rather than an indefinite duty to pay rent in commodities and services determined at the whim of the monarch. The commutation of physical rents into money-rents in the form of taxes meant that they "are not something taken from private property by the sovereign, but property is sovereignty taken collectively from the King by his tenants. The result was that pecuniary taxes became the governmental rent of land, and landed property became assimilated to the law of business freedom and security, so that, eventually, like movables, it could be bought and sold in expectation of its money values" (p. 221). In this interpretation, land taxation represents, therefore, not an exaction by the monarch but the payment of funds by owners of private property in amounts and for purposes collectively determined through representative government. The alternative historically was not the absence of taxes but feudal dues.

Here again Commons analyzes the subtle linguistics of institutional change:

> It was not necessary, of course, to change the nominal title of ownership, which, in England remained in the King. But the real owners, nevertheless, are the tenants, because the rent charges are definite taxes in terms of money, but the indefinite residuum which marks the real ownership, because it marks the orbit where the will is free, is transferred to the nominal tenants (p. 221).

CHAPTER VII. THE PRICE BARGAIN—CAPITALISM AND EXCHANGE-VALUE

Capitalism represented a new system of transactions and a new system of opportunities, a new way of living.

Commons traces the decline of the monopolistic and governmental features of franchises granted as privileges by monarchs seeking gain and advantages from their recipients. Just as baronial control of land was replaced by private property in land, the collective control of economic activity enjoyed by the guilds was replaced by relatively free and open markets.

Commons insists that the guilds, for all their collective control and practice of what he calls defensive capitalism, represented the origins of capitalism. The reason is that the guilds had been given power relative to and immune from the power of the feudal landlords.

The gilds... grew in wealth and power. Their defensive privileges became exclusive privileges in proportion as markets and commerce advanced over militarism and agriculture and increasing numbers of people depended on buying and selling for a living, where formerly they depended on command and obedience (p. 226).

When the guilds were dispossessed of their controls over economic activity, the immunity from feudal superiors (who were already being weakened in other respects) continued but was now enjoyed by individual economic agents. Thus the creation of free economic actors took two steps: immunity from the feudal lords, then abolition of the guild power which had been juxtaposed to the feudal lords. A similar process occurred in the cities with regard to both political and economic rights.

Commons articulates the "basic principle of the commonwealth," created by a combination of practice, judicial decision, and governmental reforms, as follows:

Let any person get rich in so far as he enriches the commonwealth, but not in so far as he merely extracts private wealth from the commonwealth (p. 227).

Later, economic theory and judicial temperament would demonstrate to any objective observer how complex and subjective is the distinction between enrichment and extraction and the conditions under which legislatures *cum* courts could/would "intervene." At the extreme the idea of Pareto optimality would assert that any trade was *ipso facto* beneficial to both parties and *therefore* to the commonwealth (society). But the principle stated by Commons was a manifestation of a great transformation of socio-legal philosophy, one both reflecting and reinforcing the practices and mind-set of a growing capitalism. The businessman was now in a more legally secure and opportune position:

The business man now, like the Yeoman and copyholders, could have his customs inquired into by the King's justices, and his rights and privileges asserted against private jurisdiction of both gilds and barons (p. 228).

Equally important both historically and analytically,

Capitalism entered upon its offensive stage, intent on controlling the government whose aid it had petitioned during its defensive period. Eventually its petitions became its rights (pp. 228-229).

There emerged, then, the common law courts "willing and able to convert their [the businessmen's] customary bargains into a common law of property and liberty" (p. 229).

Commons is portraying here, the reader should be aware, one facet of a broad, complex, and deep series of transformations of English society and doing so in terms of the emergence of several great bargains. One was the rent bargain, the origin of modern private property in land, with an enormous social and economic diminution of the rights of feudal landlords (the name "landlord" *is* significant) correlative with the growth of fee simple property ownership of land. Here the landlord kept their physical land but with greatly reduced social and economic power, or rights. Another was the price bargain, with the monarchy and feudal lords retaining their physical landed property (diminished as just described) but now, along with the guilds, having relatively negligible control over private economic activity in an economy of free people and not serfs, and so on. In time another great bargain was wrought out over the centuries: the landed aristocracy, including the monarch, would retain their physical land but lose much of their control over government and its policy, which were increasingly in the hands of a parliament (representative government) in whose operation the business or middle class predominated. And still later the interests of the landed and nonlanded (capitalist) property owners were challenged by the working class, and another great bargain was worked out: the owners of property retained their physical property and many of their rights but now had, through the extension of the franchise and the resulting greater responsiveness of elected politicians to worker interests, to increasingly share the goals of government policy with a wider range of interests. One result was the formation of what has been called the Welfare State, meaning thereby the passage of legislation and programs promotive of the interests of workers and others in a manner comparable in substance though not in name to the promotion through property rights of the interests of those who came to own property. All of this took centuries, the negotiation, as it were, over the Welfare State continuing to the present day.

Returning to the price bargain and the processes through which developed what has become called the free market, we see Commons again glancing at Adam Smith. He says that Smith's followers, "more than...Adam Smith himself" (p. 229), excluded the political element from their notion of a commonwealth. Commons insists that both the idea and the practice of a commonwealth in England, during the many centuries covered here, "included both the economic and the political aspects in a single concept. It was a notion both of common-weal and of participation in that weal through the possession of rights and the corresponding power to enlist the officials of government in one's behalf" (p. 229; Commons next indicates his classist perception of the classical economists who, he writes, "tended to separate the wealth of nations from the commonwealth, making the wealth of nations identical with the prosperity of but a single class within the commonwealth, the business men, upon whom all other classes depended for prosperity"). Two points: First, it is this combination of political and economic aspects, and of rights of private participation in both economy and polity, that constitutes the venue of the legal foundations of capitalism, to wit: the legal-economic nexus. And second, not all of this happened at one time. As indicated in the preceding paragraph, different groups were slowly admitted into effective membership in the commonwealth in a process transpiring over centuries.

The centerpiece of Commons's story is the growth and elevation of the common law courts. "The common law," he writes, "became the law of property, liberty *and business*" (p. 231; italics in the original). Elements of the story include the termination of the monopoly, closed shop, and private jurisdiction of the guilds; the gradual erosion of monarchical prerogative as Protestantism asserted "the right to equality, liberty and security of worship" and commerce "the right to equality, liberty and security of business. Business could not be free and secure while the prerogative exercised capricious control, especially over currency, franchises and rents" (p. 231); the establishment of an independent judiciary appointed for life; "that peculiar and outstanding feature of Anglo-American law, the subjection of officials as well as citizens to the jurisdiction of the ordinary courts of law" (p. 232); and the rise of equity law with "its control over conduct in advance of action instead of punishment after action" (p. 234). All of these were jointly important but for Commons it is the rise of equity that is the hallmark:

> Indeed, the first important field of equity was that of creating uses and trusts, which distinguish physical things from the expected transactions growing out of things. And since value does not reside in things but in these expected transactions, equity procedure at once extracts from the common-law procedure the very substance of value....The remarkable expansion of the equity jurisdiction in the Eighteenth Century reflected the rise of capitalism based on pecuniary expectations, and the corresponding subsidence of feudalism and the prerogative based on physical power. Thereafter it became possible for the courts to build up the law of business in proportion as business itself developed (p. 235).

The foregoing is the story told in Section I of Chapter VII, "The Commonwealth," the story of the rise of markets and a "business economy based on prices" (p. 231), that is, a commercial commonwealth and civilization. The remainder of the chapter, running some 47 pages, examines a variety of forms of property, forms which are, in contrast to feudalism, unique to commercial capitalism. The important point is that the courts gave legal standing and the sanction of enforcement to business devices and instruments which they need not have, and which opponents of commercial capitalism would have had them reject. In doing so, the courts confirmed, abetted, and reinforced the practices of business, all the while choosing between what it perceived as good and bad business practice. One is tempted to think that without these devices and instruments capitalism would not be capitalism. But Commons's point is that capitalism is capitalism as we know it because of the supportive and selective actions of the courts.

Commons first takes up incorporeal property, which he treats as encumbrances. Here he examines some of the legal history of certain types of promises, the law of creditor and debtor, and legal tender (legal money, which is also a form of promise and a credit instrument). He next considers intangible property, which he treats as opportunities. (Commons indicates that encumbrances and opportunities are inseparable, the distinction in part being a matter of points of time [pp. 235-237].) Here he discusses negotiable instruments, such as bills of exchange and debt instruments; goodwill; and copyright and patents;—all matters of buying and selling. Whereas these same elements enter into Commons's earlier discussions of transactions and going concerns, here they are seen as institutions critical to the conduct of a buying and selling, market-price oriented business economy whose decision makers are always looking to the future—hence value is a function of expected transactions undertaken by going concerns. The pervasive element is indicated in the first two sentences of the second section:

> The law of credit instruments passed through two stages, first, the stage of enforcement of contracts, the second the authorization of the supplementary buying and selling of the contracts themselves. The first may be distinguished as the stage of enforceable promises, or incorporeal property; the second the state of negotiable promises, or intangible property (p. 235).

A number of subsidiary themes are of particular interest. One is the already seen argument concerning the "evolution of the notion of property from the ownership of visible things to the ownership of invisible encumbrances on behavior and opportunities" (p. 237).

Second, Commons recognizes but contrasts a type of incorporeal property found in the feudal period, saying,

> but that property was not the modern relation of voluntary agreements between equals, but was lordship over physical things, or the physical products of the soil or of labor. The 'rents' of land were even a part of the lordship over lands and tenants. 'The landlord who demands the rent that is in arrear[s] is not seeking to enforce a contract, he is seeking to recover a thing.' It was only in course of time, and with the modern freedom of labor and money economy, that this 'medieval realism,' became the modern obligation of contracts between equals. The law of landlord and tenant unfolds into many varieties of the law of lessor and lessee, a special case of the law of creditor and debtor (p. 240; the quotation is from F. Pollock and F. W. Maitland, *History of English Law*, 1911).

Third, and critically important as well as illustrative of Commons's central argument about the legal foundations of capitalism, he identifies several elements of selective perception in regard to the history and theoretical treatment of money. One involves the distinction between the individualistic and public, or, alternatively, the transactional points of view. A second involves the distinction between "the *mechanism* of money and credit, rather than the behavior of judges in interpreting and enforcing promises" (p. 241). A third involves the perception "that government signified only the executive and legislative branches of government rather than the judicial branch" (p. 241). Commons's fundamental point is that money is an institution which is given legal shape and content and that economic theory has seriously neglected the legal history of money, thereby both reifying money and attenuating the understanding of what government does:

> Yet it is out of the common law, the law that standardized the customs of the people, that the legal tender quality originated, and the function of the prerogative or legislature came in afterwards to direct the judges as to the lawful standards of weights and measures, including money, which all of them should employ uniformly throughout the land in deciding disputes and enforcing promises (p. 241).

Commons's language is worth noting here: His point is not that government commands action by businessmen; it is that if businessmen want security of expectations in their dealings they will have to abide by the standards which the courts employ in deciding disputes and enforcing promises. Commons continues, in sentences which present the core of the argument of the book:

> This oversight of the Physiocrats, of Adam Smith and the classical economists, is explicable in the fact that what they mistook for the order of nature or divine providence was merely the common law silently growing up around them in the decisions of judges who were quietly selecting and standardizing the good customs of the neighborhood and rejecting the bad practices that did not conform to the accepted rules of reason. Legislatures and monarchs are dramatic, arbitrary and artificial; courts are commonplace and natural (pp. 241-242).

Commons goes on to say that

> It is also explicable in the fact that economic theory has consistently taken the point of view of individuals on the one hand and commodities on the other hand, instead of the point of view of transactions between individuals (p. 242).

The judge, says Commons, it will be recalled, is the third (or, in a different model, the fifth) part to every transaction. And the "judge...necessarily takes a public point of view, since his decisions must conform to what other judges have decided in similar disputes and to what the customs or laws of the community authorize and support. In applying the common rule he is conforming to public purpose. Hence the public point of view is inherent in every transaction, and just as much so in primitive society as in a credit economy" (p. 242).

Just what the public purpose of money comprises is a matter of evolution, says Commons. It has gone from obtaining a revenue for the king to providing a simple uniform medium of exchange for business to a stable level of prices and, possibly (the book was published in 1924) to preventing business fluctuations.

> There is thus always a public purpose in every system of money, even the most primitive, as soon as there is an authoritative decision of disputes respecting the means of payment.... This public purpose has now come to the forefront as a criterion for determining the legal standard of value and the operations of the banking system, which are the means instituted by government for furnishing and withholding credit.... Thus it is not so much the material out of which money is made, nor the mechanism of money and credit, as it is the behavior of judges in deciding disputes, that determines the measure of value and medium of exchange. It is not gold, but the legal tender attribute of gold attached to it by the courts, that determines the prices that business men shall pay for commodities, for it is that that determines the enforceability of contracts, the liquidation of debts, the assets and liabilities of a going concern. Prices are indeed 'nominal values'— they are the expectations of judicial behavior in the enforcement of promises.... [The modern economy] is a *price* economy, as the customs of business and the customs of courts actually have it (pp. 244, 245).

Fourth, Commons emphasizes the "momentous change from the common law to the business law...which converted the mere promises of one person to another into commodities that could be bought and sold on the money and securities markets" (p. 246). The feature of negotiability was long delayed because of the concepts of property as tangible objects and of contract as a personal relation. The meaning of individualism, such as it early was, changed: "While the business law in the 17th century was converting man's dealings with nature into the assets of a going concern, the same business law was eliminating the personality of individuals by converting their debts also into the [negotiable] assets and liabilities of a going concern" (p. 247). In addition, business goodwill became separated from personal goodwill (p. 268 and passim). Further as to individuals, they received their new position in the new economy gradually and by class:

> When the individual emerged out of the group it was by stages and by classes of individuals, first the landed proprietors by conquest, second the capitalists by participation in sovereignty, third the laborers (p. 249).

But not all relations were transformed into negotiable instruments, and the process of transforming those which were transformed took centuries and the "essential requirement of business practice was to convert these promises of freemen into something as nearly like money as possible" (p. 250), that is promissory notes.

> The highest and most complex type of assignability is negotiability, which consists of a promise to pay a definite sum of money, without condition, at a definite time and place. Here the personal element is as nearly eliminated as possible,...(p. 251).

Thus Commons uses the same linguistic device as earlier to reiterate his fundamental theme:

> It can be seen, therefore, why it is that modern capitalism begins with the assignment and negotiability of contracts. They accomplish two purposes, a low rate of interest and a rapid turnover of capital (p. 253).

Commons has in mind here the idea that

> negotiability...introduced...the phenomena of two opposite markets; two opposite classes of legal claims to commodities or service, and two opposing concepts of value. The two markets are the commodity markets and the money markets; the two classes of legal claims may be contrasted as commodity tickets and price tickets, and the two concepts of value are the real value assigned to commodities or labor and the nominal value expressed in prices....Historically the legal transition is the transition from bailments, which are commodity tickets, to debts, which are price tickets (pp. 254-255).

Without legally established negotiable instruments there would be no money market and therefore no capital market as we know it and, further, no capitalism as we know it.

Fifth, in his discussion of commodity and price tickets Commons takes up the relevance of bank credit as a means of creating new money. He identifies two modes of business, or "two ways of getting rich or making a profit in business." One is by increasing the quantity of goods or reducing their costs; the other is by getting higher prices without increasing the quantity of products. The former he considers productive; the latter, speculative, as ways of making a profit. Banks can lend and thereby create money to finance an expansion of real goods or to facilitate transactions involving only increased prices of goods. The private banks do not effectively distinguish between the two, being principally interested in the prospect of repayment, earnings, and in increasing deposits relative to reserves. But out of this can emerge inflation, which requires the adoption of a suitable working rule which discriminates between the two types of transaction (p. 261).

One implication of the foregoing is that, given the legal foundations of capitalism and the inextricable legal elements of all economic institutions, such as money in all its forms, the legal adoption of new working rules does not involve the intervention of government (courts and/or legislature, etc.) into situations in which it hitherto has been absent, but only the replacement of old with new working rules, the adoption of certain interests as constitutive of public purpose and not others. One reason for the relative neglect of Commons's *Legal Foundations of Capitalism* surely is its unusual and complex analysis. But another is that its central argument, with the implication just drawn, runs counter to the dominant ideology which proceeds from what Commons has been seen to identify as the individualistic point of view. Comprehension under the aegis of the dominant ideology prevents effective recognition of the continuing and fundamental importance of government. This has been supplemented by the neglect of the silent but historic growth of the common law—itself a function of the individualistic point of view—and by efforts to use/manipulate the dominant ideology to selectively advance and protect particular interests, for example, certain old working rules, while otherwise dissembling or believing that government is not fundamentally important.

As already indicated, most of this chapter is devoted to the legal evolution of the institutions of negotiable instruments, including money and debts of all kinds, goodwill, copyright, and patents. The detailed treatment of the changing legal status of goodwill and its implications for the substance of capitalism is particularly insightful. Altogether it is a complex but fascinating history, replete with subtle nuances and twists, always recounted in Commons's interpretation (his interpretation of the cases and within his model of rights, immunities, exposures, liberty, etc.) but whose basic outlines are largely straightforward and accurate. Throughout, Commons insists that "[t]he transition from concepts of physical things to concepts of business assets, could not be fully completed until the idea of ownership was shifted from the holding of physical things to the expectations of profit from the transactions of business" (p. 274). Once again, we see the combination of futurity, transaction, going concern, and the transformation of property, and so on (including the Economy/Expansion distinction [p. 282]) as the foundation of the price system, the market, and capitalism.

It is implicit in the foregoing that there are neither unique nor generic markets. Markets are what they are because of their particular legal foundations, because of the activities of private economic actors, and because of the structure of power and of other institutions which affect the formation of markets. Each of the types of markets discussed by Commons has indeed been transformed over the centuries. At each point during that period the particular type of market was more or less different from what it was at other points, and the market at the end of the period covered was dramatically different from what it was at the beginning. Indeed, at the beginning some markets, for example, for negotiable instruments and money capital, did not exist. All this is particularly evident in the case of labor markets, to which Commons next turns. In its regard, a further nuance is also evident: The meaning of a "free market" for labor has meant quite different things at different times and for different people. There is no one such thing, and what it is is in part a matter of the legal foundations of capitalism.

CHAPTER VIII. THE WAGE BARGAIN—INDUSTRIALISM

Having taken up the markets for land, commodities, money and money capital, and the legally structured relationships which form them, Commons now moves on to the labor market with the same interest in mind. Here, too, conventional concepts are seen to involve much more than one might think.

One reads this chapter, of course, with cognizance of the stature of Commons as the leading labor economist and historian of his age.

In the first section of this chapter, entitled "Individual Bargaining," Commons traces the conceptual origins and certain nuances of the right of a worker in his own labor and to choose a calling. The worker sells to the employer "his *willingness* to use his faculties"—manual, mental, and managerial—"according to a purpose that has been pointed out to him. He sells his promise to obey commands. He sells his good will" (p. 284). Neither employee nor employer are under any obligation to continue the relationship (though "Under no ordinary circumstances can the laborer be enjoined from quitting work, nor the employer from dismissing him" [pp. 284-285], what is "ordinary" is a matter of what the law provides); indeed, Commons urges that there is no single labor contract, only a contract renewed every minute and hour (p. 285); both employee and employer are continually, as it were, on the labor market (p. 286). The relation between them is not that of a right and duty but of liberty and exposure. This means that "when it is said that 'labor' is property, what is intended is that the laborer owns an expectancy dependent upon the goodwill of his employer" (p. 286). "The job is the laborer's going business... [and] jobs are a part of the going business of the employer... " (p. 286). Moreover, during the week, prior to the worker being paid, "The employer becomes a debtor, the laborer a creditor. Hence the laborer during the week is an investor in the business; usually, since the inauguration of mechanics' and laborers' liens beginning in 1829, he is a priority investor. At the end of the week he is paid his wages, not in product, but in that universal intangible property, money" (p. 287), the temporary creditor or investment relationship liquidated and the worker open to new liberties and exposures in the commodity markets.

In the second section of this chapter Commons examines several leading and indeed famous turn-of-century cases dealing with state efforts to protect labor interests, including the right to unionize and strike. The fundamental implicit theme of this section is that the economy, for example, the labor market, is a system of mutual coercion in which relative coercive power is a function of differential protection of conflicting interests by law. In balancing these conflicting interests the courts apply differential notions, or preconceptions, of public purpose, of what constitutes a person versus an association, and also of the applicability of conspiracy doctrines to economic coercion. The corporation is an association of persons but is treated by the court majority as a person and therefore not within the range of conspiracy, whereas a trade union is an association of persons and within its range, so far as the practice of economic coercion is concerned. For example, "If it is coercion to threaten to strike unless plaintiff consents to a closed union shop, it is coercion also to threaten not to give one employment unless the applicant will consent to a closed non-union shop" (p. 297).

Čommons critiques the majority opinions in these cases using his model of liberty, duty, and so on. The reader becomes aware that just as Commons has, in earlier chapters, used this model to affirm the sensibleness of the reasoning used by courts in working out the legal foundations of capitalism in a manner consonant with business interests relative to those of monarchs, here he is using that model to show how labor and business interests are treated quite differently, even though the model suggests they are analytically equivalent. The difference, says Commons, is that "the preference is given by the court to that association of persons deemed to be of the greater public importance" (p. 298). Apropos of such premises of courts, he also writes that such reasoning is not a matter of logic but "a matter of beliefs and this belief is none other than the habitual wish of the judge who decides and who...can always find precedents and logic to back up what he wishes. It is the judge who believes in the law and custom of business and not the judge who believes in the law and custom of labor, that decides" (p. 298). Thus, the corporation, which as he explains was the "child of privilege[,] has now become a privileged association of men" (p. 293).

It will be noticed that Commons affirms two things here: first, that judges have the choice between alternative precedential sequences as the stated basis of their decisions; and second, that judges' decisions are ultimately a matter of selective subjective preconceptions, beliefs, or preferences.

Of interest also is Commons's statement regarding legal selectivity in a cognate matter:

> The meaning of a corporation, like the meaning of property and liberty, has been changing during decades and centuries, and when a corporation appears in court it takes on a variety of shapes derived from different parts of its history. It is not a citizen within the meaning of the Federal Constitution but is a 'person' within the meaning of the Fourteenth Amendment. At one time it appears to be an *association* of persons, at another time a *person*; at one time it is an independent existence separate from its members, at another a dummy concealing the acts of its stockholders. At one time it is a fiction existing only in contemplation of law and limited strictly to the powers granted in the act that created it; at another it is a set of transactions giving rise to obligations not authorized expressly by the charter but read into it by operation of law (p. 291).

Judicial participation in the social construction of the economy does not need to, perhaps cannot, treat all interests equally in all matters. Where interests conflict, the courts must make a choice. A bourgeois economy will be supported by bourgeois law produced by bourgeois judges unless and until judges come to have different preconceptions and preferences. There will be one or another set of the legal foundations of capitalism. As Commons sees it, the law will absorb one set of customs or another; in these cases, either the customs of business or those of labor. (Commons is aware that each set of customs is itself an artifact and has changed over time. But the conflicts between the two sets of customs were conflicts over power, with government inexorably being used to support one interest or the other when in conflict.)

The discussion is continued in the third section, dealing with custom and law. The underlying theme is that courts have chosen the customs of business over those of labor. Commons starts with two theories of law, the one maintaining that law is *made* by the command of a superior, the other holding that law is *found* in the customs of the people. Commons's analysis effectively rejects the conventional juxtaposition. He argues that courts make law by choosing between the customs of different groups of people and in that way "reconstruct society" (p. 299). Commons writes that

> Customs are, indeed, the raw material out of which justice is constructed. But customs differ, customs change, customs are good and bad, and customs conflict. They are uncertain, complex, contradictory, and confusing. A choice must be made. Somebody must choose which customs to authorize and which to condemn or let alone.... Somebody must choose between customs. Whoever chooses is the lawgiver (pp. 299-300).

The choices are continually being made and the law is continually changed, sometimes by fiction, sometimes "by new meanings for old words" (p. 301). There is the "conflict, choice and survival of customs, according to the changing political, economic and cultural conditions and governments" (p. 302).

As for business and labor, "The customs of labor and of labor organizations are as different from the customs of business, as the customs of business were different from the customs of feudal agriculture" (p. 301). The courts have viewed labor contracts in much the same theoretical way that they have viewed commodity and other contracts but, says Commons, the relevant practices are different (pp. 302-303). This is particularly the case when it comes to collective action by workers in the form of unions. The point is that "the courts do not comprehend and sanction" the customs of unions, any more than do the capitalists" (p. 305). This is particularly the case with regard to

> what may be distinguished as the common law of labor springing from the customs of wage earners, as distinguished from that historic common law springing from the customs of merchants and manufacturers, [the former of which] consists in those practices by which laborers endeavor to achieve their ideas through protection against the economic power of employers (p. 304).

Commons next examines the convictions of workers, centering on job scarcity, job control, and the effects on other workers of one who works faster, and so forth. These convictions seem to contradict the stated ideals of business but, Commons asserts, the practices are not so different after all:

Their [businessmen's] call for more product from labor is a call for labor to reduce the exchange-value of the joint product of labor and capital in that occupation. And when value as thus reduced approaches the profitless point, the capitalist restricts the output by laying off the laborers. Restriction of output is practiced by both, but in one case it seems 'natural' and therefore right, because there is no profit; in the other case it seems arbitrary and therefore wrong because it places a limit on national wealth (p. 306).

Commons attributes the different interpretations of the same practice to a difference in underlying psychology: "The business psychology is speculative," or opportunity conscious; "The laborer's psychology is conservative," or job conscious (p. 306).

Law is therefore a choice between customs, ergo a choice between different psychologies and between different interests.

In the final section of Chapter VIII, Commons juxtaposes the business conception of free contract—which for businessmen permits the exercise of superior economic coercion, taken to be the natural state of things—to the system of "industrial government" in which labor interests are given protection against their "traditional" exposures.

In Commons's view, history repeats itself in a new context. The conservative courts have responded to "the demand for new definitions of liberty and power on the part of the aggressive laborers," thereby taking "over the protection of the liberty and power of business, just as the prerogative courts protected the privileges of the monarch and his party.... The prerogative to-day is the prerogative of business, and the common law of to-day seeking recognition is the customs of propertyless laborers developing in their own assemblies and industrial courts" (p. 307).

Commons identifies both the process and results of the continued evolution of law, with which he deeply concurs:

A common law of labor is constructed by selecting the reasonable practices and rejecting the bad practices of labor, and by depriving both unions and management of arbitrary power over the job. An amendment is gradually worked into the constitution of industrial government: 'No employer shall deprive any employee of his job without due process of industrial law, nor deny to any employee within his jurisdiction the equal protection of the common law of labor.'... Out of the wage-bargain a constitution for industrial government is being constructed by removing cases from the prerogative of management and the arbitrary power of unions and subjecting the foremen, the superintendents and the business agents to the same due process of law as that which governs the laborers (p. 312).

As an example, Commons examines the labor injunction and the correlative problem of whether policy is to be made by the legislature or the courts, in both regards the questions of legal recognition of relative coercive power and of which interest is to prevail inevitably arise.

Subsequent legislation and court decisions within the next dozen or so years after 1924 were to further the promotion of labor interests, and the reconstruction of industrial government which Commons identified and applauded. In this chapter, Commons has both established some of the legal foundations of an evolving capitalism as it came to exist and provided an intellectual legal-economic foundation for its further revision.

CHAPTER IX. PUBLIC PURPOSE

In this 75-page concluding chapter, Commons in effect asks several questions: Whose economy and polity is it? Whose interests and whose expectations are to count, and how? And what conception of public purpose is to underlie the inescapable necessity of choice exercised by the courts? One of Commons's themes, from the very beginning of the book, is that public purpose is not given by nature or by God. Although such notion has been employed as a sanctioning technique, public purpose is worked out by public decisional processes in a more or less deliberative manner. Merely identifying the problem as one of public purpose is to ask, which/whose public purpose, and thereby take the issue out of the esoteric realm of absolutist legitimation and to make explicit questions and answers that hitherto have been obscured if not intentionally obfuscated. One critical theme is that the most fundamental realm of "value" in economics concerns not the prices of goods and factors of production but the values ensconced in the working rules of a going economy and going concerns. Another theme identifies the role of individual and institutionalized discretion in the total valuation processes of society and economy.

The first section of Chapter IX, entitled "Concerns and Positions," is a carefully crafted summary of Commons's interpretation of the evolution of the economy from an agricultural to a commercial and industrial system. The reader will do well to read and outline these nine pages, relating them to the preceding chapters.

Commons continues to juxtapose the economic, jurisprudential, and legal as well as the political and social psychological aspects of developments. He traces the evolution of the institution of property. In a manner reminiscent of Adam Smith, he argues that the several stages of the Anglo-American economic system are represented by different systems of law and government, with the implication (and some of details) that changes in (and within) economic stage have involved, indeed required, changes in legal policy. Thus, for example, Commons writes that

> Since the various forms of intangible and incorporeal property cannot be created except by imposing new legal duties and new restraints on the liberty of individuals, questions were continually arising as to the reasonable scope and duration of these restraints (p. 316).

Commons's concluding point is that the modern economy is a system of private governance, with each nominally private going concern itself "indeed a government, employing its peculiar sanctions, and each individual holds a position in many governments" (p. 321). Commons writes,

> With delegations of sovereign power, property expands into an industrial government of its own, treated as a unit and even a person, although it is not a person but an industrial government. The economic power of this government begins to be recognized by the highest court in the latter part of the Nineteenth Century in the public utility and labor cases, but when its power is challenged by another industrial government, the labor organization endeavoring also to obtain sovereign powers and immunities, the court is divided.... [P]ower to withhold opportunities is economic power, and associated power is government.... In short, through the law of contracts and the law of torts the modern concept of property has evolved from the holding of things to the control of the supply of things through controlling the transactions of persons (pp. 319-320).

With each going concern a government, the determination of the use of its sanctions and the purposes to which they will be put rests "in the hands of those who primarily exercise the functions of a judiciary"—though they are not often called that, especially in nominally private organizations. Going concerns require purpose—the economist speaks of "objective functions"—and "It is therefore in the decision of the judicial functionaries of each concern in interpreting their working rules that the economist must look for the concern's purpose, that is the 'public' purpose of the concern. In the Anglo-American political concern [i.e., government], this public purpose has been evolved under the names of classification and due process of law" (p. 321). Commons treats classification and due process in the next two sections.

In the second section, Commons explains the growth of income through the increasing efficiency of the totality of people in an economy, arguing that individual efficiency has likely decreased. This growth of income has come about through human action, technology, and changes in the working rules. First, "the proportioning of [complementary and limiting] factors in a national economy is not the blind proportioning of blind forces of nature, but is the proportioning of inducements to willing and unwilling persons" (p. 323). Second, "this mechanistic economy of nature, as Smith sorrowfully acknowledged, has been greatly interfered with by the collective power of political and industrial governments.... [C]ollective action of political and industrial governments has reproportioned considerably the limiting and complementary factors, and obtained a different national result from that intended by nature as interpreted by Adam Smith" (pp. 323-324). Third, the "reproportioning has kept on according to the purposes of those who controlled the governments. Not Adam Smith but William the Conqueror was the founder of Anglo-American political economy. Adam Smith started the theory, but William started the economy. Nor did Smith start the whole of the theory" (p. 324)—here Commons points to the work of legal theorists and judges, and again emphasizes the evolving separation of public purpose from the private purposes of the sovereign, which is to say, the evolution of the fields of property and sovereignty.

Fourth, a corollary to the third point is that the distribution of the increasing income has been effectuated according to the ability of individuals "to pull a larger share out of the total increasing national efficiency" (p. 322). On the one hand, Commons rejects what he considers to be the mechanistic and aprioristic theorizing of Adam Smith, as well as later productivity-based distribution theory; on the other hand, he rejects Karl Marx's class exploitation theory;—both in favor of a nonnormative "appropriation" theory in which distribution is a function of the power and values represented by the working rules, with a focus on both those in a position to control government and the choices of the interests to which government gives its protection, and without a rendering of normative judgment.

Commons argues that government is used to determine which individuals and which classes will have the opportunities comprehended under the name of freedom and the immunities and exemptions from duties going under the name of Liberty—classifications analytically fundamental for Commons. In undertaking and achieving such determinations, government is changing the proportioning of inducements. The identity of those who control government has changed, and with it the public purposes: "The widening of the suffrage introduced additional participants in formulating the collective will. The definitions of property and liberty were enlarged to include both the private will of the propertyless laborer and the collective will of corporations and other going concerns, each defined, supported and enforced by the collective will of the nation" (p. 325).

The crux of every formulation of public purpose is "what is deemed...public policy" (p. 325). Commons combines several themes when he writes that:

> Quite correctly here, as elsewhere, the courts endeavor to escape this unruly horse [of Public Policy] by seeking some external rule fixed in the nature of things that does not change with changing valuations. But try as they may they cannot escape valuing consciously or unconsciously, by logic or habit, the relative importance of the human interests at stake...the allowable amount of pressure...the relative importance assigned to persons and classes of persons (pp. 325-326).

The last sentence quoted is very important. Herein Commons points to the ineluctable necessity of judicial choice (and of governmental choice in general). Its significance is due in part to the popular preference for a depoliticized definition of reality, the view (together with the invocation of supposedly transcendental principles—which themselves would foreclose choice) which Commons is at pains to rebut.

Commons also stresses that government action always selectively enhances and restricts different private interests. He argues that the question is *not* private versus public purpose, but *which* private purpose will government be used to support because *it* is "deemed" (p. 325) to have a public purpose. His example is government taxing and spending:

> The taxing power 'may not be used for private purposes.' But it always is used for private purposes and can be used in no other way, for its effect is to reduce the field of freedom and liberty for the taxpayer and enlarge the field of freedom and liberty for all who are benefited by the tax. The question always is, not, *What* is a private purpose over against a public purpose? but, Is the private purpose *also* a public purpose, or *merely* a private purpose? (pp. 326-327).

The former question misstates and misleads; the latter points to the actual effective choice, given the inexorability of government choice.

A corollary to the foregoing is given by Commons in his statement that "*all* private business and jobs are affected with a public interest [and not just "public utility companies" long considered—"by way of historical accident" (p. 328)— to be businesses affected with a public interest] in so far as the collective powers are directed to their protection or furtherance against superior power of others" (p. 327, italics added). The hegemonic ideology induces one to perceive that such a statement is statist in seemingly rejecting the *private* nature of business and jobs. But it is precisely Commons's argument that all private powers, immunities, and so on exist by virtue of their legal definition, assignment and protection, and the use of government by one class or another for that purpose, cultural mythology notwithstanding.

Commons's principal argument in this section is to emphasize

> the process of classification and reclassification according to the purposes of the ruling authorities, a process which has advanced with every change in economic evolution and every change in feelings and habits towards human beings, and which is but the proportioning and reproportioning of inducements to willing and unwilling persons, according to what is believed to be the degree of desired reciprocity between them. For, classification is the selection of a certain factor, deemed to be a limiting factor, and enlarging the field of that factor by restraining the field of other limiting factors, in order to accomplish what is deemed to be the largest total result from all (p. 329).

The key to this process is what is "deemed" or "believed" to be in the public interest, on which basis nominally private rights, opportunities, and so on are defined and redefined—and not some mechanistic transcendental external rule.

Commons approaches the same point in a different way. He acknowledges that only private activity is wealth-producing. Governments "do nothing but proportion inducements, and individuals do the rest. But they may waste the commonwealth by bad proportioning, may enlarge it by good proportioning" (p. 330). However, whether growth of output, as a result of changed proportioning, augments the total welfare "is a matter of opinion and judgment and depends on the relative human values attributed by the determining officials of government, at the time, to those who are benefited and those who are burdened" (p. 330). This is the same point made within modern welfare economics when it is said that there is no unique Pareto optimal result, only results specific to particular sets of entitlements. It is precisely Commons's point that changing the preeminence given to capital interests to also include labor interests as property, that is, treating labor as a limiting rather than subordinate complementary interest, means that a change takes place in what constitutes "good proportioning" relative to "bad proportioning"—that is, a change in whose interests are to count in determining the entitlements which underlay the actually achieved Pareto optimal result (p. 330).

The legal foundations of capitalism thus includes the "history of efforts to work out fundamental principles of classification which shall permit new proportioning of the national economy without unduly disturbing the old" (p. 331). The legal concept brought into play here is, of course, "due process of law." But what constitutes due process (and also equal protection) and duly or unduly disturbs the past in matters of legal change are matters of judgment. It is the exercise of judgment that is at the core of both legal decisions and legislative determinations seeking to comport with some notion of what is "deemed" or "believed" to be due process of law.

Section three treats the working rules of going concerns, notably the notion of due process of law. Commons begins by noting the double meaning of words frequently encountered in legal theory. "Words," he says, "are symbols or signs by which mean convey to each other not only interesting ideas but also inducements to act" (p. 331). He rejects the idea of "a mechanical unfolding of ideal concepts of liberty, justice and law" (p. 332), such as was advanced by Hegel, in favor of a concept of "an historical process brought about through the decision of disputes between members" of the political going concern (p. 333). He distinguishes between law as justice and law as commands, and between law as purpose and as process, between, that is, due procedure of law and due purpose of law. In the former, the court is interested only in the process by which legislation was passed, and so forth, and whether it comports with the court's understanding of what the constitution and/or common law requires in the way of settled and just procedure; in the latter, in the substantive content of the law and whether it comports with the court's understanding of the substance of certain rights and of public purpose. In both respects, the question is legal change of law, or which change is to be permitted and which not. On the one hand, traditional usage must be followed so as to preclude arbitrary and capricious treatment; on the other, no one has a vested property interest in any rule of law so as to preclude change of law. Most of Commons's discussion has to do with questions specifically of procedure and whether changes of procedure comport with the underlying rationales of past procedure. Change of procedure requires consideration of public purpose.

Such questions were increasingly important in matters relating to the conflict between capital and labor. They centered on "the distinction drawn between property right and personal right, the former having to do with the exchange-values of property, the latter with rights that do not immediately involve exchange-values, or prices. At some points property rights are deemed to be more important, at other points personal rights, and the difference of opinions between justices is largely a difference as to which, in the particular case, is the more important for the *due purpose* of law" (pp. 337-338).

Ultimately these were matters of judicial review; that is, the courts would make the final determinations. The courts would determine not only whether due procedure was followed but also whether a right purpose was intended (p. 341). Moreover, by judicial interpretation federal judicial review would apply to both federal and state legislation (pp. 340, 342). Commons traces the relevant history of the concept of due process, concluding with the addition of substantive to procedural due process, the former being concerned with "substantive justice," with the "rights *that are deemed important by the court*" (p. 341). Established property rights, or what the courts considered as established property rights, thus were given a privileged position relative to what it considered personal rights (pp. 341-342). In this manner judicial review is a mode through which rights are formed and reformed, under the rubric of protecting due process of law—as part of the continuing working out of the legal foundations of an evolving capitalism.

In section four, entitled "Due Process of Thinking," Commons notes first that the changed definition of due process elaborated upon in the preceding section represents the amendment of the constitution by the courts (p. 343). The upshot of the change does not, however, change the situation that "It is the working rules of government which determine the direction in which the collective power shall guide behavior." That is what government does, willy nilly. The new definition of due process identifies or defines certain conscious discretion by the courts. The key determination is that "Certain directions [of guided behavior] are deemed beneficial, others detrimental.... Purpose governs the working rules." This means, once again, that the court is involved with answering the key question: "What, then, is beneficial, and what is detrimental?" (p. 343).

Courts have to think this out, hence the phrase "due process of thinking." Among other things, Commons says that courts inevitably classify to give differential weight to different facts, including the determination of inclusion and exclusion. Courts are searching for both truth and justice. "[D]efinition is classification according to the importance of the facts" and is therefore "also valuation" (p. 347). Precedent is "the instrument of classification." Indeed, "Precedent is classification, and classification is the equal treatment of all who belong to the same class" (p. 346). The problems are that classification must be made in relation to purpose, that different classifications can be made for different purposes, and that substantive inequality impinges upon questions of equal protection (p. 345). (At one point Commons notes that certain cases "permitted choice of working rules" through the changed meaning of due process. It might be more accurate to say that these cases made unmistakably evident what had been the case all along [p. 344].)

Not surprisingly, given the analyses of earlier chapters, Commons returns to *futurity*. He starts by considering the weighing of facts. Facts are matters of collection and classification but both imply "a purpose for which the facts are selected." Moreover, although the "immediate purpose of definition is instrumental to an ultimate purpose," the "ultimate purpose is the total of all the expectancies to which each fact or class of facts contributes." Thus does Commons refer, first, to "the ultimate feeling of value, the emotional process of valuation that tinges all definitions" (p. 349); second, "an emotional valuation of qualities and faculties in the process of social life" (p. 348); and third, to futurity: "Purpose is anticipations of the future, and pulls forward" (p. 349). Public purpose is a matter of values and expectancies and thereby of behavioristic psychology. Commons continues this section with certain behavioral principles representing for him a sevenfold "process of thinking" (p. 351). Several reflect the foregoing discussion. Two examples are:

Ideals are ideas projected into the future by means of symbols (p. 349).

Valuation is the feeling of relative importance for the future, not of ideas, but of the expected behaviors which are their content...(pp. 350-351).

So far as the legal foundations of the economic system are concerned, "Due process...passes judgment upon the use of power in suppressing or liberating personality" (p. 351). In other words, due process—the way authoritative decision makers render and deploy the concept of due process— structures legal and economic power in the future.

Commons argues that "due process of thinking scrutinized the purposes and distinguishes correct habits of thought from the incorrect;....So that, while mere process of thinking is the process of habits, ideals, definitions, investigations, classifications, valuations and behavior, *due process of thinking, which is due process of law*, is the process of correct habits, right ideals, true definitions, sincere investigation, reasonable classification, reasonable value, and justice; whereas its opposite, undue process, is perverse habit, wrong ideals, double meanings, partial investigation, class legislation, confiscation and injustice" (pp. 351-352). Commons must not be understood as thinking that due process of thinking is a matter of finding ontological or epistemological truth. In his view, the process is one of working out the meanings and selective applications of these terms and concepts on the basis of what judges and others "deem" and "believe." Just as the immediate purpose of definition is *instrumental* to the ultimate purpose of the total of all expectancies, the process is *pragmatic*:

the concept of due process of thinking, to be derived from the reasoning of the courts because they deal with actual cases as they arise and at the same time seek to explain and justify their opinions in the public interest, is neither a concept of caprice nor of universal reason. It is the truly pragmatic process of inclusion and exclusion of facts as they arise, of classifying the facts as they themselves and other judges have classified them, of investigating and valuing all of the facts through listening to arguments of interested parties. In short, due process of law is the *collective* reasoning of the past and the present, a process of reasoning to which the just judge feels himself as firmly bound as though it were a superior bodily presence commanding him (p. 352).

The modern mind might consider Commons's portrayal of "the *collective* reasoning of the past and the present" a rather esoteric and metaphorical proposition. But for Commons it gives expression to the working of things out through the legal process, a court at once looking both backward (and sideways) to the work of other courts and forward to the world it is helping to make. The crux in practice is legal change of law, including change of the applications of received legal concepts, change in the concepts themselves (such as property, liberty, etc.), and change in the balancing of interests given effect thereby through court decisions and explicated in the majority and minority opinions in particular cases.

Section five, entitled "Discretion," continues the preceding analysis, arguing that ultimate discretion is exercised with regard to the meaning of public purpose, specifically with regard to the substance, as distinguished from the procedure, of law. Due purpose, writes Commons, has to do with "what *ought* to be the law of the land." Government officials have "power that is not unlimited. They are bound by ideals. Due process is ideal process. It is what *ought* to be rather than what *is* or *was*. Regard must be had to the *substance* rather than the *form*" (p. 353). As to the basis and social function of due process/due purpose,

Where, then, shall we find the substance of the law? We shall find it in the habits and ideals of those whose definitions are final in determining the law. This is Discretion. The field of Discretion is the field of Power and Immunity...(p. 354).

The ideals, being the ideals of "those whose definitions are final in determining the law," are those of the judge, especially of the highest court.

His views may not be very 'idealistic' in the opinion of other people, but that is because their habits and ideals are different from his. They are idealistic *for him*, for they are in the unfinished future that he is bending towards (p. 354).

So the role of the exercise of the discretion as to the substance (due purpose) of law is the social construction of the future, the critical role of the judge.

All agents of government exercise a will which, within their range of authorized discretion, is "the state-in-action"; their individual fields of discretion are the fields in which their "will is the collective will." "The will of the state is the will-in-action. It is discretion, and discretion resides wherever there is power (Freedom) an immunity." Their will is the will of the people, but only "[w]ithin the limits of reversal by the court." The Supreme Court is the end of the line, "the place where pure reason is supposed to lodge," but "[i]t, too, has its field of power and immunity. There the habits, ideals, definitions, classifications, valuations of its members are the will of the people-in-action." Within its field of freedom and immunity the court has "legislated by definition," changing the meaning of due process of law, property and liberty, and, for example, thereby changing the distribution of authority between state legislatures and federal courts (p. 355). Changes in definition "have the twofold effect of permitting the legislatures to legislate and permitting the court to legislate....[i]n each field of power and immunity thus redistributed by definition..." (p. 356). Such changes in definition, Commons writes, "are of course not arbitrary. They spring from new conditions. Yet they are discretionary" (p. 356).

The attribution of changes in definition to changes in condition seems to be a narrowing argument. For if definitions are matters of valuations and ideals, changes in the membership of the judiciary can mean changes in the identity and values and ideals of "those whose definitions are final in determining the law" without changes in conditions, and, furthermore, changes in conditions themselves must be evaluated and selected. However, that attribution is not followed through by Commons, who has several different points to make, points which identify the wide range of discretion but do not constrain its overall exercise in governance:

> The collective will...is no longer a merely capricious unaccountable will of a personal sovereign, but it is a will that proceeds by deliberative process of law....A new definition is a new valuation of facts, a new valuation is a new classification, a new classification is a new proportioning of inducements in the national economy, a new proportioning is legislation, and legislation is a change in the working rules of the concern. Legislation resides wherever discretion resides, and the collective will is not the will of the legislature alone, but is the habits, ideals, definitions, investigations, classifications, valuations, discretion and behavior of judges and executives who have official power and immunity in formulating the working rules (p. 356).

Commons concludes this section with an interesting and important example of how majority and minority opinions in a case approached the question of reasonable rates for a railroad, both positions attempting to constrain administrative discretion but differing in recognizing the range of discretion (pp. 357-359). For Commons,

> Probably these metaphysical and mechanistic conclusions are required in order to conform to the Eighteenth Century attempt both to separate government into legislative, judicial

and executive branches and to separate the human will into will, intellect and action. They
tend to preserve the primitive notions of a complete dualism of the objective and subjective
world. The objective world is the world of facts, the subjective is the world of feelings,
emotions, caprice (p. 359).

Commons establishes his position by quoting a law review author about
delusion through the illusion that, in such matters, "there is a fact which can
be discovered if we are only persistent enough in our search for it, and which,
once it is found, will provide a mathematical solution of all rate-making
problems" (p. 359). In "reality," says Commons, "facts are facts as our habits,
investigations and purposes deem them to be facts" (p. 359). It would seem,
therefore, that for Commons, changing definitions can arise from new
conditions but conditions can be variably experienced and evaluated,
depending upon purposes and values. That is what ultimately is at the core
of the role of "public purpose."

The final section of Chapter IX, and therefore of the book, is entitled
"Economic Theory of Going Concerns." For Commons, the economy, as a
going concern, is not a mechanical allocation of resources. It is a process of
working out the purposes of life and part of that process involves government
by a theory of value "in which individuals and classes of individuals count
according to what is felt to be their relative importance for public purposes"
(p. 360). There must be working rules governing whose interests are to count.
In determining those working rules authoritative decision makers must have
recourse to some notion of public purpose, including some "sense of fitness
and unfitness, or common sense and habit" (p. 359), all of which is, at point
in time, more or less subject to change. In any event, according to the
authoritative "appreciation of relative importance" for public purposes,
individuals "get the assistance of officials in the form of rights and liberties,
and the restraint or neglect of officials in the form of duties and exposures.
So that instead of an 'organic' theory of the state based on duty, or a 'contract'
theory of the state based on liberty, we reach what may be distinguished as
an *economic theory of going concerns based on the authoritative proportioning
of inducements in a world of limited resources*" (p. 360, italics added). Thus
is established the institutionalist proposition that markets do not allocate
resources; allocation is a function of the working rules which proportion
participation in the economy and thereby structure markets and determine
whose interests count (p. 361).

For Commons, this economic theory of the state is empirically accurate,
because it is

the theory of a going concern with its going business, having its roots in the past, its behavior
in the present, held together by the hopes of peace, wealth, virtue and the fears of violence,
poverty and vice, through the control of which collective action proportions the
inducements to individuals to participate in the burdens and benefits of collective power.

In short, the economic theory of the state is the theory of proportioning inducements to willing and unwilling persons in a world of scarcity.
...Ethics and economics are thus inseparable, for each proceeds from the principle of scarcity (p. 361).

Commons believes that "properly interpreted," this was the view of Adam Smith, and that "it was only by picking out and abstracting that part of his theory which exalted individual initiative and criticised governments for suppressing initiative, that his successors...distorted his notion of the wealth of nations" (p. 362). A "return to the true spirit of Adam Smith" would recognize the fundamental and inevitable role of government in the proportioning of inducements, in seeking, that is, "the best proportioning of inducements by the state to useful and useless persons" (p. 363), as "useful" and "useless" are understood by those whose decisions are final.

But along with that, Commons recognizes that the state is not the only active decision-making process. He writes of

the way in which courts and legislatures have recognized and endowed with power and immunity the industrial governments which organize, marshal, and manage armies of producers for mass production. They, however, also are collective wills animated by a collective purpose, and proportioning also by their working rules, like the state, inducements to willing and unwilling persons to participate in their collective power. Thus in descending circles of proportioning and reproportioning, the collective power of the nation is delegated to subordinate collective powers, and they in turn to individuals, held together by thinking alike.
It is this thinking alike that constitutes collective purpose (p. 363).

The economy, therefore, is a vast system of governance, decision making, or field of action delineated by matrices of power, liberty, exposure, immunity, duty, and so on, as determined and redetermined through on-going processes. There is the state, but there is also the corporation, as well as the trade union, all participants in the system which is what it is and becomes because of its legal foundations.

Apropos of empirical standing, Commons not unexpectedly but profoundly both rejects and explains

the metaphysical notion that there exists somewhere an objective world of rights and duties superior to the actual rights and duties,...[which] goes along with the metaphysical notion that there is somewhere an entity 'the state' apart from the officials who determine and execute the will of that state. These metaphysical notions have, indeed, a powerful influence on men's minds, simply because man lives in the future but acts in the present. Thus constituted, he projects outward into a world of ideas his hopes and fears, and gives to his expectations a local habitation and a name.
Yet these ideas are but ideals—they exist, but they exist in the mind. They exist because man craves security for his expectations, and could not act at all as a rational being without the feeling of security....When his rational expectations are gone the savage

in him takes possession. No wonder he fills the sky with deities and entities—they are
his hopes.

But the real world of rights and duties about him is the collective will expressed in working
rules necessitated by the scarcity of resources. His 'freedom' is his power to command the
officials according to those rules, who are both the instruments of that will and the actors
who determine what that will shall be when it acts. They, too, like him, move toward their
habits and ideals, and respond, according to those habits and ideals, to his call for help,
if needed. To that extent he enjoys 'freedom' as well as liberty, for he has the aid of collective
power to give effect to his will.

At this point, however, where this power ends his 'disability' begins, for there the collective
power ceases to come to his aid. And there also his right ends and his exposure to the
liberty of others begins (p. 364).

All this characterizes both the official government of the state and the unofficial
but no less effective government of the corporation and other nominally private
organizations and associations. In both cases, special attention must be paid
in Commons's system to those "who are both the instruments of that will and
the actors who determine what that will shall be when it acts."

Because of the acceptance of the practice or institution of judicial review,
the courts have a somewhat hegemonic position. The judge is distinguished
by his "greater deliberation... in making up his mind.... The supreme courts
are placed most remote from the individuals whose interests are at stake, where
they can review the general principles, and consequently their majority and
minority opinions expound at length the grounds on which their conclusions
rest." But, says Commons, "Seldom do their differences of opinion turn on
the enumeration of facts... Their differences turn on what they deem to be the
importance of the facts." And these turn on the individual justice's "sense of
fitness and unfitness arising out of habit and custom," which "differs as widely
as human character" and is responsible for "the differences of opinion in the
majority and minority opinions of courts and the evolution of definitions and
classifications" (pp. 365-366). But always "the state, in reality, is the officials
in action; their action is the organization of violence according to due process
of law; and due process of law is the working rules of officials.... [S]ecurity
[of interests] is... a choosing in advance by officials of the direction in which
they will afford security" (p. 367).

Commons thus identifies three different standpoints from which
classifications can be formulated and on the basis of which the economy defined
and policy promulgated. These may also be comprehended as modes of
discourse. One is the "standpoint of competition of individuals and concerns"
(p. 367). A second is the functional standpoint with regard to the perceived
functions performed by different individuals and groups, such as the
entrepreneur and the capitalist. The third is that of the going concern, which
"includes not only the competitive classification of land, labor, capital and
entrepreneur, and the personal combination of these factors in the jobs and

positions of individuals, but also that authoritative proportioning of factors through inducements to persons, which constitute political, industrial and moral government" (p. 368). Commons's model of immunities and exposures, and so forth, has meaning principally with regard to the third, though most social discourse is in terms of the first and second.

The first two modes of discourse tend to be more aprioristic and mythological. Thus Commons calls attention to

> certain ontological mysteries which attend notions of a collective will, springing from that twofold weakness of the human mind which creates abstract images endowed with souls and identifies what *ought* to be with what *is*....
>
> Generally, it will be found that what is intended is that sovereignty *ought* to be the Will of God or the Will of the People, and this idea is expressed as an entity living apart from the actual state which evidently does not meet that ideal; or that the corporate will *ought* to be a human soul but is a bloodless entity different from the human beings who act in its name (p. 371).

Evidently Commons was motivated to make these remarks, and comparable remarks found elsewhere in the book, by two things: first, his adoption of an objective (nonnormative) and non-teleological model of legal-economic organization and evolution; and second, by his perception that most other people are operating not only within the first and/or second of the three standpoints discussed just above but also in subjective and normative, indeed typically highly charged, terms. The reader has to understand both the details of Commons's analysis of the legal foundations of the economic system and its ontological and epistemological status.

Commons acknowledges the social role of "these ontological mysteries," in a manner reminiscent of Vilfredo Pareto's principle of the social utility of falsity. Commons writes:

> the mystery is so far removed from the actual that it can accommodate all kinds of wishes without being discovered. In this way these mysteries have a certain pragmatic value, for, in the name of God, or the People, or the Corporate will, the particular official or agent can do many things which he would not do in his own name. He can always say that he has no discretion in the matter, and that, while as an individual he would do differently, yet etc., etc. (p. 372).

This perception by participants "undoubtedly has a degree of accuracy," says Commons. But changes occur, often with great difficulty in overcoming the mysteries, after "the ontological mystery is partly dissolved, and it is seen that the will of the concern is what the concern does, and what the concern does is what its functionaries do" (p. 372). The reader will recall that Commons took such an empirical and secular approach in his treatment of the formation and operation of the working rules and in other respects as well.

Commons also examines the practice of these ontological mysteries in the face of new varieties of facts. These predetermined absolutes have been revised through the device of changing the definitions of such terms as property and liberty by a court which "enjoyed a degree of immunity,... no superior authority that could prevent the change in definitions, or give to that change a different slant." These changing definitions revise the mode of discourse and both permit both (1) adjustment to and revision of the socially constructed reality and (2) psychic balm, a sense of the predetermined to accompany the reality of change:

> A change in definitions is such a simple and natural way of changing the constitution from what it is to what it ought to be, and the method is so universal and usually so gradual in all walks of life, that the will of God, or the will of the People, or the Corporate will, scarcely realizes what has happened. The method is, indeed, that common-sense device whereby man can go on believing in unchanging entities, and yet be practical (p. 373).

Correlatively, Commons is interested in indicating how selective perception has distinguished between individual rights and collective action through the modern state. Commons does so in a manner that demonstrates the extremely limited interpretive power of any body of economic theory which is predicated upon that distinction. After recalling that it was "the tightening of procedure which gradually converted the prerogative of the King into the sovereignty of the citizen," he remarks that it worked so smoothly

> that, when legal and economic writers in the 18th and 19th centuries began to think about it they identified the sovereignty of the citizen as one of the natural rights of man. This power of man to require officials to do his bidding in conformity to the working rules of the concern became even one of the 'faculties' of the human will, a capacity or ability of the individual to act, like the ability to plough, or eat, or think. The actual state, with its actual officials, seemed to be unnatural, a merely coercive power interfering with and overriding the natural liberty of man to use his faculties as he pleased, rather than the collective power by which man's will is made effective. The best that the state could do was to let man alone. Yet these collective powers, exercised on behalf of individuals through the responsibility of officials to them, in accordance with the accepted rules guiding their actions, are the main instruments of modern industry, for they are the source of those encumbrances and opportunities which constitute the incorporeal and intangible capital by means of which feudalism was displaced by capitalism and slavery by liberty (p. 373; see also p. 385).

Commons's legal-economic model is thus used once again to indicate the legal foundations of the economic system, especially of capitalism. Contrariwise, economic theory has neglected, even negated, the exercise of collective will through judicial and other governmental determinations of public purpose. By taking both the economic system and individual rights as "given," economists have finessed the fundamental operation of government. This applies to the theory of value, which not improperly focuses on the determination of price but is incomplete if it omits the operation of the values ensconced within the working rules. Commons applauds modern physical science insofar as it avoids metaphysical explanatory factors and settles upon simple mathematical statements, calling it a "mathematical agnosticism." But he believes that economics and other social sciences should be volitional in character, with the volition being that of human beings acting both individually and collectively—and in the process exercising control over the economy, combining the principles of mechanism and scarcity, the latter encompassing decisions as to the proportioning of resources and of control.

For Commons, volition and purpose characterize the economy. "Economic phenomena, as we know them," he writes, "are the result of artificial selection and not of natural selection" (p. 376). He rejects those theories, both physical and evolutionary, which have "attempted to get rid of the human will and to explain economic phenomena as the working out of natural forces, either foreordained or blind" (p. 376; included in the latter category is the non-teleological evolutionary economics of Thorstein Veblen, the other founder of institutional economics, whose rejection of teleology was of the same kind that Commons rejected). Political economy, in Commons's view, deals with "purposeful control over physical nature" and "over human nature," each according to "working rules changed from time to time, but always intended to control the actions and transactions of the participants" (p. 376). The subject matter of political economy is the "habits, customs and ways of thinking of producers, consumers, buyers, sellers, borrowers, lenders and all who engage in what we name economic transactions." Political economy thus understood evolved as "[t]he desirable customs were selected gradually by the courts, the undesirable customs were progressively eliminated as bad practices, and out of the whole came the existing economic process, a going concern, symbolized by a flux of prices, and operating to build up an artificial mechanism of rules of conduct, creating incorporeal and intangible property quite different from the unguided processes of nature" (p. 377). "Thus," Commons writes,

> a volitional or economic theory starts with the *purpose* for which the artificial mechanism in question was designed, fashioned and remodeled, and inquires, first, whether that purpose is useful or useless, legitimate or illegitimate, ethical or unethical, right or wrong (p. 377).

The "artificial" element is the human will's "own ultimate purpose accompanied by an intermediate or immediate instrumental purpose of obtaining control of the limiting factor, through control of the mechanism" (p. 378). The phenomena of political economy are the outcomes, in addition to the actions of individual buyers and sellers, "of rights of property and powers of government which have been fashioned and refashioned in the past by courts, legislatures and executives through control of human behavior by means of working rules, directed toward purposes deemed useful or just by the law-givers and law interpreters" (p. 378). The task of the economist is to uncover the limiting factor in particular situations, examine its legal bases, mode of operation, and possibilities for alteration. This must be done with due regard for what Commons calls the principles of timeliness, anticipation, and caution, the principles which Commons says "distinguish a volitional theory from a mechanical theory. Each looks to the future but describes action in the present" (p. 386). Futurity is important because of human volition and purpose.

Commons next considers various aspects of value and cost, in terms of ultimate purposes and intermediate and immediate goals. Real cost and real value are juxtaposed to their psychological, that is, volitional or purpose-laden, alternatives. Individual and social perspectives are also juxtaposed. Earlier arguments are restated with regard to value and cost. Meaning by "principle" the adoption of certain lines of action, Commons writes that

> The value principle, looked upon, not as a quality intrinsic in commodities nor in the relation of man to nature, but as a social principle of inducement and an individual principle of anticipation, is none other than that expected power of persuasion or coercion over others which induces performance on the economic side, and gives rise to claims of rights and liberties on the property side. On the other hand the cost principle, looked upon as a social principle of resistance and an individual principle of caution, is that subservience to others or service to others, which on the economic side is the resistance to performance and on the property side is a duty or exposure corresponding to the right or liberty of others (p. 382).

(Although Commons does not consider the matter here, his discussion is compatible with the utility theory of value, except that the utility theory does not go as far as did Commons's theory in recognizing the role of collective action in proportioning opportunities and so forth, in part through the values ensconced in the working rules, thus determining whose interests, or utilities, were to count.)

Commons returns to the topics of the going concern and the working rules. Here he again rejects the conduct of economic theorizing solely on the basis of individualistic mechanics, preferring to emphasize the principle of scarcity and the role of collective action in proportioning inducements, and so on as the mode of exercise of volition and purpose, especially public purpose. Commons seems to consider narrow, but does not reject outright, the view that "the propertied classes always control the government since it is they who own the tools, cattle and machinery, and their ownership is safeguarded only by control of government" (p. 383). He prefers, as has been seen earlier, a broader conception of sovereignty and a more complex legal-economic model of relationships.

In any event, to the principles (as he calls them) of mechanism and scarcity, Commons would add that of the working rule. These are in addition to the secondary principles of "anticipation or inducement, caution or resistance to inducement, and timeliness or acting upon the limiting factors at that time, to the degree and to the extent that they are deemed to be effective in accomplishing the purpose intended," which "action implies the principle of mechanism in that it signifies getting control of the *strategic part* of the mechanism, and it implies the principle of scarcity in that it signifies a due proportioning of the *quantities* of the several factors contributing to the mechanism" (pp. 384-385). "But," he writes,

> it implies, above all, the principle of purpose, looking toward the future, of which anticipation, caution and timeliness are its behavioristic and measurable dimensions, but of which the ethical and economic consequences foreseen are its driving force (p. 385).

"Liberty," he repeats, "is the individual's absence of physical coercion," though not the absence of coercion through markets. But there is also the determination of whose liberty is to count:

> public purpose is that of giving to the individual by means of common rules binding on all under similar circumstances, a power of calling on government to give effect to his will (p. 385).

The economic system is suffused with public purpose, such that both the anarchistic notions of man's will and of property must be rejected. Governments have changed the nature of property and the domain of the individual, in part by determining the area over which the bargaining activity of individuals can take place and in part by proportioning the factors over which the state has control. "This proportioning of inducements, by means of working rules, to individuals and associations is *Political Economy*" (p. 387). Political economy necessarily includes elements of both the natural economy of nature's resources and the economy of scarcity over both of which human individual and collective volition is exercised and purpose directed. Political economy includes the directing of the natural economy, of mechanisms, to the goals identified and selected through the economy of scarcity. Political economy therefore also necessarily includes economics (narrowly conceived), ethics, and law. Political economy involves

> the proportioning, by means of the working rules of going concerns, of persuasive, coercive, corrupt, misleading, deceptive and violent inducements and their opposites, to willing, unwilling and indifferent persons, in a world of scarcity and mechanical forces, for purposes which the public and private participants deem to be, at the time, probably conducive to private, public or world benefit (p. 388).

A theory, therefore, of the legal foundations of capitalism requires a broader and deeper theory than that of traditional economics. And Commons believes that he has here provided the beginnings of such a theory.

EARLY INSTITUTIONAL ECONOMICS:
ADDITIONAL MATERIALS FROM
JOHN R. COMMONS

INTRODUCTION

The following materials of John R. Commons continues the collection already published in *Archival Supplement 4*. The same introductory remarks apply to these documents. In general, the documents were given to me by Edwin E. Witte upon his retirement from Wisconsin in 1957 and are now published, so far as I know, for the first time (which does not mean that similar ideas may not have been published, many years ago, in other forms). Amendations in the handwriting of Commons have been incorporated without identification. Only minor stylistic editing has been introduced. Square brackets indicate my additions; parentheses are Commons's.

The documents will interest a variety of readers. They represent the several major fields in which Commons worked: labor, institutional economic theory, and (what is now called) macroeconomics.

Reasearch in the History of Economic Thought and Methodology,
Archival Supplement 5, pages 63-119.

The manuscripts of *Bank Credit, Economic Cycles,* and *A. Aftalion* date from at least the early 1920s, and could have been written earlier.

Bank Credit must be read with several things in mind: the state of monetary and banking institutions then in existence; the state of monetary and banking theory as it then existed; Commons's own set of interests and mode of theorizing, that is, the prism through which he examined and defined economic phenomena; and the respects in which his analysis was, in retrospect, ahead of then-current thinking. Much the same applies to *Economic Cycles* and *World Depressions.*

Passages in *Notes on Analytic and Functional Economics* are key to Commons's theories of the legal-economic nexus and law and economics in general. Other passages, here and in *Economic Cycles,* are indicative of Commons's view of the role of conceptions as tools for use in the study of reality, rather than a specification of reality itself—important material on which is also present in *Economic Cycles.* Functional analysis can be analyzed in varying dichotomous terms: pure and applied, positive and normative, deductive and inductive, and single and multiple variables. Also present is a model of moral (non-legal), legal and market decision-making and therefore a model of the organization and control system of the political economy— inclusive, too, of both deliberative and nondeliberative decision making.

Although the manuscript of *World Depressions* refers to diagrams, none accompany my copy of the text. Among other things, one finds here recognition of the Keynesian idea of profit margins as a function of tension between falling wage rates versus inadequate effective demand.

Present in *Economic Cycles,* in the discussion of B.M. Anderson's work, is material pertinent to subtleties of the evolution of utility theory and, related thereto, the conflict between individual free will and subjectivity and the "scientific" desire for absolutist determinacy. Commons's distinction between the noun Value and the verb Valuing is very important in this and other regards.

The original documents will eventually be deposited in the Commons Papers at the Wisconsin State Historical Society/University of Wisconsin Library.

Warren J. Samuels
Editor

THE LAW OF COLLECTIVE BARGAINING

(Personal. Not for Publication) [Inscribed in pencil in
upper-right corner: October 20, 1920 and "JRC personal"]

Will you kindly look over the following suggestions for an act, and comments
on the same, designed to meet the Coppage and Hitchman cases, and return
the same with comments and criticisms to J. R. Commons, University of
Wisconsin, Madison, Wisconsin. Should be pleased if you would cite cases
sustaining or conflicting with the suggestions.

Rough Draft of a Bill

SECTION I. As used in the following sections the term "Association of
Capitalists" shall mean any partnership, mutual or cooperative company, or
any corporation, or any affiliation of two or more associations of capitalists,
either with or without the purpose of profit, either domestic, interstate or
foreign, operating in the state of Wisconsin, for the purpose of owning, buying
or selling property, commodities, or the products or services of labor, or for
the purpose of mutual assistance in establishing rules, usages or understandings
that shall prescribe the rates of wages, hours of labor, or other conditions,
affecting directly or indirectly the contracts of master and servant, employer
and employee, to be entered upon by its members or by non-members similarly
situated as employers of labor.

An "Association of Labor" shall mean any mutual or cooperative association
for the purpose of mutual benefit without profit, or any organization of laborers,
employees or intending laborers, or employees, or any affiliation of two or more
associations of laborers, for the purpose of mutual assistance in establishing rules,
usages or understandings that shall prescribe the rates of wages, hours of labor,
or other conditions affecting directly or indirectly the contracts of master and
servant, employer and employee to be entered upon by its own members or by
non-members similarly situated as laborers, servants or employees.

A "person" shall mean any individual, whether laborer or capitalist, acting
for himself or as a member, agent or representative of respectively any
association of laborers or association of capitalists.

SECTION II. Every person shall be deemed to have an inalienable right
to become a member of any association of capitalists or association of laborers,
on such terms as said associations may prescribe, and any and every contract
or understanding whatever, express or implied, by which any person agrees
that he will not become a member of any association of capitalists or of
laborers, is null, void and of no effect, as being against the public policy, hereby
declared, of promoting the free organization of associations of capitalists and
associations of laborers.

SECTION III. It shall be lawful for any person or any association of capitalists, their members, agents or representatives, to refuse to employ any laborer, or to require by by-law, rule, understanding or usage, its members to refuse to employ any laborer, on the ground that said laborer is a member of an association of laborers; and to refuse to deal and to require its members to refuse to deal with any person, or any association of capitalists or association of laborers, their members, agents or representatives, on the ground that they employ or deal with other persons members of any association of laborers. And it shall be lawful for any association of laborers to prescribe by by-law, rule, understanding or usage, that none of its members shall enter into any contract, express or implied, with any association of capitalists or with any member, agent or representative of such association, and to prescribe that none of its members shall work with any person not a member of said association of laborers, or of any affiliated association of laborers.

SECTION IV. Any person or persons damaged in any respect by any person, any association of capitalists or any association of laborers in violation of his or their right, as defined in Section II, to become a member or members of any association of capitalists or any association of laborers on such terms as such association may prescribe, shall have a right of action, jointly or severally, in law or equity, against such person, association of capitalists or association of laborers, except in all cases where such damage is inflicted by the exercise of the rights of such persons or associations, as defined in Section III of this act.

SECTION V. This act shall be deemed to apply only to contracts, express or implied, of master and servant, employer and employee, and not to any contract, express or implied, relating to tangible or intangible property, to products, or commodities, except as such contracts relating to said property, products or commodities may be permitted, restrained or prohibited under the provisions of Sections 000 to 000 of the statutes. [Antitrust law and agricultural products. [In original - ed.]]

Comment

This proposed draft of an act is designed to meet the decisions of the Supreme Court in the Coppage and the Hitchman cases. The draft is based on the supposition that those cases went off, first on a failure to recognize the public purpose of labor organizations while recognizing the public purpose of capitalistic organizations; and second on the failure to provide in the Kansas law, declared unconstitutional in the Coppage case, and on the failure to recognize in the Hitchman case the reciprocity and equal treatment of rights and duties between associations of capitalists and associations of laborers. Sections II and III are intended to bring out both the public purpose of labor organizations along with capitalist organizations, and to provide reciprocity and equal treatment in their dealings with each other. Sections IV and V are intended to restrict the act to the relations of employer and employee and to distinguish this from the anti-trust acts which pertain to buyers and sellers of commodities or property.

Public Purpose. The public purpose of both classes of associations is intended to be brought out by first, the right of every person to belong to any association. Second, the prohibition of contracts not to belong to any association. Third, a positive statement of public policy, though I recognize this is not usually incorporated in statutes.

Goodwill and Freedom of Association. The Court in the Hitchman case proceeded to deny the right of a labor union to solicit peaceably the employees of the Hitchman Company on a mistaken analogy to the goodwill of a business. The goodwill of a business is a matter of high public policy, because it is a great incentive to build up a business; but the value to the public of this incentive consists altogether in the fact that the expected customer is wholly free, without penalty, hardship, or the violation of any contract, to leave the merchant who enjoys his patronage and to transfer his patronage to another merchant. This freedom of the customer induces the merchant to keep his custom by good service, and not by relying on the power of the state to enforce contracts. If the customer is tied up by a contract, so that he cannot leave and so that it is illegal for the competitor to solicit him to transfer his patronage, it ceases to be goodwill, and becomes a compulsory patronage, similar to a franchise, exclusive patronage, or contracts of serfdom and peonage, where the owner retains patronage, not by better service than competitors but by the power of the state. Now the Hitchman case tied up its employees by such contracts, express and implied; consequently the analogy of goodwill, on which the decision turned, was bad. Sections II and III above are suggested as necessary in order to apply the correct analogy of the legal concept of goodwill, as between associations in respect of their power to solicit the free patronage of laborers.

At the same time, it is already held by the Supreme Court that an employer may refuse to hire a worker because he is a member of a union, and also that a union may require its members to refuse to work for an employer because he hires non-union men. In other words, the employer may run a closed-non-union shop and the union may strike for a closed-union shop. This principle is sound, for the reason that it recognizes the freedom of association of both, and equal reciprocal treatment of both. It is thought best, however, to state the principle clearly, as in Section III, because the principle was not recognized in the Kansas statute declared unconstitutional, and especially because it enables us to draw clearly the line between that false notion of goodwill which consists in tying up a laborer by contract which it is illegal to interfere with even by persuasion (Section II); and that true meaning of goodwill which is .the right to refuse to deal with one person, and the accompanying right of a third person (usually but not necessarily a competitor) to persuade him to deal elsewhere. In the Hitchman case there was no violence or threats of violence—it was merely persuasion of which the union was found guilty. The persuasion was persuasion to break a contract which tied the laborer to his job as against the solicitations of the union representatives, though not as against the solicitations of other employers; and it is this kind of contract against the persuasions of a labor union that is to be declared illegal (Section II) and thus place the union on the same footing of goodwill as a competing employer.

Damages and Injunctions. Section IV is suggested notwithstanding full recognition of the fact that it permits actions in damages and injunctions against labor unions. But it is intended to limit these actions by prohibiting actions where unions inflict damage by refusing to work with non-union men. And this is the main thing. It also preserves the principle of reciprocity and equal treatment by allowing the same right to employers. The fact that the courts do not sustain actions against employers who inflict damage on unions by refusing to employ union men, while at the same time they support actions against unions who inflict damage on employers by refusing to work with non-union men, can be explained only on the theory that the court recognizes a public purpose in capitalist associations but no public purpose in labor associations. They do indeed recognize the abstract right of both to refuse to hire or refuse to work, which is the right of each to inflict injury on the other; but in the one case this is privileged, since it is not followed by damages, in the other case it is not privileged, since it is followed by damages. Sections II, III and IV, taken together, attempt to carry out the principle of reciprocity and equity of treatment, not only to the abstract right, but to the actual consequences of exercising that right.

Furthermore, unions must choose between two evils. The courts already have practically incorporated unions by making them subject to damage suits and injunctions as though they were incorporated. Section IV recognizes this hard fact and attempts to restrict the action for damages at the point where it blocks the whole union program, and does so by the simple device of treating unions exactly as employers are already treated.

Farmers' Associations. Section V seems necessary in order to meet the effort of farmers' cooperative associations to secure the same advantages as labor unions. It seems to me that the two should be separated, and a different, perhaps accompanying act, or additional sections of this act, should be devoted to farmers' associations, for they are, by the definition of Section I, classed as associations of capitalists, dealing in commodities and not dealing in the services of laborers. I recognize the political expediency of combining the two, but this would require redrafting the above sections.

NOTES ON ANALYTIC AND FUNCTIONAL ECONOMICS

May 1926 (To be Revised)

(These notes should be read in connection with my Legal Foundations of Capitalism (1924); Law and Economics (Yale Law Jour, Feb. 1925); Anglo-American Law and Economics (mimeograph) and Reasonable Value (mimeograph)

In analyzing the various factors that have been taken into account by the several schools of economic thought for the past 150 years, and then bringing these factors together in a functional relation it will be found that we have to do with five functional relations which may briefly be characterized as scarcity, efficiency, force, custom and futurity (Yale Law Jour; Reasonable Value). Each of these functional relations may be separated, both in thought and practice, from the others, by distinguishing what, for us, is the ultimate science on which each rests, and then, by analysis and experiment, developing each separately within its own field. In other words, each of these functions rests on separate distinguishable sciences, and, for this reason, from the standpoint of economics as a whole, each may be distinguished as an analytic science, but the connection between it and economics may be described as a functional science.

Thus, Force rests on the ultimate human relation of violence, which when organized as a going concern, yields the analytic sciences of military science, politics and analytic jurisprudence; in short the analytic science of sovereignty. When these sciences, however, are functionally related to the other four, then we have Force functioning in the field of economics, and here we deal, not with the technique of, say, analytic jurisprudence, but with Functional Jurisprudence—not with the technique of Politics or the technique of the organized force of military science, but with functional politics and the functional relation of force to the science of economics.

Likewise Scarcity rests on the ultimate relation between the wants of living creatures and the limited resources available for satisfying wants, but scarcity, in its functional relation to economic science, operates within the variable interactions of efficiency, force, custom and futurity.

Efficiency, from the analytic standpoint, is the technology of all the sciences, from astronomy to psychology, but, from the functional standpoint, it determines and is determined by the other relations of scarcity, force, custom and futurity.

Custom and Futurity, from the analytic standpoint, are the physiology, biology, psychology of habit and consciousness, but from the economic functional standpoint they are the repetition of transactions and the expectations of future transactions modifying the form and dimensions of present transactions.

Economic science, then, has two problems of methodology, namely, analysis and function. Analysis takes economics into the field of other sciences, and how deeply it shall go into those fields is a question of the particular issues involved. Function picks out from each analysis the interaction of each upon all the others. And the distinction, as a matter of methodology, will lead us to distinguish the Newtonian, or analytic method of science, from the Darwinian, or functional method of science.

I. Force

John Austin separated by analysis the functions of sovereignty from all other social sciences, by separating moral law from jural law, and defining the latter as "the aggregate of rules set by men as politically superior or sovereign to men as politically subject." This distinction separates law from economics as well as from morals and likewise from all questions as to the sources of law in custom and the expected social consequences of law. If this analysis is carried out and sovereignty is separated from all other social relations, then sovereignty is the organization of the physical force of the community and law is the set of working rules commanded by political superiors to political inferiors according to which violence is organized. Unorganized violence is anarchy, but organized violence is the monopolized physical force of the community commanded by superiors who compel the obedience of inferiors. It is the social relation of force specialized as the military, political and juristic relations of sovereign and subject, state and citizen, sheriff and defendant, and so on. This specialization is accomplished through the organization of subordinates, to be known as officials, such as executives, generals, armies, sheriffs, policemen, who direct and physically execute upon the subjects the will of the sovereign; and it is the expectation of these managerial transactions of sovereign and citizen, with their sanctions of physical force entrusted to sheriffs, policemen and armies that constitutes that going concern which, in its later developments, we name the state.

An analytic science of sovereignty requires its subdivision into three sciences— military science, politics and analytic jurisprudence. Military science, in its comprehensive and historical sense, would show how the physical violence of the community, is extracted, specialized and organized apart from the other forces of society, and this would include the two general aspects of conquest and order. Historically this would go back to tribal organization, war chiefs, conquest of Indian tribes, etc., and end with the modern world wars and the high specialization of standing armies, constabulary, police force, sheriffs and constables for the maintenance of order and execution of process of law. It would thus include the two types of instrumentalities employed, the personal instrumentalities of armies, policemen, sheriffs, detectives, and the physical instrumentalities of fortifications, ships, jails, penitentiaries, guns, ammunition and clubs.

The analytic science of politics, on the other hand, would show the procedure by which the commands of the sovereign are formulated and then conveyed through subordinates until they reach the judiciary [penciled question mark alongside in margin, and word "judiciary" underlined in pencil] who make findings of fact on which the executives execute the commands, where the details belong to military science and police organization. Historically this science of politics would go back to tribal councils and come down through the feudal organization, the absolute monarchies with their system of legislation by courtiers, concluding with the modern constitutional governments, legislatures, lobbies, political parties and propaganda, with their physical equipment of legislative halls, executive mansions, political headquarters, newspapers, platforms and soap boxes.

Finally, analytic jurisprudence, in its comprehensive meaning, deals with the procedure by which the general rules of a sovereign, addressed to all individuals or particular classifications of individuals, are reduced to individual commands of a judge [the words "jury" and written in pencil above "judge"], directed to a sheriff, constable, or policeman, as to how and how much the physical force of the community shall be employed upon particular individuals who have come within the jurisdiction of that specialized physical force. Historically, analytic jurisprudence would go back to tribal organizations or despotisms where the legislative, executive and judicial procedure was not clearly differentiated. It would include martial law, civil law, criminal law, and other specializations, and would come down through the delegation of judicial powers by a monarch to his local or itinerant judges, ending with the modern separation of an independent judiciary in England and a supreme judiciary in America.

It is to be noted that none of these sciences, whether military science, politics or analytic jurisprudence, as such, has anything whatever to do with problems of justice, expediency, ethics, policy or any justification whatever of any particular use that is made of the physical force of the community. They are simply sciences of the technique of procedure in the organized employment of violence within a community, and, as such, have no functional relation whatever with any other aspect of social life. They deal with this instrument of force organized for efficiency, and not with the ends or consequences sought to be obtained by use of the instrument. Thus they are analytic and not functional sciences. If the military scientist, or the military man, runs over into a discussion of any function which physical force performs on behalf of any interest whatsoever, he becomes a politician, jurist, economist, or propagandist, outside the specialty of his own military science. So, if the political scientist goes outside the technique of procedure in formulating and communicating the commands of sovereignty, he goes over into the field of morals, ethics, economics. Likewise, the analytic jurist is concerned only with a special detail of the social relation of Might, belonging to the field of what is described as adjective law, [question mark in pencil in margin alongside] which is the mere technique of procedure, or process of law, distinguished from so-called substantive law, which is Due Process of Law. Substantive law is functional jurisprudence dealing with the social ends and consequences of judicial decisions, but analytic jurisprudence is the technique of procedure, from the point where a general rule has been issued, to the point where individuals are physically brought into court, compelled to testify, and the sheriff is instructed to execute the judgment. The legal conditions ["adjective and substantive" in pencil in margin], distinguished from the economic or functional conditions upon the occurrence of which the court asserts jurisdiction and sets in motion its executive officers with their physical force, are merely technical circumstances recognized in the procedure as "operative facts," and they end with the legal consequences of physical compulsion, distinguished from economic or social consequences, at the hands of similar executive officers with similar physical compulsion. [In margin: "Conditions: Act: law, proce[dure]. Result: writ]

There is here no question of the social or economic functions of the judiciary, either as to the social origins or social aims or consequences of judicial process, and hence no question of justice or injustice, morals or economics, and no question of right or wrong except as contained in the metaphorical statement that obedience to the commands of the sovereign is right and disobedience is wrong. Yet obedience and disobedience are neither right nor wrong—these are functional terms derived from ethics or custom or subjective opinion. Analytic jurisprudence deals only with commands [question mark in pencil alongside in margin; words "conditions" and "precedent" in pencil above], obedience and disobedience, regardless of whether they are ethically wrong, or economically good or bad.

A certain person, for example, performs an act or neglects to perform an act, in disobedience to the general command in question. This act or neglect is deemed by the court to be an "operative fact" in that it sets up, in the person of some one else who alleges—not that he is injured, for that is a functional concept—but who alleges that the general command has been disobeyed—or in the person of a public prosecutor—who alleges not that the public is injured but that the sovereign command has been disobeyed [question mark in pencil in margin]—a legally recognized authorization to require the court to act. This act of the court sets in motion the physical force of sovereignty, by way of bringing in the parties and witnesses and ends in a decision guided by the aforesaid general rule, accompanied by an order ["writ" in pencil above] addressed to the proper executives requiring them either to impose or not impose the physical force entrusted to them, to the extent and in the way directed by the court.

The late Professor W.N. Hohfeld distinguished two terms, in common use among analytic jurists, that indicate this procedure of sovereignty in the decisions of disputes arising between private citizens, and while the fitness of his terms has been contested, yet their meaning, as he uses them, is plain. The terms are Power and Liability. A person claiming that a general command has been violated by another person has the power, by which is meant the legally recognized authorization, to bring a suit in court, whereby the court is required, according to the rules that govern procedure, to bring in the defendant and witnesses, conduct an investigation, punish perjury, make a decision based on findings of fact and law, and issue an order to the officers of the court. Thus the term power indicates, not that the plaintiff is an injured person, nor that he has rights that have been violated, but that he has a "right of action" in that he is a functionary of the court, authorized, as a prosecuting witness, to set the juristic procedure of sovereignty in motion.

Opposite to Power is Liability. Liability is the situation of the defendant who is compelled to submit to the decision and order of the court in that he must or must not perform the act ordered or forbidden, on penalty of the exercise of force by the officers of the court. Thus the measure of the authority of the plaintiff, metaphorically known as his legal capacity or legal ability or "power," is simply the extent of his authorization as a functionary of the court to require the physical force of sovereignty to be brought into action, and this power is exactly the same thing as the liability of the defendant upon whom this physical force is exercised. Thus we have the legal correlation and equivalence of power and liability, which are the two sides of the identical physical force of sovereignty.

But this so-called power, which is simply an authorization to set the physical force of sovereignty in motion, goes further than a suit asking for a penalty or compensation on account of violation of a general rule of the sovereign distinguished as Remedial Powers. It also includes authorization of the citizen to issue specific commands or instructions changing the legal relations of himself or other persons, which commands then are enforced as though they were the general commands of the sovereign himself. These may be named the substantive powers of the citizen. When a citizen, for example, accepts an offer and then creates a contract, or when he makes a will or appoints an attorney or agent, he thereby issues instructions to the courts and officers to use the physical force of the community, if necessary, to enforce the contract, recognize the appointment, transfer the title, or execute the will. This substantive power of instructing the court what to do is correlative and equal to the liability of other persons, but in the use of their substantive power the term liability may indicate benefits, instead of penalties, conferred on other persons.

These benefits and injuries, however, belong to functional jurisprudence and not analytic jurisprudence. These remedial and substantive powers of the citizen are for him an important function which he expects sovereignty to perform for him, but from the standpoint of analytic jurisprudence the courts enforce his commands not on behalf of the citizen but in compliance with the general rules of the sovereign. This contract, or agency, or will, if it thus conforms to the general commands, becomes then the grounds on which either himself or another party obtains the aforesaid remedial power of authorization to bring a suit and set in motion the aforesaid acts of physical force, imposing a penalty or compensation on account of violation of the general commands. The special command of the individual is thus deemed to be a general command of the sovereign.

Thus the juristic meaning of power, as used by Hohfeld in strictly analytic jurisprudence, is the authorization granted by the sovereign to the subject, on the occasion of an operative fact, to set in motion the physical force of the sovereign, and thus execute the will of the subject, wherever the latter is legally authorized to bring suit or to create such new legal relations as contracts, wills, agencies or transfers of title. And the juristic meaning of liability is that some physical force of the sovereign employed, or expected to be employed, upon a subject who disobeys the general rules of the sovereign, including the specific commands of himself or other subjects which conform to the general rule.

If, on the other hand, the court decides that there is no disobedience of a general rule including an authorized specific command of a citizen, then evidently the sovereign physical force is refused on behalf of the plaintiff by the identical act that refuses to employ that force upon the defendant. This negation of sovereign physical force is logically expressed by the negatives, no-power, no-liability, but to it the terms disability and immunity have been technically ascribed by Hohfeld in the terminology of analytic jurisprudence.

The question, however, has been debated whether these terms of negation are actually legal concepts,[1] since they are a _denial_ of the use of sovereign force, and if legal concepts signify only the _use_ of physical force, then, logically, the not-using physical force is not an act of sovereignty. If we say that a certain thing is "no-man," then we cannot, of course, say at the same time that it _is_ a man. So if we say that a certain procedure is no-sovereign-act-of-physical-force we cannot say that it _is_ a sovereign act of physical force. A not-man is anything else in the universe except a man, and a no-power-no-liability is anything else in the universe except sovereign-physical force. From this analytic point of view, it follows that only the terms power and liability, and not the terms disability and immunity, are legal terms, indicating solely the legal conditions which set in motion the physical force controlled by the court (power), and the legal consequences resulting from the use of that force (liability).

It is evident, however, that the analytic jurist as well as the laws and constitutions which use the correlative terms disability-immunity, do not have the whole universe in mind, as might be the case if they employed only the terms no-power-no-liability. They do have in mind a specific person who has "no-power," that is, a specific person who is not permitted to use the force of sovereignty as an instrument in carrying out his will against another person.

If he is permitted to use that force he has a legal power and the opposite person is under a legal liability—if not permitted to use it he is under a legal disability and the opposite person thereby enjoys immunity. Hence "disability" is not the mere negation of power in the logical sense of contradiction, but is the refusal to permit a specific person to use that power against a other person, in which case the latter enjoys that highly valuable result of functional jurisprudence—immunity.

It will thus be seen how impossible it is to separate the functional aspect of jurisprudence from strictly analytic jurisprudence. And this is simply because sovereignty does not stand alone in its analytic nakedness but it is an organized instrument of physical force which individuals endeavor to use in order to enforce their own will upon the wills of other people, or which they endeavor to prevent other people from using in their efforts to enforce their will on self. Sovereignty is an instrument of private purposes, like an axe or a gun, and its functional significance turns on who can or cannot use it, and how far and when he can use it, for himself or against others. If individuals can employ this instrument then they are deemed to have legal power (privileges in the 5th and 14th amendments); if they can prevent others from employing this instrument, then they have immunity. Sovereign privileges and immunities are the two desirable economic instruments, privileges indicating the power of self to impose the physical force of sovereignty, to which others are thereby liable, and immunities indicating the disabilities of others to impose that physical force on self. It is simply because sovereignty is an instrument and not an entity, that analytic jurisprudence has not been worked out logically by Anglo-American jurists but has always terminated in a functional jurisprudence.[2]

Thus functional jurisprudence is the instrument of which analytic jurisprudence is the technique. The business man, laboring man or economist must not, and indeed, cannot fully grasp the technicalities in all their complexity, but he is concerned with the use that is made of the instrument in obtaining economic results. He is concerned with the privileges or powers, in the sense of ability to make a contract, draw a will, appoint an agent, transfer titles, bring a suit and get a judgment; thus imposing his will on others; and he is concerned with immunities, which are the disabilities of other persons to impose their will on him, through the instrumentality of the community's organized physical force.

It is this functional relation of law to economics that converts the powers, liabilities, immunities and disabilities of jurisprudence into the assets and liabilities of business. The liabilities of a business concern are the money values of the debts which are, at the same time, the assets of other business concerns, in that, if necessary, other concerns have a legal power to get a judgment and execution upon the indebted concern. Thus they are properly named "incorporeal property" in that they are the reciprocal relations of legal power and legal liability employed in the enforcement of contracts.

But the assets of the concern are not only the money values of these debts enforceable by an order of the court imposing upon other persons the positive acts of performance in paying the debt—the assets are also the market values of expected orders of the court, if necessary, imposing on other persons the negative acts of avoidance or forbearance. These are the so-called rights in rem ["Hohfeld?" in pencil above the line], known as the tangible property of buildings, lands, machinery, and the intangible property of goodwill, patents, rights of access to market, and so on. Yet the terms rights and property, as thus used, belong to functional jurisprudence and not analytic jurisprudence. Analytically they are the expected power or authorization of the citizen, as a functionary of the court, to require the physical force of sovereignty to impose acts of avoidance or forbearance upon any person who might trespass on the property or obstruct the access to markets or infringe on the complainants' market by taking away his customers or laborers, by forbidden methods of obstruction or infringement. As a consequence of these forbidden acts the tangible and intangible property is both created by law and has a market value, and the power to obtain the aid of sovereignty to enforce avoidance and forbearance on others in general, is consequently reckoned as business assets. Thus the assets of business are, in part, the expected Legal Power of the citizen, authorized as a prosecuting functionary of the court, to require the physical force of sovereignty to be employed in requiring those acts of performance, avoidance and forbearance of other people, which economically constitute their liabilities, and his assets. The expected acts of performance are, from the functional standpoint, the incorporeal property known as debts, and the expected acts of avoidance and forbearance, also from the functional standpoint, are the tangible property and physical goods and the intangible property of access to markets.

But the assets of a business concern are not only the legal powers to give special commands enforceable at law, or, as a prosecuting witness to get a judgment and execution against other persons; they are also the inability of other persons to get a judgment and execution against the concern. From the standpoint of functional, though not analytic, jurisprudence, this is the disability of other persons and the immunity of the business concern. Disability, from the analytic standpoint, is simply the negation of power, that is, the denial to the complaining witness that he has authority, under the circumstances, to set in motion the physical force of sovereignty, and this is the same as a denial of liability, that is, it is an immunity of the concern against whom the complaint is made. Functionally, this immunity from the physical force of sovereignty is one of the big assets of business, equally great with the legal powers (privileges). While legal power is ability to get a judgment and execution against other persons (or to transfer to other persons by sale or will the power to get such a judgment), legal immunity is the disability of other persons to get a judgment and execution against self. To the extent of this disability of others, which is the immunity of self, the business concern possesses that which, in its functional aspect, is economic liberty. Reciprocally, one's own disabilities are a limitation on his own assets, for they signify, either his legal inability to give specific commands enforceable at law, or his inability to get judgment and execution on other persons. If he cannot make contracts and appoint agents or transfer titles, or get the court to award judgments requiring acts of performance, avoidance or forbearance on the part of other persons, evidently, to that extent, his disability reduces his assets.

Thus, from the standpoint of functional jurisprudence, distinguished from analytic jurisprudence, the assets and liabilities of business are the function of force enlarging and limiting the economic opportunities, economic power and economic competition of business. The assets are the legal powers to use force and the legal immunities from the use of force—known in the constitutional law of the Fifth and Fourteenth Amendments as Privileges and immunities— the powers (or privileges) being the legal ability to get the physical force of sovereignty to require performance, avoidance or forbearance on the part of others, and the immunities being the legal disabilities of others to require performance, avoidance or forbearance on the part of self.

The deductions from the limits to these assets are the liabilities and disabilities of the concern, the liabilities being the power of others to require the force of sovereignty to compel the positive performance of paying debts, which of course is a deduction from assets, and the disabilities being the inability to require by the force of sovereignty, performance, avoidance or forbearance on the part of others, which is evidently a limitation of assets.

Finally, it is these same assets and liabilities that constitute the capital and capitalization of economic theory. These economic concepts require the introduction of other functions, operating along with sovereignty, the first of which to be noted is scarcity

II. Scarcity

Analytic economics has to do solely with the functions of scarcity just as analytic jurisprudence has to do solely with the function of violence. Its highest development has been that of the so-called psychological, especially the Austrian economists. The "economic man" of those analytic economists is an abstraction of scarcity, just as the jurisprudential man of the analytic jurists is an abstraction of force, from the other social relations of man, as well as from its own functional relation to the other functions.

Each function has, indeed, its basis in the self-interest of man that arises from scarcity of resources relative to wants, but sovereignty is the ["organized" lined out in pen] pursuit of self-interest by way of organized violence, and economics is the pursuit of self-interest by way of organized production and exchange. If priority were to be given to one or the other of these abstractions from the social mass, the priority might plausibly be assigned to sovereignty, because production and exchange cannot be conducted without the law and order maintained by organized physical force. But priority cannot be assigned. The relation between sovereignty and economics is functional. Each modifies the other. Historically superior men made their living by conquest so that slavery and serfdom were the types of economics that functioned with the corresponding types of sovereignty. The relation is just as intimate and functional in modern times, though each is differently organized, such that the powers, liabilities, immunities and disabilities of the jurists become the assets and liabilities of business and the capital and capitalization of both business and economics.

The analytic economics of the classical school took scarcity for granted, and it was the hedonic school that analyzed and perfected its formula. They extracted, specialized, isolated and organized the scarcity relation of wants to resources, leading up to the procedure of a modern market, just as the analytic jurists did for the violence relation of superior to inferior, leading up to the procedure of a modern court of law. It was the elaboration of this universal function of scarcity, similar to the elaboration of the universal function of force, that created the so-called exact science of economics, with its equilibrium of demand and supply, resulting in changes in price and the details of this equilibrium appeared as the theory of diminishing utility, increasing disutility, marginal utility, complementary goods, rent surpluses, and so on.

This field of inquiry is properly designated analytic economics, for its essential method consists in eliminating all other functions under the name of "friction," the inference being that friction was something extraneous to the pure science of economics and would be eliminated if all individuals were perfectly free, infinitely intelligent, and absolutely equal. In other words, the exact science of economics eliminated the "frictions" caused by sovereignty, custom and futurity, by assuming that the latter were not only constant, but also operated equally upon equal individuals, and then worked out the formula of scarcity along with differential advantages occasioned by differences in efficiency of individuals and differences in the productivity of nature's resources.

This analytic economics is of course essential, for the principle of scarcity operates in all transactions, but when it is functionally linked up with the principle of sovereignty, then it is no longer an exact science but is an expectation of that interaction of scarcity and force known as the social relation of assets and liabilities, as well as the interaction between individuals and concerns of varying legal and economic situations and varying legal and economic powers, distinguishable as the scarcity relation in its several dimensions of opportunity, power and competition.

These varying functional relations may be set forth in the following formula in which B and B' are buyers and S and S' are sellers:

Force Relation	Scarcity Relation	Force Relation
	Opportunity	
Power	B (competition) B′	Liability
Disability		Immunity
	Power	
Immunity		Disability
	Competition	
Liability	S (opportunity) S′	Power

III. Futurity

Analytic psychology may be, for our purposes, divided into two branches, physiology and expectation. Physiology should explain the nervous structure and the repetitions of stimulus and response known as habit, while expectation would be explained as the capacity to modify present behavior in consideration of future happenings. The corresponding functional psychology, for economic purposes, is the custom and volition.[3]

We have to do here with the latter, which is merely expectation operating as a function which modifies present acts in view of expected acts. The expected acts to be considered are the sovereign acts of courts of law and the individual acts of buyers, sellers, et al. Hohfeld, in his analytic jurisprudence, develops eight concepts from the usages of the courts, indicating that they represent that number of jural positions occupied by individuals with reference to other individuals. I submit, however, that from the standpoint of functional jurisprudence, for economic theory, these may be reduced to four present expectations of which the other four are the expectancies. The present expectations are the four social positions which he names right, duty, privilege and no right, but which from the standpoint of their functioning in economics, may be named right, duty, liberty and exposure. These correspond to the four expected juristic positions, from the analytic standpoint, namely Power, Liability, Immunity and Disability. In other words, the four legal positions of individuals in their transactions known as rights, duties, liberties (no-duty) and exposures (no-right) are the economic expectations of judicial and executive acts of sovereignty to which the individual stands related in the four possible positions of power (privilege), liability, immunity and disability.

This suggestion conforms to what has already been said respecting assets and liabilities, which are such on account of expected scarcities and expected powers (privileges) and immunities. But the present tense of these future powers and immunities is the rights and liberties of business in the field of economic opportunities, economic powers and economic competition.

This suggestion, I shall attempt to experiment with upon the illustrative cases and interpretations set forth by Corbin.[4] The experiment requires two lines of inquiry. First, whether the concepts of right, duty, liberty and exposure may correctly be considered to be functionally the present equivalents to the expected powers and liabilities, immunities and disabilities; and Second, whether, if Hohfeld had applied his analysis to cases in what I shall call political law, as well as private law, he would have found it more convenient to have reserved the terms power, liability, immunity, disability for political law and the terms, right, duty, privilege (liberty) and no-right (exposure) for private law.

1.   Equivalence of Present Rights and Future Powers.

Corbin lays the foundation for this distinction in his definitions of "operative facts," "evidential facts," "legal relations," "intellectual conceptions," and "societal consequences." An operative fact is "any fact the existence or occurrence of which will cause new legal relations between persons. A clear distinction" he continues, "should always be observed between physical phenomena and the legal relations consequent thereto. The former are in the world of the senses, the latter are intellectual conceptions...An evidential fact is any fact the existence or occurrence of which tends to prove the existence of some other fact...Evidential facts may themselves be operative as well, but need not be...When we state that some particular legal relation exists we are impliedly asserting the existence of certain facts and we are expressing our present mental concept of the societal consequences that will normally follow in the future."

It is here submitted that the only pragmatic or realistic meaning which can be given to the term "intellectual conception" is that of expectations of what will happen. From the scientific standpoint of a disinterested observer, an intellectual conception is a formula indicating the relations between parts or between the parts and the whole. But from the pragmatic standpoint of the person who is actually engaged in transactions, his intellectual conceptions are his mental formula of what may be expected to follow if he acts or does not act in such or such a way. Now it is his acting in such or such a way that constitutes an evidential fact or an "operative fact."

Corbin designates an "operative fact" as a "physical phenomenon" in the "world of the senses." But, from the standpoint of the persons engaged in the transaction, it is a physical phenomenon carrying with it an expectation, and an expectation, if consciously formulated, is exactly an expectation of that judicial behavior which the analytic jurist indicates will follow an "operative fact." If, for example, a person sells a house or makes a contract, or a will, or employs an agent or laborer, he "causes new legal relations between persons" in the sense that, from his standpoint, he expects the courts will enforce his will as indicated. [In margin: Give a 3rd person right to set court in motion—i.e., probation.] What he does in all these cases is to indicate, by a physical act, his will that the titles to goods shall be acquired, transferred or modified, and the "new legal relations" are those expected changes of ownership, title, or property. His will thus expresses by a physical act an evidential and operative fact for the court, but for him, the physical act is performed because he expects that the court will act, if necessary, in conformity to what the evidence shows he expected when he performed the act.

Now what he expects is that the courts will recognize him as having a power and other persons as having a correlative liability, that is, the courts will recognize his act as an "operative fact" and thereby will enforce his will in the matter. Or he expects that the courts will not recognize it as an operative fact, in which case he expects that no other person will be able to set the law in motion to prevent, restrain or punish him. What he here expects is immunity for self, correlative to the disability expected for any other person who might be concerned in the matter.

It is apparent, then, that the terms "operative facts" and "evidential facts" can be looked at from either the analytic or the functional standpoint. From the analytic standpoint operative and evidential facts are to be looked upon as creating new legal relations distinguished as new powers, liabilities, immunities and disabilities, which have to do with the use of sovereign physical force; but from the functional standpoint of private citizens, engaged in transactions and looking forward to the expected acts of sovereignty, these same present transactions are the daily facts which constitute the whole of their economic behavior and which, from the standpoint of expected physical force, are their present legal rights, duties, liberties and exposures.

It follows that all operative and evidential facts, from the standpoint of participants in economic transactions, are, at the same time, "intellectual conceptions" of the expectations by the participants, of those powers, liabilities, immunities and disabilities, that the parties will enjoy or suffer at the hands of those who exercise the force of sovereignty. And it is to these expectations of the way in which the law will determine their relations to each other that the functional legal terms, rights, duties, liberties and exposures, are appropriate. Rights and liberties are expectations of powers and immunities, while exposures and duties are expectations of disabilities and liabilities.

Corbin's language lends color to this interpretation based on the principle of Futurity, for he says, "When we state that some particular legal relation exists, we are impliedly asserting the existence of certain facts, and we are expressing our present mental concept of the societal consequences that will normally follow in the future. A statement that a legal relation exists between A and B is a prediction as to what society, acting through its courts or executive agents, will do or not do for one and against the other. If A invades B's house, we are able to predict that the police will eject A, that a court will give judgment for damages, and that the sheriff will levy execution. We say that B had a right that A should not intrude and that A had a duty to stay out. But if B had invited A to enter, we know that those results would not occur. In such cases we say that B had no right that A should stay out and that A had the privilege of entering.[5]

Here it will be seen that, if we convert the terms no-right and privilege into their functional economic equivalents, exposure and liberty, then the terms, rights, duties, liberties and exposures, are the present expectations of the future powers, liabilities, immunities and disabilities, that A or B would enjoy or suffer if the matter came to trial in court on the evidence of the operative facts of entering the house with or without permission.

Here, also, we distinguish between "legal consequences" and "economic consequences." Corbin's "societal consequences" are intended to signify "society" in the sense of the organized function of force, operating through courts and executives, but this is properly to be distinguished as "legal consequences" to which the analytic terms powers, liabilities, immunities and disabilities may property be restricted. Economic consequences, however, are intended to signify "society" consequences in the sense of the function of scarcity operating in the threefold relation of competition, opportunity and power (prices), and to these "societal consequences" the functional terms, rights, duties, liberties and exposures may properly be applied. Legal consequences are merely the use of force without regard to social consequences; but economic consequences are the social consequences of scarcity resulting from the legal consequences. Both are "societal," but legal consequences are the expected use of society's physical force at the hands of the sheriff and others, while economic consequences are the expected resultant use of scarcity at the hands of buyers, sellers, borrowers, lenders and others. Legal consequences pertain to analytic jurisprudence, but economic consequences to functional jurisprudence. Both are indeed expectations but the one is expectation of society's use of force, the other society's use of scarcity, and the two are functionally interdependent in all economic transactions.

It remains to inquire whether the other illustration given by Corbin can similarly be reduced to this functional relation of futurity existing between the present acts of citizens and the expected acts of sovereignty. It may be conceded that, from the technical standpoint of analytic jurisprudence, Hohfeld's eight terms have a useful coordinate relation, for they are similar to the coordinated concepts of Salmond and Terry. The question, however, which is here sought to be answered from the functional standpoint, is whether the four terms of present expectations can be broadly enough defined to be made equivalent to all the meanings of the four terms of future acts of sovereignty expected. That is, can the present rights, duties, liberties, exposures, as seen by participants in transactions be considered the parallel equivalents of the future powers, liabilities, immunities, disabilities, as seen by the analytic jurists? This is a question of terminology useful for the correlation of law and economics, and is not a question of objective reality, for even the technical terms of analytic jurisprudence are mere intellectual conceptions designed to help the analyst think clearly, and whether they fit or do not fit the objective reality is largely a question of what part of reality we are interested in.

Corbin gives four illustrations in popular terms, each of which we shall endeavor to convert from analytic jurisprudence to the functional jurisprudence of scarcity and futurity.

"1. If we determine that A may conduct himself in a certain way he has a privilege with respect to B and B has no-right that A shall not so conduct himself."

The term privilege here employed has a valuable technical meaning in private law, but it is also, along with the term "immunity," a very important term of constitutional law (political law) and hence we reserve the term privilege for that system where we consider it to be equivalent to the term power, as elsewhere used by Hohfeld and Corbin. In place of the term "privilege" we substitute the functional economic term "liberty," in the sense of no-duty, as the equivalent of Hohfeld's private law meaning of privilege and the correlative of his private-law "no-right." This term "liberty" is not employed by Hohfeld for the apparent reason that its historic associations connect it with the private activities of business or labor, but it is exactly on account of this functional significance for economics that "liberty" is preferable to "privilege." Legal privilege is analytic, but legal liberty is the functional equivalent for economics.

Now the functional relation in jurisprudence, which is parallel to legal liberty and is that expected relation of which legal liberty is the expectation, is simply the expectation of immunity, the expectation that the physical force of sovereignty will not be employed against the individual, in that he performs no "operative fact" that sets up in any one else a legal power to set the wheels of law in motion against him.

If this change from the analytic term privilege to the functional term liberty is made, then all the more should a change be made from Hohfeld's analytic "no right" which in strictness has neither jural nor economic significance (Kocourek, Pound) to the functional term "exposure." For, if a person B "has no right, that A shall not so conduct himself," then B is evidently exposed to either a benefit or a damage if A does "so conduct himself." But if the exposure is a damage, because he has no-right, the evident meaning is that he may expect that he cannot obtain the aid of a court to prevent the damage or get a judgment for damages and order the sheriff to levy execution. This is none other than the expectation of disability, which is the expectation of no-power. This is a highly important economic relation, for it signifies that the conduct of the opposite party, A, is "privileged" when it comes to a trial in court, and it is exactly this "privileged" conduct that is meant when we speak of "free competition" or economic liberty. For free competition causes immense damage to competitors, by depriving them of customers or laborers, compelling them to cut prices, go into bankruptcy, and so on, all of which occurs, in part, because the competitors have no-power to get a court to prevent the competition or give damages. The colorless analytic term "no right" is none other than the very colorful functional term "exposure" to which every business man and every workingman knows he is subjected by his inability to get a court of law to stop or mitigate the competition that distresses him.

We have thus used the functional term "liberty" in place of the technical analytic term "privilege," to indicate that absence of duty in matters of economics which we call opportunity, power and competition, and it is apparent that the correlative term exposure to damage by virtue of that liberty or competition is the functional economic equivalent of that liberty. Thus legal exposure is the present economic situation parallel to an expected legal disability and correlative to that liberty of others which is their expected immunity.

2. Corbin goes on: "It we determine that A must conduct himself in a certain manner he has a duty to B, and B has a right against A."

What we have said above will serve to explain also this proposition. If B has a legal right against A, it means that in a transaction with A he has a present expectation that he will have in the future, if occasion arises, a legal power to bring a suit against A and get judgment and execution. Thus the legal right of B is his present expectation of future legal power, and the correlative legal duty of A is his present expectation of a future legal liability, should the suitable operative facts occur.

3 and 4. Corbin's analytic use of the terms power, liability, immunity and disability is as follows: "If we determine that by his own voluntary act A can Change B's legal relation with A (or with x), A has a legal power and B has a liability. If we determine that A cannot by his own voluntary act change the legal relations of B, then A has a disability and B has an immunity."

It will be noted here that Corbin, following Hohfeld, has changed his principle of classification from that which determined his analysis in 1 and 2. In the illustration of rights, duties, privileges and no-rights his principle was, What may the parties expect if the present rights come to a trial in court? The terms, right, etc. are predictions that a court will or will not give judgment, etc., in which case the right of one is equal to a correlative duty to act or to forbear on the part of the others. In other words the expectation is that of the relation of plaintiff and defendant in a trial court. There is here, therefore, a correlative duty. But in numbers 3 and 4 there is no correlative duty—there is simply a power to change legal relations by selling and buying, borrowing and lending, making a will, creating an agency, etc. The term liability, therefore, is employed because there is no duty, correlative to a right—there is only a power to change legal relations, and the term liability signifies, not a duty enforced in court, but an expectation that his legal relations will be changed by the acts of buying, borrowing, hiring, and so on.

This change in one's legal relations is a change in his expectations of the judgments he may expect to get in a trial at court, that is, a change in his expected powers, liabilities, immunities, and disabilities, resulting from changes in ownership. It is the distinction we have sought to make by the terms remedial powers and substantive powers, with their correlatives and opposites. Remedial powers are powers to get a judgment in court, but substantive powers are powers to authorize other people to get judgments in court. Both are in the future, and the present expectations of both are the rights of the present with their correlatives and opposites. But, in the case of remedial powers the expectations are immediately those of a certain judgment in court if the present expectations are violated, while in the case of substantive powers, the expectations are those of a different judgment in court, owing to a different set of rights brought about by a change that has voluntarily been made in the expectations of the parties.

This so-called change in legal relations is a new set of instructions directed to the court by the parties, and hence a new set of remedial powers that may be expected if a violation of the new set [of] expectations occurs. Whatever technical names may be given from the standpoint of analytic jurisprudence, it would seem, that from the functional standpoint, the term rights, duties, liberties and exposures are appropriately fitted to the expectations of both remedial and substantive powers, liabilities, immunities and disabilities. From the remedial standpoint a legal right is an expectation of power to get a certain set of judgments for the violation of existing rights or liberties, but from the substantive standpoint a legal right is an expectation of power to get or authorize others to get a different set of rights or liabilities. What is meant is that from the functional standpoint, rights have been transferred, or modified, as when goods are bought and sold, when money is borrowed and loaned, when labor is hired and fired, etc.

Another consideration may be noted. The term "power" has come into use recently as a substitute for what Bentham (followed by Holland) called "divestitive" facts, or "transitive" facts. Their economic significance, like the economic significance of Hohfeld's equivalent term "power," is simply transfers of ownership. From the functional standpoint this is the "right" or "liberty" to buy and sell, etc., which could not be enjoyed if the physical fact of transferring goods were not accompanied by the legal fact of transferring title to the goods. Thus what the new term "power" signifies is that Bentham's and Holland's term "transitive fact"—the physical fact of delivery of goods—is now looked upon as an "operative fact" in that it calls into being a "power" of the seller or buyer to transfer the title of ownership.

The predicament, however, arises, that there is here no liability of any private citizen to the use of force, correlative to the power to have force used if necessary in order to sanction the transfer of title. Yet it is submitted there is a correlative—it is the liability of courts, sheriffs, and similar officials, and the power of the citizen is none other than this liability of the officials to execute his will in the transfer of goods and alienation of title. This legal relation between citizen and official belongs, however, not to private law but to what we distinguish as political law.

2.   Private Law and Political Law.

The second question which we raised above was, Whether the terms power, liability, immunity, disability, are better to be reserved for the field of political law, leaving the terms right, duty, liberty, exposure for private law. We employ the term "political law" to indicate the law governing the relations between officials and citizens, contrasted with private law governing the relations between citizens. In continental jurisprudence the equivalent term is "public law," and on the continent this term has a precise meaning because it is the law of administrative courts. But in the Anglo-American system, the disputes between public officials and private citizens, since the Revolution of 1689, have been subjected to trial in the same courts as those which determine the disputes between private citizens. Hence the term "public law" with us is reserved for the rights of the general body of the people as against individuals. This is not what we mean by political law. We mean the equivalent in general, though not in detail, with the continental public law, and also the law of our written constitutions.

Thus political law, in the American system, may be considered to include three types of reciprocal rights in the sovereign relation between officials and citizens.

1.   The rights, etc., of citizens relative to executives who enforce the physical sanctions of sovereignty, all of which may be illustrated in the office of sheriff. This is the law of executives.
2.   Rights, etc., of citizens relative to trial courts and appellate courts where the investigations, findings of fact and interpretations of law are conducted, upon which the sheriff is authorized to act. This is the law of tribunals.
3.   Rights, etc., of citizens relative to any official arising out of the provision of written constitutions. This is constitutional law.

The functional economic significance of this analysis may be seen in the many cases of dispute arising out of the relations between employer and employee, corporations and customers, etc. In order to analyze this functional significance and connect it up with analytic jurisprudence I shall build upon the circumstances of two illustrative cases, one arising out of the employer-employee relation (accident compensation), the other out of the buyer-seller relation (Pittsburgh Plus).

An employee claims compensation or damages on account of accident to be paid to him by his employer. His claim, so far, is merely a moral claim, since his only method of enforcing it against the will of his employer is by the consensus of opinion of those whose goodwill the employer feels bound to retain. There are five separate groups with five interests somewhat separated, to whose expected goodwill this employer might feel obligated. There are his fellow-employers as competitors, or other employers similarly situated respecting this employer-employee relation. Second, the consumers of his products whose goodwill he desires to retain. Third, the goodwill of the fellow-workmen, who are similarly situated with the one who makes the claim. Fourth, the goodwill of bankers, usually known as good credit. To which must be added, fifth, a favorable attitude of the legislative, judicial and executive officials of government.

These goodwill relations are evidently economic as well as moral. If they were solely moral relations then the proper term applicable to them would be good opinion rather than good will. If the employer is sensitive to the mere opinions of others, he is probably not a successful business man. For the sanction to which he then feels bound is only the nominal penalty of losing a part of the conflicting good opinion of employers, customers, employees and bankers. But if the loss of this good opinion begins to cost him the loss of customers, or employees, or business, or credit, then their good opinion begins to have that economic sanction which changes the dimensions of his assets and liabilities, and is therefore known to him as goodwill. Goodwill is the scarcity function of good opinion. It adds the economic sanctions of profit and loss to the moral sanctions of a good man. Good will is business, good opinion is morality.

Thus goodwill is the expected repetition of profitable transactions, but it is quite inseparable from the hoped-for good opinion of those whose transactions are profitable. It is apparently for this reason that juristic writers, in their distinctions between "positive morality" and "positive law," overlook the distinction between good opinion and goodwill. Pollock,[6] for example, following Austin, describes positive morality as "a rule set by an indeterminate body of men," and criticizes the analytic jurists who refuse to give to it the name of "law," because as they say, it is not re-enforced by the command of a political sovereign and the sanction of physical force. According to them, says Pollock, a primitive village community, wholly governed by "custom," would not be governed by "law" in the sense of positive law, and he suggests that we have here a "scientific law" rather than a "positive law."

Properly speaking, however, a scientific law has no sanctions—it is the mere repetition of events without any penalties imposed by the group, for violation of the uniformity of repetition. If "positive morality" sets positive laws to human beings, it must be because an alternative of obedience or punishment is set up by the group for each individual within its jurisdiction. If this punishment or sanction, is mere loss of good opinion—a strictly moral penalty—it is probably ineffective, because the individual can go on making his living or profits just the same. But if the economic penalty of loss of goodwill is added, then, according to the economic circumstances of the individual, it may have much greater coercive power than even the legal penalties of physical force. Or rather, under circumstances of great scarcity, where the opportunities for livelihood are limited, the economic sanctions may be so powerful as to dispense with the need of physical sanction.

This was evidently the case with primitive village communities, where the physical sanctions, though not wholly removed, were but dimly in the background. The scarcity of resources was so pressing that that was enough to compel everyone to conform to the customs, or perish. It is only in modern periods of abundance that the economic sanctions seem to retire, and the physical sanctions of sovereignty seem to be the only sanctions of "law." The analytic jurisprudence of Austin, which eliminated all economic sanctions under the generalization of positive morality, could not arise in periods of scarcity—it was an outcome of the wealth of England after the Eighteenth Century. In village communities it was not the will of a sovereign that made law, but the scarcity sanctions of fellow communists.

This generalization does not stop with village communities. It underlies much of the gild regulations prior to the period of Abundance, and, indeed, has been set forth by Loria and others to indicate the economic reasons for the abolition of serfdom and slavery, since, with the modern occupation of available natural resources the scarcity sanctions of the wage system may profitably be substituted for the physical sanctions of slavery.[7]

Similar considerations apply to the modern importance of goodwill as an asset of business. The supplies of materials, of labor, of credit, of consumer's purchasing power, are limited, and hence the economic loss by a falling off in profitable transactions is an increasingly powerful scarcity sanction, the avoidance of which is obedience to that "indeterminate body of men" whose expected patronage is known as goodwill.

If we examine the way in which this modern goodwill operates as the main asset of business, the examination will throw light upon the notion of "positive morality" as "a rule set by an indeterminate body of men," and thereby upon the concept of law in general. It certainly is not a "rule" in the sense of a "command" by a superior addressed to an "inferior." Yet it is to be distinguished from the individual transactions, that is, the mutual inducements, occurring between an employer and his individual employees, customers, fellow employers, bankers. Goodwill is more properly to be described as the expected repetition, duplication, variability and choice of transactions with others. By repetition is meant the continuance of present transactions. By duplication is meant both the expansion of the going business and the acquisition of new customers, laborers, et al. to take the place of those who drop out. By variability is meant the host of individual and cumulative changes in transactions arising from changes in any or all the elementary functional conditions of efficiency, scarcity, force and futurity. By choices is meant the policy of the business concern looking towards the future and adapting itself to these repetitions, duplications, variabilities and futurities.

Out of these four dimensions of transactions arises the modern concept of a going concern. A business is a going business if its participants expect that it will have a repetition and duplication of existing profitable transactions and will be able to maintain itself in the face of the many changes continually occurring in the social relation of efficiency, scarcity, force and expectation with their changes in production, marketing, legislation and judicial decision. It is to these expectations of profitable transactions that the three terms, Good Will, Custom and Sanction are applicable.

While the term "goodwill" has popularly been restricted to the goodwill of customers, yet the idea contained in the term is the same as that contained in the expectations of a labor market, a market for materials, a money market, and the expectations of favorable treatment by competitors and by legislatures, courts and policemen. Customer's goodwill is a special case of general goodwill and general goodwill is good opinion plus economic gain or loss.

Also the term custom; while this term has obtained in jurisprudence a technical legal meaning, yet even there its scope is always a matter of judgment in particular cases. The legal meaning is a special case of the universal trait of human nature upon which all expectations of the future are based, namely the expected repetition and duplication of behavior similar to its repetition and duplication in the past.

Now it is this repetition and duplication that constitutes Sanctions. An individual transaction is personal and even arbitrary, depending upon the personalities and economic and legal positions accepted by the parties. To these the term Inducements is applicable. But if these individual transactions are multiplied, repeated and not too highly variable, then they lose their personal and arbitrary character and become that "rule" set by an indeterminate body of men, which is not a "command" of a superior to an inferior, but is simply this expected repetition and duplication of inducements. To this [the] term sanctions is applicable, for the term refers, not to the inducements of individuals, but to the inducements of groups. Sanctions are the expected repetition and duplication of inducements, and the different kinds of sanctions and their differences in induciveness depend upon the different kinds of groups and the different instruments which they employ, the two principal ones being scarcity and force.

Thus the so-called "command" of analytic jurisprudence, derived as it was by Austin from the modern supremacy of the legislature, becomes a subordinate item, and the so-called "rule" set by a superior to an inferior, becomes merely the expected repetition, duplication and variability of the inducements which similar groups are expected to practice. It is a "rule" not because it has been commanded but because it is expected. This expected behavior of groups is the group sanction, and the expected limits which these sanctions impose on individuals in their transactions are their rights, duties, liberties and exposures, enforced partly by the expected moral sanctions of good opinion, the expected economic sanctions of goodwill and the expected physical sanctions of good government.

The defect, however, with the sanctions imposed by an indeterminate body of men is in their variability, their uncertainty as to the future, and their lack of cumulative power. For this reason, the two devices of organization and adjudication have been historically contrived in order to bring precision, promptness and efficiency by converting unorganized sanctions into organized sanctions.

Here, again, is another phase of that "positive morality" which analytic jurisprudence properly enough excludes from positive law, but it is not mere "morality," it is organization of the economic sanctions of Scarcity where positive law is the organization of the sovereign sanction of Force. Goodwill rests upon the sanctions imposed by an indeterminate body of men, by which is properly meant that the sanctions are unorganized. If these indeterminate bodies are able to accomplish an organization with power to regulate the acts of individual members, then, of course, their variable economic sanctions can be concentrated into a single concerted act. And if they go still further and authorize representatives to act for them as directors, general managers, business agents, tribunals, and so on, then their concentrated economic sanctions can be set forth as something to be more surely and accurately expected in the future as a ground on which individuals may be made to feel obliged to act now so as to avoid that threatened application of the sanction.

This again, according to the tenets of analytic jurisprudence, belongs to the field of positive morality and not to the field of positive law. Pollock pointed out the fallacy of those analytic jurists who set up the contention that the absence of a command of sovereignty is equivalent to a command to do what there was no command not to do. Applied, however, to the subject of concerted and organized economic sanctions which we are here considering, the absence of a legal command not to organize an association for concerted action, is complete only when there is a collateral command addressed to third parties not to interfere with the contracts or understandings by which the members agree to act in concert, as well as a collateral refusal to give injured parties a remedy at law. Pollock's dialectic answer overlooks the functional position of positive law as an instrument which individuals and groups reach out for when they seek to have the physical force of sovereignty employed where their concerted economic force is inadequate. Organized economic sanctions must have the aid of sovereignty, if not for the purpose of enforcing their understandings, at least for the purpose of preventing third parties from interfering with their own enforcement. These are matters to be dealt with when we come to the law of association under the subject of political law.

Returning to our illustrative case of an employee claiming compensation for an accident, there are five conceivable organizations that might be called into being for the use of economic sanctions relative to that claim:—an employer's association, a buyer's association, a seller's association, a banker's association and a labor union. Instances can be found where these several types of association are actually functioning, and they are therefore all to be comprehended in any complete analysis of the functioning of organized economic sanctions.

When, however, these associations have established themselves, such that the sanctions can be imposed promptly, there arises the need of tribunals which shall determine in particular cases the rights, duties, liberties and exposures of individuals in expectation of the powers and immunities and their opposites, which each shall have through the application of the organized economic sanctions. It is these tribunals that give greater uniformity to the sanctions and thus convert them from variable arbitrary and personal decisions, into that certainty of expectation which indicates the transition from custom to common law. In this way at least two systems of so-called voluntary adjudication have arisen in recent years, employing solely the scarcity sanctions, namely, labor arbitration and commercial arbitration. These may become compulsory arbitration, so-called, which merely signifies that the state consents to add its sanctions of force to their sanction of scarcity.[8]

We now come to political law proper in the sense of expectations of the physical sanctions of force and this we distinguish as the law of executives, the law of tribunals and constitutional law. If, in our illustrative case, the worker, who claims compensation against the will of his employer, cannot obtain the same either as a personal favor, nor by the unorganized economic sanctions of goodwill or the organized sanctions of collective bargaining and voluntary arbitration, he may evidently "go into politics" and perhaps get the legislature to lay down a rule giving him power to require the courts or administrative quasi-courts, to investigate and make findings of fact and interpretations of the law in his case. Austin speaks of these rules as "commands" issued by a politically superior to a politically inferior. But in America laws and constitution are not so much commands as they are expectations of court decisions. Under the American system of separation and independence of the legislative, executive and judicial branches of government, it cannot be figured out just what the law or constitution is until a court has decided the cases that come before it. The people and their lawyers do not look to the so-called commands issued in the past, they look to what they may expect the courts and executives will do relative to the particular transactions they are contemplating. They look forward to the sanctions and not backward to the command. Constitutions and laws are what the courts are expected to order the sheriff to do. They are dead letters from the start and rise to life only in the expected decisions of the courts and acts of the sheriff and police.

[In margin, the statement: "How about a case which may fit into several dif[ferent] rules?" not in Commons's handwriting.]

We begin, therefore, with the powers and immunities of the sheriff, and endeavor to discover what happens under the designation "due process of law." The sheriff's powers are his authorizations to use force and are contained in the writ or other process delivered to him out of the court. If he exceeds these powers or neglects to exercise them, he is liable as the case may be, to fine or imprisonment upon conviction, and is liable to an action at the suit of any party aggrieved, for damage sustained, in addition to the fine or imprisonment. In the case of certain judgments in civil action, the writ is even delivered to the plaintiff or his attorney, who then has the legal power to control the sheriff in levying execution, and the sheriff is bound to obey his instructions, but is not bound if, in his judgment, the instructions of the plaintiff will produce a greater sacrifice of property than the accompanying injury to the plaintiff on account of disobedience of the latter's instructions. He may require an indemnity bond from the plaintiff to protect him harmless against liability which he may incur for these acts done at the plaintiff's request.

If we arrange these various relations between citizens and sheriffs, as Hohfeld has done between citizens, we shall have the formula:

Citizen	Sheriff
Power	Liability
Disability	Immunity
Immunity	Disability
Liability	Power

The power of the citizen (privilege in the constitution) is his authorization to require the sheriff to use force against another person, and the correlative liability of the sheriff is his liability to action and damages in disobedience of these requirements. The sheriff's immunity is, of course, his absence of liability to plaintiff or defendant as above indicated, and this, in the case of the plaintiff, is his disability to require the use of force against the defendant. Reciprocally the same and other citizens have certain immunities, deducting from their liabilities, and these are the disabilities deducting from the powers of the sheriff to use force against the citizen.

These reciprocal relations have been worked out historically at great length and in detail, mainly by way of the decisions of the courts at common law, and it is not necessary to specify their many applications.[9] It is enough to notice the functional results that citizens may expect from these relations and to devise an appropriate terminology. The central point is the sanction, which is the expected authorization (power) of the sheriff to use force upon citizens, or the ise of force upon the sheriff himself, by other executives authorized to imprison or levy execution upon him.

The exercise of this sanction in a particular case has arisen out of a suit instituted by a plaintiff on the ground of disobedience of law on the part of a defendant. In other words, it has arisen out of an alleged right of the plaintiff to issue a command and the correlative duty of the defendant to obey the command. If the rightful command was not obeyed, that became the operative fact upon which the plaintiff acquired the power to require the sheriff to use force in order to compel obedience. To the defendant therefore is submitted the alternative, obedience or force. Obedience is the fulfillment of duty, force is the alternative sanction which he can avoid by obedience.

Thus, on analysis of what happens in process of law, we find that it is a choice of alternatives, and the term "liability" correctly signifies this opportunity of the defendant to make a choice between obedience and force. In ordinary language, however, this is not looked upon as a "choice." It is looked upon as "no-choice." He must obey or be forced to obey or pay damages if he does not obey. Yet the very statement of these contingencies indicates that he does have a choice. A liability is an expectation of obediences or force. What happens is that the choice is an alternative submitted by a superior to an inferior, whereas the customary concept of choice is an alternative submitted by equals. The one is coerced choice, the other is equal choice.

It is for this reason that we distinguish managerial transactions from bargaining transactions, corresponding to the distinction between sanctions and inducements, and the distinction between superiors and equals. All transactions are based on choices of alternatives by the participants in contemplation of expected consequences. But their economic differences turn on the presence, distance, absence and power of the several parties to the transaction. In our typical formula of a bargaining transaction there were two buyers and two sellers, indicating the three relations of opportunity, competition and economic power (price), as follows:

Opportunity

B   (Competition)   B'

Power

Competition

S   (Opportunity)   S'

If, from the standpoint of S, there is but one buyer, B, or an ineffective buyer, B', then B can force down the price that S receives, depending on their relative economic power. But S's power is limited by the competition of S', and if there is no such competitor present, or if he is an ineffective competitor not able to make an offer at a low price, then the power of S is likely to be greater, to the extent that he is relieved of this competition. Then, if both B' and S are absent altogether, the bargaining is that of an isolated relation between B and S unmodified by the opportunities and competitions that either might enjoy or suffer from equal access of others to the alternatives offered.

There are thus two types of bargaining transactions, the isolated and the competitive. In the isolated bargaining there are two parties, in the competitive bargaining there are four parties. Hence in the isolated bargaining each of the two parties, B and S, is submitting alternatives to the other, the alternative being, accept the offer or suffer the loss of non-acceptance. The relative power of the two is the relative injury to each of non-acceptance. It will thus be seen that the constituents of the alternatives are different in the isolated and the competitive transaction. In the latter the alternatives of gain and loss are offered through third and fourth parties having access to the market. In the isolated case the alternatives of gain and loss are offered by each of the two parties to the other.

But suppose that one of the parties, B, is in control of a physical force which the other does not control, the alternative then which B submits to S is, accept my offer or suffer my violence, whereas S can only submit the alternative to B, accept my service or quit your violence. The relative power of the two is the relative injury of non-acceptance and violence, and to this is appropriately given the name, managing transaction. It is managerial in that there are but two parties to the transaction, and that one submits to the other an alternative of suffering greater injury than he would suffer by performing the service, while the other cannot submit a similar alternative to the one. The managerial transaction and the preceding isolated transaction are both isolated, but the managing type differs from the bargaining type in that the alternatives are between scarcity and force, whereas in the bargaining they were between two degrees of scarcity.

So far, this managing transaction is pictured as isolated and not yet "institutionalized." It is slavery, but not the institution of slavery. It is merely a case of alternative inducements, without the sanctions of an institution. If next the inferior is not able, by calling upon the sheriff, to require the latter to prevent the superior from using violence, then his disability is the immunity of the superior. And if, at the same time, he is prohibited by the sheriff from using violence, and the one is authorized to call upon the sheriff, if necessary, to prevent his use of violence, then the liability of the latter to the authority of the sheriff is the power of the former to require the sheriff to use force and thus submit the alternatives of obedience or force at the hands of the sheriff. This is the institution of slavery supported by the sanctions of force, authorized by the group, and the managing transactions thus sanctioned are those of overseer and slave.

But the so-called "sanctions" of law are evidently not the actual use of force by the sheriff—they are the expected use of force implied in the authorization and obligations of the sheriff to use force if called upon, and since these authorizations and obligations are put into motion by the citizen, they are technically the reciprocal powers, liabilities, immunities and disabilities of the slave-owner, the slave and the sheriff. The slave has no privileges (powers) or immunities, indicating that the sheriff has correlatively no liabilities or disabilities, in relation to him, but also indicating that the owner has powers and immunities correlative to the liabilities and disabilities both of sheriff and slave. Thus the "sanctions" are not the actual use of force, but are the expected alternatives set forth within this meticulous analytic detail of authorizations and obligations. The sheriff, with his authorizations (powers, minus disabilities) and his obligations (liabilities minus immunities) to use force is the instrument by which the owner, in his managing capacity of overseer, is able to add the sanctions of organized collective force to his own inducements of managerial force. The sanctions and inducements are not the force itself, but are the expectations of the authorized use of force, and it is these expectations that constitute the rights and liberties of the owner and the duties and exposures of the slave.

If we take the next step in our analysis of historical and functional jurisprudence, we find it in the court decisions that followed the adoption of the Fourteenth Amendment which made the slaves citizens of the United States and prohibited any state making or enforcing any law abridging the privileges or immunities of such citizens. Here the term "privilege," if it is exclusive of "immunities," signifies the legal power to set in motion the judicial and executive officers in the exercise of remedial and translative (substantive) powers. This signifies that the exercise of force is eliminated except as exercised by the sheriff according to the process of law available to other citizens. Since the courts have enlarged this meaning of citizen to include corporations, which are associations of stockholders, bondholders and bankers, operating as a person through their managers and superintendents, for whom the use of force is prohibited, the inducements and sanctions now permitted turn on the use of scarcity instead of force, and the labor relation is changed from that of overseer and slave to that of foreman and worker. The two types of transactions operate, namely managing and bargaining transactions, but the sanctions and inducements are changed from force to scarcity. In the bargaining transactions the laborer is a seller and the going concern is the buyer, and the transactions are classified as similar to all other bargaining transactions, such as commodity transactions with other concerns, credit transactions with bankers, landlord and tenant transactions, etc. Here the principle of legal equality of access governs all participants and the resulting economic opportunities, competitions and powers are measured in the prices, whether it be the price of labor, commodities, of credits or of land and the lease of land.

This bargaining transaction, in the case of the labor relation, is that of employer and employee, but the managing transaction is that of foreman and worker. If we distinguish the bargaining from the managing transaction, there are four points of difference:

1. The bargaining transaction of employer-employee involves four parties, two competing employers and two competing employees, but the managerial transaction is isolated in that it involves only two parties, foreman and worker.

2. In the bargaining transaction a price is determined, the price of labor which is the money-income of the employee and the money outgo of the employer, the product-income of the employer and product-outgo of the employee. This is the relation of scarcity. But in the managerial transaction, it is the output of labor that is determined relative to the input of a quantity of labor, so that the relation is one of efficiency. The income-outgo relation is a price determined by scarcities, but the output-input relation is a quantity of product determined by efficiency of management.

3. In the bargaining transaction the parties are dealing with each other as individuals and the alternative expectations which they offer are properly designated inducements. In the managing transactions the foreman is the representative of a group of capitalists, partly owners, and partly creditors, and the alternative expectations which he submits to the worker are properly designated sanctions, since they are the alternatives of output or dismissal by a group of associates. Each kind of transaction is founded on control of scarcity, but the bargaining transaction is here named a scarcity inducement, since it is a relation between individuals, while the managing transaction is named a scarcity sanction since it is a relation between a group and an individual.

4. The legal powers and immunities of the bargaining transaction are the expected use of force by the sheriff or police to permit access to markets, even against consent of any of the parties; but the legal powers and immunities of the managerial transaction are the expected use of force by sheriff or police to prevent access without consent. The former, considered as present expectancies, are the legal rights and liberties of a market, but the latter are the rights and liberties of ownership. The former permits individuals to employ the inducements of scarcity in their bargaining transactions; the latter permits a group to employ the sanction of scarcity in its managerial transactions.

With these four distinctions in mind between bargaining and managing transactions it is apparent that the 14th Amendment brought about a transition from the inducements and sanctions of force to the inducements and sanctions of scarcity. Of course, the changing conditions of scarcity of labor output relative to expected prices to be paid to the employers by expected consumers, determine the relative strength of the inducements in the bargaining transactions and the relative strength of the sanctions in the managing transactions. In a period of unemployment, with a scarcity of jobs on account of expected scarcity of consumers' purchasing power, both the inducements to accept low wages and the sanctions to increase labor output are strengthened.

And they are weakened in periods of abundance. Public policy also enters to change the strength of the inducements and sanctions of scarcity, as seen in protective tariffs, immigration restrictions, taxing policies, and so on.

It is apparent, too, that a change from scattered employers to concentrated and integrated industry brings with it changes in both the inducements and sanctions of scarcity. The scope of managing transactions is enlarged and the organization of management is concentrated in the hands of superintendents and foremen, the sheriffs and under-sheriffs of industry employing the sanction of scarcity where the historic sheriff employed the sanction of force.

This analogy is permissible in that it follows the judicial process of reasoning by analogy in the functional process of adapting the older rules of law to changing economic conditions. The terms property, liberty and due process of law have been thus enlarged during the past fifty years (see Anglo-American Law and Economics) and it is, in fact, a rounding out of these enlargements by a similar process of reasoning by analogy that finds the similar industrial powers and immunities of the foreman employing the sanction of scarcity where formerly were employed the sanctions of force. When the terms privilege and immunity are enlarged from the physical sanction of the emancipated negroes to the scarcity sanctions of going concerns employing thousands and hundreds of thousands of workmen, the logic of the analogy is incomplete until the analogy between the sanctions of scarcity employed by the concerns and the preceding sanctions of force is also completed. Moreover, recent movements to regulate the sanctions of the foremen in industry are quite parallel to the historic process of British constitutional and common law in regulating the sanctions of the sheriff. What happens is that, with the arbitrary sanctions of force subjected to stable expectations, the arbitrariness of the sanctions of scarcity is being similarly reduced somewhat to stability.

LAW OF TRIBUNALS

In the historic case of the sheriff, this has occurred by inserting Tribunals between the sheriff and the citizen. Maitland's historic statement has frequently been quoted;- "the whole history of English justice and police might be brought under this rubric—the Decline and fall of the sheriff."[10] From a time when he was the "first man of the county" representing the monarch, he has become a subordinate of the court whose findings of fact and writs addressed to him determine his authority and obligations in the use of force. (This and constitutional law to be developed.)

We thus reach the functional and analytic distinction between substantive law and adjective law. Substantive law is the expected adjective law which regulates the use of force. And when the functions of scarcity are added to that of futurity and force, substantive law is the expectation of the sanctions of adjective law which determine the economic sanctions of management and the economic inducements of opportunity, competition and power of individuals, and it is these expectations that constitute their reciprocal rights, duties, liberties and exposures. [Alongside this paragraph in margin is a question mark in pencil.]

Within this threefold functioning of force, scarcity and futurity, there is as yet no ethical function of right or wrong, good or bad—there is solely the interaction of the three functions, force, scarcity and futurity. It requires an additional function, custom, to introduce these further modifications. This will be considered after further notes on efficiency.

IV. EFFICIENCY

Analytic technology may be considered to include all the physical and biological sciences, from astronomy to industrial psychology and scientific management with their engineering applications, regardless of the functions they play in the social organization. But functional Technology, which utilizes these sciences for individual and social purposes, resolves itself into those managerial transactions which constitute efficiency. Analytic technology is the field of the various sciences and their engineering applications, but functional technology is the social function of efficiency. For efficiency turns on the legal relations which determine the type of managerial transactions, from slavery, serfdom and tenancy, to the modern industrial management of superintendents, foremen, and free laborers. And of course efficiency has its functional relation to scarcity, for the relative efficiencies of different industries have their part in determining the relative scarcity or abundance of their output. Analytic technology is worked out from the standpoint of man's manipulations of the forces of nature regardless of their social origins or social consequences, just as analytic jurisprudence is worked out from the standpoint of violence regardless of social origins and consequences, and analytic scarcity from the standpoint of wants and resources regardless of social origins or consequences. (The discussion of efficiency will require distinction between differential efficiencies and differential scarcities, bearing on Ricardo's theory of rent and the differential productivities of agriculture and machinery. See Reasonable Value, mimeograph.)

V. CUSTOM

John C. Carter, agreeing with Sir Frederick Pollock, in 1890,[11] made an illuminating criticism of Austin's doctrine of sovereignty, which, referring to our distinction, was in fact an appeal for the substitution of functional jurisprudence for analytic jurisprudence. Carter said: "Law is not a body of commands, imposed upon society from without, either by an individual sovereign or superior, or by a sovereign body constituted by representatives of society itself. It exists at all times as one of the elements of society springing directly from liability and custom. It is therefore, the unconscious creation of society, or a growth.... It is only for exceptional instances that judicial tribunals or legislative enactments are needed. In those cases where the customs are doubtful or conflicting, the expert is needed to ascertain or reconcile them, and hence the origin of the judicial establishment.... New customs, new modes of dealing, must be contrived to meet new exigencies, and society by the unconscious exercise of its ordinary forces proceeds to furnish itself with them. But this is a gradual and slow process attended with difficulty and loss. Another agency is needed to supplement and assist the work of society, and legislation springs into existence to supply the want."

We may go even further than Carter in asserting the functional relation between custom and law. Not only the common law, which is definitely ascribed to an origin out of custom, but also the constitutions and statutes themselves are gradually changed by judicial interpretations and changes in the meanings of words, these changes being ascribable to changes in the customs of business. This may be seen in the changes in meaning of the Constitutional terms, property, liberty and due process of law, which changes in meaning have changed the constitution to conform to the changing customs of business. In this respect, new customs are continually arising out of the credit system, the marketing system, the prevailing legislation and prior decisions of courts, the changing methods of production, and hence both the origins and the consequences of these customs are functionally related to sovereignty, scarcity, futurity and efficiency.

This functional significance of custom is to be distinguished from the analysis of custom, as an isolated fact of human nature. As such it belongs to that behavioristic science of psychology which traces habits back to the physiology of living organisms and shows itself in the repetition of acts that have been found by heredity and experience to be preservative of the life and welfare of living creatures. In these lower living creatures habit is but the repetition of the stimuli and response characteristic of life, and connecting physiology with psychology. But when these repetitions rise to the level of human actions of a being that uses tools and language, then these habits become the repeated practices and transactions motivated by the inducements of individuals and the sanction of groups. This is custom, and it is the expectation of these repetitions of inducements and sanctions that constitutes all social institutions, including all economic institutions.

(Develop the relation between custom and ethics and morality. See Anglo-American Law and Economics.)

VI. NEWTON AND DARWIN

Modern economic science has been found to turn on the functional relations of these several analytic sciences, and the question of how they can be functionally related is the leading question of methodology. Each of the five functions, in its own abstract field, may be and should be carried out to the greatest possible perfection by those scientists who devote themselves to each, without regard to that functional relation which it bears to the others. But when the functional relations themselves are the subject matter of investigation, then a method must be devised whereby all of the functions shall move along together, modifying each other as they go.

There have been invented in modern science two methods of investigation, the Newtonian and the Darwinian. The Newtonian method consists in isolating from all other attributes of nature the single attribute of the attraction which every particle in the universe has for every other particle. Without asking what or why respecting this attribute, Newton worked out the universal laws of motion resulting from it, in the form of equations applicable to every motion from stars to electrons, and Einstein made these laws more precise by means of mathematical devices invented since the time of Newton.

It was this Newtonian method of exact quantitative science, isolated from all other attributes that the classical school of economics adopted and the hedonic school perfected. The single attribute thus isolated was the activity of man impelled by the relation of wants to the limited amount of controllable resources available for the satisfaction of these wants. In other words, their economic theory was the universal function of scarcity, and its elaboration as an exact science reached the Newtonian conclusion of a changing equilibrium of the forces of demand and supply resulting in changes in prices, and the details of this equilibrium appeared as the theory of marginal utility, final utility, complementary goods, rent surpluses, and so on.

This analytic economics is, of course, essential, and must be understood before any step can be taken to convert it into the functional economics, just as the other analytic sciences must be understood before they can be functionally related to the analysis of scarcity.

It is a difficult matter to determine just where functional economics separates from analytic economics. It depends on the subject matter in hand. In a question of alleged discrimination, for example, we have a practice that interferes with that prompt operation of supply and demand, which abstract economics calls for. What happens is that the facts of scarcity and the facts of custom or law are operating functionally each upon the other. But if we endeavor to take all of these factors, none of which operates in isolation, then it is that the Darwinian methodology is the method applicable. Darwin's is indeed a functional method, distinguished from analytic method of science, and is therefore suited to a science where the actual process under the influence of many variable factors is being examined, rather than an isolated process that can perhaps be separated from all variable factors.

Darwin starts with Heredity, which from the analytic standpoint is a science of physiology, but from the functional standpoint of Darwin's problem of the Origin of Species, is merely the repetition of structures and habits.

He finds that this repetition, however, is not always identical, a fact whose explanation belongs again to physiology, but for Darwin, who seeks its functional significance, it is summarized merely as variability.

Next he finds the fact of multiplication, or duplication, of individuals, beyond the possibility of obtaining enough subsistence for all, and, while this is also in its analysis a problem of physiology, yet from Darwin's functional standpoint, it becomes simply the variable relation of scarcity resulting from a pressure of population upon limited resources. The functional significance of scarcity resides in the activity of struggle for existence in opposition to a competition with other individuals and species. Thus scarcity, from the analytic standpoint, is a science of physiology, but from the functional standpoint in the origin of species, it is opportunity, power and competition among all living creatures.

It follows that some individuals survive and others perish young, so that heredity is subject to a selective process, and this selection is found to occur under two variables, artificial selection where the mind of man selects and protects the creatures whose variabilities suit his purposes, and natural selection where those individuals whose variabilities give them an uncivilized advantage are the ones who survive.

The whole of these functional relations between many variable factors is summarized as the survival of those best fitted to survive under all the circumstances, and consequently a process of change is going on.

Thus the Darwinian method is a functional method comprehending all the variable factors, instead of an isolation method restricted to only one of the many functions involved. It can be summarized as an historical process of repetition, variability, duplication, conflict and selection.

If we seek to apply this method to the Origin of institutions as Darwin applied it to the Origin of Species, distinguishing it from the Newtonian method, we must seek to develop, as did Darwin, not the analytic sciences on which the science of economics is builded [sic], but the functional relations of the subject matter of those analytic sciences in their modification of each other. It is not technology that we are concerned with but the managerial transactions which utilize technology in the way of increasing or decreasing efficiency. It is not sovereignty that we analyze separately from economics, but sovereignty insofar as the use of force modifies and is modified by the changes in scarcity, efficiency, expectations and customs. It is not custom as physiological habit but custom as a variable social relation of practices and transactions in the various dealings of people with each other. It is not psychology as a study of the capacity to see into the future, but psychology as the specific functional modification of inducements and sanctions held out to those persons and by those persons who act in the present with regard to expected consequences.

These various functional relations would seem to be brought together in the formula of an expected repetition of transactions, the concept of a transaction being so formulated that all the variable factors are so related to each other that a change in any one occasions a change in all the others.

It is evident, however, that this functional relation assumes a problem different from that set up in the analysis of each of the factors. With Darwin the problem was the origin and progress of the different species of living creatures, and the corresponding problem in economics is the origins and progress of the institutions for producing and acquiring wealth. Political Economy is national economy, and a national economy develops by the repetition, duplication, variability, conflicts and artificial selections of transactions, each of which is affected by the variable factors of efficiency, scarcity, custom, force and expectation. (Develop the several types of artificial selection of customs (practices and transactions) by courts, associations of business and labor, etc.)

WORLD DEPRESSIONS

[Inscribed in upper-right corner: May 9, 1931-J.R.C.]

I have drawn two curves on this chart, one for the United States and one for England, to represent the average changes in wholesale prices of commodities during 140 years, from the beginning of the French Revolution in 1790 to the present year of a dozen revolutions and dictatorships. These wholesale prices are the prices received by employers from the sale of their products, out of which they pay wages, rent and interest, leaving to themselves, if possible, a margin for profit. These curves of price changes are the Economic Backbone of World History for 140 years.

The French Revolution lasted 25 years, from the States General of 1789 to the battle of Waterloo in 1815. It was followed by another thirty-five years of European oligarchies, dictatorships and falling prices, so that the Revolution and its effects lasted 60 years.

From the chart we may expect that history is repeating itself, and that [the] world is in for perhaps another 40 or 50 years of revolutions, dictatorships, economic depression and unemployment, following the world war of 1814.

During the 25 years of the French Revolution and the Napoleonic dictatorship, the charts show a remarkable war prosperity, caused mainly by the enormous issue of bank notes in England, with the resulting huge profits of employers and no unemployment. During the next 35 years, from 1815 to

1850, during which time England returned to the gold basis by retiring the excess of bank notes, the world-wide fall in prices and consequent unemployment culminated in the revolutions of 1848 in Europe and the Chartist uprisings of unemployed labor in England.

America was as yet a frontier nation, and its policy of conquest through to the Pacific furnished an outlet for the unemployed of the Atlantic states, the depressed farmers of the Middle West and the immigrants from Europe. The wildcat banks of 1832 collapsed in 1837 as shown by the chart, and the protective tariff of 1840 afforded temporary relief against the prolonged depression of industry which was heading in Europe towards the revolutions of 1848.

Suddenly the gold discoveries of 1849 began to show their effects the world over, with increased profits and full employment, but with the over-expansion that collapsed in 1857.

Not until the American Civil War, which was our great Revolution and confiscation of property, did industry start up again with a new war prosperity, stimulated by enormous issues of paper money which sent prices rapidly up to the peak of 1865. This inflation added to Europe's supply of gold by the export of American gold, and the chart shows that in Europe the gold prices of commodities rose, with increased prosperity in all except the cotton industries which were deprived by the war blockade of their raw material.

Then came another sweep of falling prices with slight recoveries in 1872 and 1882. This fall in prices began first, with the rapid retirement of paper money in America, then the demonetization of silver by Germany in 1873 followed by other countries until 1897. This was the period of world-wide unemployment, the rise of socialism in Germany, the Greenback, labor, and populist parties in America, the general railway strikes of 1877 and 1894, the nation-wide coal strike of 1897.

Then, with the establishment of the gold standard and the rich discoveries of gold in South Africa, along with the cheap process of extracting gold from the rock a mile deep, the price movement started up on another period of 20 years, with short recessions in 1904, 1907, and 1914, and, by the aid of the paper money and new bank credit of the world war, prices reached their peak in 1920.

Then the third great slump in prices, with the retirement of paper money and bank credit, the return of former gold countries to the gold standard, the adoption by former silver countries and by impoverished countries of the gold exchange standard, the absorption of surplus gold by the United States, France and India, and the falling off of gold production in South Africa.

With this economic backbone of world history for 140 years let us consider the main theories of causation, of remedy and even of revolution that have followed along its curvature.

Modern economic theory started with the debate between Ricardo and Malthus during the fall in prices and the great unemployment and depression of industry that followed the battle of Waterloo. Malthus declared that the causes were to be found in the inability of consumers to purchase the products which had been produced, and his remedy was a protective tariff and the employment of labor on public works and on the improvement of landed estates, where the product would not come upon the competitive markets and cause a further reduction of prices. Laborers as consumers would thereby receive a larger share of the total product at the expense of taxpayers, capitalists and landlords.

This theory of increasing the share of labor as a means of preventing unemployment was carried to its limit by Karl Marx in 1848, who proposed that the share going to capitalists and landlords in the form of profit, interest and rent should be wiped out altogether, and that labor alone should receive the whole product. Today Soviet Russia points to the fact that, by following Karl Marx, they have no unemployment while millions are unemployed in capitalistic countries.

The doctrine of Malthus was restated by Rodbertus in 1837 to the effect that laborers do not receive a sufficient share of the total purchasing power to enable them to purchase back all that they have produced. Hence an accumulation of unsold goods known as overproduction or underconsumption, and consequently unemployment and business depression. In this form the doctrine has been taken over by the socialists and trade unionists, and finds its post-war statement in the theories of Foster and Catchings and others, to the effect that there must be a different distribution of wealth in order that consumers may have more purchasing power and capitalists less purchasing power.

On the other hand, the doctrine of Ricardo turned on the margin for profit instead of the share of profit. The cause of the depression and unemployment after 1815 was found by him in the obstinacy of laborers who refused to accept lower wages and thus permit employers to retain a margin for profit, without which they could not afford to employ the laborers. If laborers, who were then wholly unorganized, would accept lower wages, corresponding to the fall in prices, then the employers would employ them and start up industry again.

This doctrine of Ricardo has been the doctrine of capitalists and the older economists for a hundred years, until, since the war, the doctrine of Malthus, Rodbertus, the socialists and trade unionists have, for a time, been accepted. The argument runs that mass production requires mass consumption and the latter can be provided only when wages are high. If wages had been high enough during the past ten years then the laborers could have purchased back what they produced, and unemployment would have been prevented.

It is evident, however, that during the past eighteen months, when prices are again falling at the average rate of about one per cent per month, manufacturers are returning to the doctrine of Ricardo, and they are holding that, although they greatly regret it, yet wages must be reduced enough to afford a margin for profit before they can afford to start up again and employ the unemployed. They are taking the laborers back, but at reduced wages.

Hence the present-day world is again distracted by the same issue that divided the founders of political economy 115 years ago. It is the issue of the share of profit versus the margin for profit. On the one side is the argument that the share of profit in the world's industry is so large that consumers cannot buy what they have produced. This leads to a redistribution of wealth, and ends in revolutions and dictatorship.

On the other side is the argument that the margin for profit is too small, and this leads to the world-wide unemployment, reductions of wages and the long hours of work, which foment strikes, revolutions and dictatorships. The dictatorships are of two kinds, the dictatorship of the proletariat in Russia and the dictatorship of landlords and capitalists in Hungary, Italy and other countries. It is the issue of Communism versus Fascism.

It must be admitted that Europe is again plunging towards one or the other of these revolutions. America will, of course, be involved. The premonitions are the world-wide fall of prices, the tariff wars, and the inability to get a reduction of armaments.

The most important remedy now before the world is the Bank for International Settlements, known as the Young Plan, with headquarters at Basel. Its importance is in the fact that its Board of Directors brings together the heads of the main central banks of the world.

However, it is unfortunate that the Federal Reserve System cannot be represented on that Board of Directors. America controls some 40 percent of the world's monetary gold, and no action of the Bank for International Settlements can be taken without paying particular attention to the independent policy of the Federal Reserve System. And, on the other hand, the Federal Reserve System cannot be free to act in stabilization of American prices, as it did in 1923, if such stabilization should jeopardize the maintenance of the gold standard in Europe.

Thus in 1924 to 1927, the policy of the Reserve System was controlled by the efforts to help England to return to the gold standard, with a resulting extraordinary cheapening of credit, followed by excessive overproduction of commodities and inflation of stock prices in America, culminating with a crash in 1929. Since that time there has been a fall in American prices of commodities equivalent to one per cent per month for 18 months, with even a greater fall in England and Europe.

Evidently the Federal Reserve policy must be one of cooperation with the Central banks of Europe, if the gold standard is to be maintained and if the excessive rise and fall of prices is to be prevented.

But here the jealousy of the American people and the fear of entangling alliances with Europe compels the Reserve System to do underhanded and surreptitiously by private conversations, what could be done openly before the whole world if the Federal Reserve System were represented on the Board of Directors of the Bank for International Settlements.

This fall in prices, which might be prevented if America would participate in the International Bank, is an impressive lesson on the conflict of a hundred years between the theories of the share of profit and the margin for profit. It is estimated, for America, that the share of profit is 25 per cent of the national income, while the share of interest and rent is about 15 per cent, leaving only 60 per cent as the share for wages. Evidently if Labor gets only 60 per cent of the national product then labor cannot purchase back all that is produced.

The practical question is, If Labor's share had been more than 60 per cent of the national income and the share of profits less than 25 per cent would the higher wages and smaller profits have prevented the unemployment of the past 18 months?

The question is entirely different when we turn to the margin for profits. I estimate, from the federal reports on income taxes, that the medium margin for profits in years of business stability is an average of about 3 per cent on the gross sales of manufacturing corporations. In other words, for every dollar of earnings obtained by these corporations, they expended, on the average, 97 cents in order to get it. This margin ranged from an average of 6.7 per cent in 1919 to an average loss on sales of 3.3 per cent in 1921 and an average loss of 1 per cent on sales in 1924.

Consequently, a fall in prices of only one per cent per month is a reduction 33 times as great in the margin for profit if the margin is 3 per cent of the selling price. Even if the margin for profit is 10 per cent of the selling price, a fall of one per cent in prices is a fall of 10 per cent in the margin for profit.

It does not work out exactly this way, because employers simply stop production and lay off their employees. What therefore appears to be a lack of consuming power on the part of laborers, and is known as underconsumption, is simply this reduction in the margin of profit by falling prices, and the consequent inability of employers to hire labor.

On the other hand, an average rise of one per cent per month in wholesale prices—which was less than the rise in 1919 and 1923, as shown on the Chart means an increase 33 times as great in the margin for profit, if the margin is 3 per cent of the average selling prices. Consequently employers hire more laborers, and what appears to be overproduction is mainly the result of an increase in the margin for profit 10 to 30 times as much as the rise of prices.

For this reason the world-wide fall of prices, or the world-wide rise of prices, depending on the instability of the gold standard and the lack of cooperation of the Central Banks of the world, is the most important of the world-wide problems of prosperity and depression, of employment and unemployment. In capitalistic countries it is the expectation of profit that makes possible the employment of labor and the payment of interest and rent. Business enterprises are working on very narrow margins for profit, and although the share of profit in the national income may be 25 per cent, yet the margin for profits may average only 3 per cent of the sales value of the product.

It follows that the most important of the present problems is the world wide stabilization of the purchasing power of money.

For this reason I look for a repetition of the world history from 1815 to 1849, and from 1865 to 1897. It is well known that there is a falling off of the world's rate of increase in the gold supply. A very serious shortage is predicted by the year 1940.

But even more important are the results of banking policy in the United States and France. These countries now own about 60 per cent of the world's monetary gold supply, a much larger amount than is needed to support their credit structure. The French and American people have acquired a strange fear of the loss of this gold to the rest of the world, although this loss is the only means by which other countries can acquire gold and thus reduce their excessively high rates of interest and discount which are now depressing their industries.

Although the cost of interest, as often pointed out, is only one or two per cent of the total cost of production of commodities, yet interest may be 20, 30 and even 200 per cent of the margin for profit. And it is the margin for profit that decides whether industry shall go on or stop. Europe is compelled to keep interest rates higher than American rates, or else lose their gold to America and abandon the gold standard.

Equally important are the payments of war debts to the United States. These amount to $240,000,000 per year, payable in gold or in our own public debt. The European countries can pay these debts only by selling their own exports of commodities to the rest of the world, and thereby acquire the credits with which to purchase the gold or the American securities. With the falling off of foreign markets these European countries are forced to sell their exports at continually lower prices in order to obtain the given amount of gold and securities. Already, since the settlement of the debts, their export prices have fallen about 20 per cent, which means an increase of 25 per cent in the quantity of commodities which they must sell abroad in order to pay their debts to America.

The United States is in the position of a great creditor surrounded by impoverished debtors, and forcing them to sell their possessions at bankrupt sales in order to pay immediately in gold or its equivalent.

But America is at the same time a seller of its own products to these same impoverished debtors and to the rest of the world where they are competing with us. We are compelled therefore also to sell at prices 20 per cent lower than the prices prevailing when the amount of the debt was agreed upon, five or six years ago. It is not an exaggeration to estimate that probably the loss to American farmers, manufacturers and laborers, by these falling prices, is more than ten times as great as the amount of gold or gold credit which we require Europe to pay each year.

If this catastrophe should occur in private business the creditors would get together and either scale down the debts or declare a moratorium until such time as the debtors would be able to pay. But in foreign affairs we insist on our rights. In this case the burden falls mainly on Germany, and is driving that country to Communism or Fascism and the repudiation of war debts.

Our own huge war debt has been reduced about one-third, but if we consider the fall in prices since 1920, the burden of the remaining two-thirds on the taxpayers is greater than was the whole burden at the prices of 1920. And if the prices continue to fall the burden on industry and agriculture will continue to be greater than the amount saved by further reducing the debt.

If America would cancel the war debts of Europe outright then the other countries would cancel theirs. This would be perhaps the most effective step towards restoring international confidence in the willingness of America to help them recover from their present downward plunge.

In lieu of these efforts towards recovery, America is forced into the practice of dumping—this means that we sell our manufactured and farm products to foreign countries at lower prices than those charged to American consumers. The practice of dumping is now an avowed American policy, where formerly it was condemned. Even the Farm Board congratulates farmers that domestic prices are higher than world prices for the same commodity.

This accounts in part for what seems to be the absurd effort of all countries, except England so far, to raise high protective tariffs or even embargoes, against other countries. What they are doing, however, is trying to keep prices as high as possible at home but dumping their surplus at low prices abroad. The efforts of Europe to bring about a reduction of these tariffs, although enthusiastically agreed upon at Geneva, proved utterly futile when the delegates returned to their own countries and faced their own parliaments and people.

These high protective tariffs in times past have nearly always been enacted in periods of falling prices, like the American tariff of 1840, the German tariff of 1876, the French tariffs and the American tariffs of 1899, 1921 and 1929. They are the legitimate protest of the people against the falling prices which always show themselves first and most severely in the prices of exports and imports. Protective tariffs, against which the League has strongly protested, cannot be expected to be reduced during a period of world-wide falling prices.

The outlook is dark for the future. We see a slight recovery in the spring of 1931, owing to the fact that inventories are being exhausted. But soon the world-wide forces will drive towards another fall in prices below the present levels, and so on indefinitely.

America really controls the world situation, by refusing to cooperate with Europe. During the past years of apparent prosperity we did not care. But during these years of world-wide depression and unemployment the American people may perhaps begin to think about the obstructive part we are playing not only against Europe's recovery but against our own recovery. It is not merely a matter of joining the League of Nations, or the World Court, or reducing our tariffs, or reducing armaments. These are worthwhile educationally, but they will not seriously be listened to until the American people are convinced, by their own prolonged depressions, unemployment and strikes, that they are standing in the way against their own and against world recovery.

I do not know that it will be possible to get them to understand the international movement now going on, amongst economists, financiers, and publicists, for restoring the world price level to the level of 1926 and stabilizing the purchasing power of gold as nearly as possible at that level. And if they do understand its necessity and its reasons, I do not see that they are willing to trust the Federal Reserve System as a member of the Bank for International Settlements, or to release Europe from debt payments. These are the reasons why I think we are in again for the thirty to forty years that will repeat the world history after the battle of Waterloo and the surrender of Lee at Appomatox.

A. AFTALION*

[Undated]

Aftalion in his analysis of the periodic cycle eliminates money as a factor in its causation by considering the circulating media a constant and adequate measure of exchange value. "The fall of the final utility," he writes, "finds its expression in the fall of the price" (Vol. II, 297). "If the money has remained constant" it measures the marginal utility of merchandise. "It is this hypothesis that we have made in the preceeding reasoning. We have declared that overproduction diminishes the final utility of commodities. We have added that this diminution entailed the lowering of price. It is thus by implication that we admitted the constancy of the monetary factor, or the absence, more or less, of movements in this factor which one could make carry the responsibility of the cyclical fluctuations of prices" (Vol. II, 297).

Proving to his own satisfaction that the monetary explanations, either from the quantitative or marginal utility of money theories, could not explain the cycle, Aftalion had of necessity to explain it on a basis of the variations in demand and supply of commodities. He then disposes of demand by relegating it to a subordinate or secondary position and makes it dependent on supply. Under-demand was to him merely the old under-consumption theory dressed up in monetary clothes (Vol. II, 237). It would be an exaggeration to say that the oscillations in the price level were due to dualistic causes, demand and supply, and thus account for the periodic crises (Vol. II, 238). To say this would be to overemphasize the importance of demand. The demand cycle is due to revenue, revenue in turn is a result of the prices of production which issue from supply of consumption goods. Thus demand is dependent on supply and rises and falls in the cycle with supply (Vol. II, 238). Demand is merely an effect reacting upon its cause (Vol. II, 239), and re-enforces its influence. The economic cycles would occur periodically without fluctuations of demand (Vol. II, 239), "but without the fluctuations in the supply, neither crises [n]or periodic cycles would be observed" (Vol. II, 239). The alternation of over-production and under-production explains all that is essential in the phenomenon of the cycle. The variations in the supply are the initial and determining factors; the motor of the whole mechanism. Demand rhythm plays a subordinate part, as a repercussion of the supply and merely intensifies the cycles that were caused independently of it (Vol. II, 239).

The monetary and demand factors being thus eliminated or subordinated the only possible cause left to explain the businesss cycle is the variation in the supply or supplies of commodities. The supplies of commodities and the psychological demand of the people (to distinguish from a commodity demand) determine the price level. "The manner in which the general superabundance of commodities acts upon their price is not different than— when it is a question of particular commodities" (Vol. II, 273). Aftalion then proceeds to give the marginal utility analysis of the exchange value of all commodities. As the volume of goods or supply increases, the marginal utility of the units of supply decrease, population remaining stationary. This increase and decrease in marginal utility means a rising and falling price level when measured in money. This rising and falling price level is the business cycle. Looked at from the standpoint of society, then, the cycle is dependent upon a sort of social marginal utility that is dependent in turn upon the supply of consumption goods that emerges from the technological productive process. The rise and fall of the exchange level or price level is due simply to the rise and fall of the marginal utility of consumption goods offered on the market (Vol. II, 274, 275).

It will be seen that Aftalion, like Malthus, based the business cycle on marginal utility or what Malthus called "intensity of demand." In Aftalion's case the marginal utility was social and based on the satisfactions derived or satisfactions expected from consumption goods. In Malthus's analysis the "intensity of demand" was confined to the capitalists or landlords and was dependent on their rate of profits or love of ease. Aftalion ignores the relation of the profit motive to the business cycle. His analysis is in reality a commanded value barter economy theory as money plays a colorless part in his exchange process.

* All references are to "Les Crises Periodique de Surproduction," Paris, 1913

BANK CREDIT

[Undated]

Bank credit introduced a wholly new element into the valuation process, namely the valuation of promises. In a precious metal economy the price level is determined by the relative supplies of two independent variables, the supply of precious metals and the supply of commodities. (Supply means rate of supply, i.e., the quantities offered in exchange, i.e., "velocity of circulation," and we may use the term "volume" instead of "supply.") In the paper money economy, likewise, the two variables, volume of money and volume of commodities exchanged are independent. The difference between the two economies is simply the difference that in the precious metals economy both the volume of money and the volume of commodities exchanged depends upon two independent technological processes, while in the paper money economy the volume of money depends on a volitional process and the volume of commodities upon technological processes.

In either case, the volume of money has no dependence whatever on the needs of business. The needs of business may be designated the volume of transactions, that is, the quantities of commodities actually sold at the prices actually agreed upon. Volume of transaction is therefore the volume of exchange values at which business men are making their sales of commodities. Precious metals are mined regardless of how much money is wanted by the world, i.e., regardless of the volume of transactions, and paper money is issued by the fiat of government regardless of how much of it the business community needs at the prevailing prices.

But in a bank-credit economy the bank notes and bank deposits are issued by bankers only upon the request of the business man and the bankers limit the volume of issues with reference to the fact that these issues are their promises to pay legal tender money on demand. He can make a greater profit by issuing a greater volume of them but if he issues too great a volume compared with his supply of reserves he may not be able to meet his promises to pay on demand. Hence the supply of bank credit is not an independent variable like precious metals or paper money but is a dependent variable, depending for its volume on the two other independent variables, namely the volume of transactions and the volume of precious metals or paper money from which the banker expects to obtain his supply of legal tender which is his means of paying on demand. Thus, while in the case of precious metals or paper money either the mining industry or the will of government creates the supply of money, regardless of the volume of transactions, yet in the case of bank credit it is the volume of transactions that creates its own supply of money.

Three fallacious analogies have often seemed to conceal this peculiar reversal of the quantity theories of value: first, the analogy of bank credit to commodities; second, the analogy of paper money to bank credit; third, the analogy of the rate of bank discount to the rate of interest on capital.

1. Bank credit is a promise of a banker to pay lawful money on demand, yet it is a most peculiar promise because it circulates like money and has "general purchasing power" like money, and is, in fact, like almost any other commodity, in this respect. Very often it is even said to be a "store of value," that is, an embodied value, like gold or silver. But this is a pure physical analogy. Bank credit is nothing but a negotiable promise which has been made by common law and statute into something as nearly like money as possible. The analogy to a "store of value" is good enough for ordinary daily business but for a quantity theory of value depending on "demand and supply" it is misleading, because its supply is created outright at the time when there is a demand for it. It is not an independent store of value—it is a function of the process of agreeing on valuations in the process of transactions. The only proper physical analogy to precious metals would be to suppose that the volume of gold consisted of new grains of gold freshly mined, lasting from 30 to 60 days, then disappearing into the air to be replaced if necessary by new gold. The actual volume of gold, however, is indeed a store of value that does not perish, but the volume of bank credit is a wholly new volume every 90 days. In short, it is not a volume of commodities at all—it is a volume of negotiable promises to pay a legal tender on demand, created daily and perishing daily, but given in exchange for business men's promises to pay the banker a legal tender within 24 hours to 90 days. It is wholly a phenomena [sic] of the legal order of private property, that is, of the volume of transactions, and not of the technological order of production, supply and demand.

2. Paper money has always (?) been issued as a promise to pay on demand by a government or by a national bank authorized by government, and hence it seems to be like a bank credit which is a promise of a private banker to pay lawful money on demand. But this paper money has usually three qualities not possessed by bank credit. It is receivable by government in payment of debts (taxes) owing to government; it is the standard adopted by courts in assessing damages and penalties in suits at law, and it is also adopted by courts as the standard of value in the enforcement of contracts. Bank credit possesses none of these qualities. Our national bank notes and federal reserve notes (?) have been given partly these qualities and in-so-far are paper money rather than bank credit. Hence paper money, if receivable for taxes and accepted by the courts, has an independent means of getting itself into circulation—is, in fact, a "forced circulation," that is, "lawful money," by the action of government and courts. But bank credit can get itself into circulation only through the confidence of the community that the banker will pay this lawful money on demand. Its volume is a <u>voluntary circulation</u>. Furthermore, paper money is re-issued regardless of the needs of business as shown by the volume of transactions and hence is like the supply of precious metals, "a store of value,"

having the most essential of all values in modern business, that of paying taxes, damages and debts. But bank credit when once retired is never issued again—another and a different promise is made by the business man to the banker and by the banker to the business community. Bank credit is truly a promise to pay on demand and nothing more, but paper money, like precious metals, is the thing which the banker promises to pay.

3. The rate of bank discount on the loan of "money," like the rate of interest on the loan of capital, is a cost of carrying on business, and is paid by the business man to the banker exactly as he pays to other business men and laborers the prices at which he buys their commodities and services or pays to bondholders interest on their investments. But it is a very different kind of service. The other costs are paid for a part of the existing supply of commodities, labor and capital, which are independent variables, whose quantities are not determined by the business man himself, but the bank discount is a payment to a banker for the use of his reputation of solvency in the community. The bank credit given by the bank is a guaranty by the banker to the community that the business man, within the next 90 days, will pay his promises to the bank. Commercial banking is primarily an insurance business in which the bank discount is an insurance premium limited by the alternative rates of interest that the business man would be compelled to pay or sacrifice if he borrowed the same amount of money as a "working capital" or kept the same amount of his own money on hand as a working capital.

The extent to which the banker can thus guarantee the solvency of his customers is bound up with the extent to which he himself can expect to command the lawful money which he promises to pay on demand in lieu of the business man himself keeping it on hand. The banker must look ahead at least 30 to 90 days and calculate his probable ability to keep and get lawful money to pay out on demand. He has three sources—(1) the amount of his reserves on hand, (2) the amount of securities which he can sell and of promises of business men to pay in 30 to 90 days, and (3) the amount of lawful money in the country. Any material change in any one of these affects his probabilities of maintaining a safe ratio of reserves to demand liabilities. The limits are elastic, but they <u>are limits,</u> and within these elastic limits the volume of bank credit which he can issue is highly elastic. Hence the rate of bank discount, which is the rate of premium which the banker charges for insuring the solvency of his customers, must be changed up or down according as any one of the above three sources of his own ability to pay on demand affects the ratio of his reserves to his demand liabilities.

This variable rate of discount is what business men know as the "value of money" and it is analogous to a rate of interest on the loan of capital. But the commercial banker is not primarily an investment banker—that is, he is not primarily a middleman between investors and borrowers who lend and borrow capital, he is an insurance middleman between buyers and sellers on [of?] short time promises; and what he insures is the prospective ability of business men to pay their short-time debts in lawful money. He is strictly a dealer in lawful money, not a dealer in real estate, commodities, or any physical capital which earns an income and pays a profit, or rent, or interest on true capital.

Hence, while the analogy of the rate of discount on money for 30 to 90 days to the rate of interest on capital is good enough from the standpoint of the costs of conducting business and earning profits out of which to pay the discount or interest, yet from the standpoint of the peculiar character of the banking business, the rate of discount is not a rate of interest, it is a rate of insurance on the probability of business men's ability to obtain lawful money within 30 to 90 days in consideration of the banker furnishing them with an equivalent of lawful money now acceptable to other business men from day to day. It is just what business men say it is, "the value of money" which they need at once in proportion to the volume of current business transaction, whereas their own ability to obtain that money is not expected until 30 to 90 days afterwards.

Hence the volume of bank credit is not a volume of a commodity created independently of the needs of business, but is a volume of current insured promises of business men to pay lawful money in which the prices agreed upon by business men in their daily transactions, that is the volume of current exchange-values, is insured by the banker for 30 to 90 days after the insurance is taken out and the premium has been paid in advance. Hence it is not the volume of two independent variables, the volume of commodities and the volume of bank credit, that are exchanged against each other as it is in the case of money, but it is the very exchange-values or prices which business men agree upon in their transactions that actually create the volume of bank credit from day to day. This can be seen if we describe the three principal ways in which bank credit is created.

1. Commercial bills
2. Line of credit
3. ?

Economic Cycles

[Undated]

Two questions arise in any attempt to classify theories of economic cycles according to a single fundamental principle (as distinguished from an enumeration or a grouping of theories), namely the question of the theories of value underlying the theories of cycles and the question of the standard measure of value. Does the theory of the author in question turn on his theory of value or upon an ideal of what is the important feature to be attained by means of a standard of value? The two problems may be distinguished as the scientific problem of the cause, regulator or measure of value and the pragmatic problem of deciding upon a convenient, just, or reasonable standard of measurement of value. However much the theories may have differed on the scientific problem of the nature of value they have usually treated the other question of a standard measure of value as something apart and belonging to a different field either of convenience or justice.

Now, there are two great systems of measurement running through all sciences and their applications, which may be distinguished as the measurement of quantities and the measurement of forces. In the measurement of quantities the standard of measurement must always be of the same kind as the quantity measured, as when length is measured by a standard unit of length and so on. But in the measurement of forces the standard cannot be of the same kind as the force to be measured, since the force itself is known only by the amount of work it does. Hence the standard of measurement consists in the selecting some one measurable resultant of the force which is deemed to vary in quantity as the force varies in energy, as when the expansion and contraction of mercury in a tube is selected to measure changes in temperature out of the millions of other changes in other substances caused by changes in temperature.

It was Malthus who first introduced into modern economic theory the idea that value is a force that induces individuals to act in certain directions rather than other directions. This concept of value was smothered for many decades under various concepts of value as a quantity of a certain substance embodied in commodities, either the embodied labor or the intrinsic use-values of nutrition, warmth or shelter afforded by commodities, which characterized the theories of the classical economists and the Marxian socialists.

The hedonic concepts of diminishing utility or increasing disutility introduced by Gossen, Jevons and the Austrian economists, might have led away from these concepts of embodied value were it not that the hedonic school became in fact a "neo-classical" school, identifying the feelings with the commodities, or rather making the intensity of feelings a function of the quantity of commodities. The concept of value still remained a quantity concept, and all the physical concepts of quantity of value of the classical economist and socialist remained as before, embodied in commodities, although the mathematical treatment changed from arithmetic functions to geometric functions and the differential calculus.

It was not until Anderson, in 1906?, by the aid of a more modern psychology, resurrected unknowingly Malthus's idea of value as a social force inducing action of individuals, that the concept of value as a force instead of a quantity, began to emerge again from a century of embodied value. Yet Anderson used this fruitful concept to create another entity of embodied value, which he named "absolute value," and which therefore had the peculiarly unscientific faculty of changing its dimensions in one direction at the very moment when individuals are acting towards it as though it had a change in the opposite direction. Thus, if the exchange-value of money rises, individuals who have money can purchase more goods in general than before with the same quantity of money, but if Anderson's "absolute value" of money rises it may be that individuals can purchase a less quantity of goods in general than before. A rise in the absolute value of money may be a fall in the exchange-value of money, and the prices of goods in general measured in money may rise while the value of the money which measures them is also rising. Anderson evidently retained the embodied value idea of earlier economists. The explanation is doubtless to be found in the infatuation of the noun Value, which misled all the theorists of embodied value. Had Anderson substituted the verb, Valuing, for the noun Value he could hardly have made this mistake and would have carried out consistently his fruitful concept of value as a social force inducing action of individuals. We then should have had conformity to the well-known behaviour of individuals who act as though the value of money had increased when it will buy larger quantities of goods and as though it decreased when it will buy a less quantity of goods. In fact, from the standpoint of value as a force inducing people to act there is no such thing as Value—there are millions of people valuing, and consequently there is no absolute value, nor embodied value as a quantity; there is only a force which we can know only as we can measure its results in the actual valuing process. Value is what value does, just as electricity is what electricity does, and we know it only as we can compare the different quantities of work which it does.

Hence the concept of measurement is two-fold, whether applied to quantities or forces. We first compare quantities of the same kind or forces of the same kind; then, by custom or law, agree upon a standard unit by means of which we can more accurately agree with each other as to the quantities or forces compared. Comparison is unstandardized measurement, measurement is standardized comparison. In either case we take for granted that there is something absolute, essential or fundamental, back of our comparisons, but we also take for granted that it cannot be known except by comparisons and measurements. And then, when we do make comparisons and measurements, we find, if we have correctly isolated the quantity or force measured, that we can more or less control its operation for purposes which we deem important.

It is for this reason that the primary classification of theories of economic cycles herein proposed will distinguish between those theories of value which make value a quantity, which we shall name theories of Embodied Value, and those theories which make value a force inducing human action, which we shall name theories of Volitional Value.

There is often, as just suggested in the case of Anderson, a mingling of the two concepts, and in such cases the classification will be made on the point of whether or not the whole tendency of the author is towards the Embodied Value group or towards the Volitional Value group. And the test will usually be found in the concepts of the purpose which the author deemed most important to be attained in establishing a standard of value.

This distinction between embodied value and volitional value appears in the distinction made by Laughlin between normal credit and abnormal credit. Speaking, of course, of bank credit he says: "Normal credit is the coinage of goods, or property, into present means of payment (in terms of the standard, e.g., dollars of gold) in amount no greater than the value of the marketable goods, or property, owned by the borrower.... In short, the process, at bottom, is an exchange of goods against goods, facilitated by the exceedingly efficient forms of credit provided by credit institutions.... Credit has been the evolution of a refined system of barter, enabling goods to be exchanged against goods. When looked at generally, all bankable goods form the supply, and at the same time the demand.... Hence normal credit can have no general effect on values and prices, after a time long enough to permit temporary fluctuations of price to spend their force."[12]

On the other hand, "abnormal credit is built upon error, delusion, or fraud; and sooner or later its falsity is sure to be discovered. Abnormal credit is speculative; and illegitimate speculation e converso may be defined as the use of abnormal credit.... Credit men and banks are daily trying to distinguish between normal and abnormal credit, the one being sound, the other unsound; and yet externally they act alike.... The operations of abnormal credit, with only a few exceptions, provide the materials for a commercial crisis.... Changes of prices arising from illegitimate speculation must, of course, be dealt with wholly by influences regulating, or restrictive of, abnormal credit and overtrading. This, however, is a study of human nature working under great tension in the world of trade and commerce, which is not within our present purpose."[13]

Thus, it will be seen, normal credit is defined as that in which demand and supply rise and fall equally so that the general level of prices is not changed, and this definition corresponds to the embodied value concepts of Ricardo, Karl Marx, Proudhon and John Law.

On the other hand, abnormal credit is defined as the errors, delusions, optimism, over-trading, fraud, maladjustment of supply and demand, growing out of the psychology of human nature, with which a theory of embodied value is not concerned, and this, too, corresponds exactly with the explanations offered by Ricardo, Marx, Proudhon and John Law.

Contrasted with this are the volitional theories, beginning with Malthus, repeated by Aftalion and more or less developed in the theories of Juglar, Sprague, Fisher, Mitchell, Cassel and Hansen, who finds in this capricious and deluded human will itself a natural law of expansion and contraction, of optimism and pessimism, which instead of being outside the economist's purpose, is the subject matter of the theory of value.

Purposes of a Stable Standard of Value

The stages of development and the sub-classifications of the Embodied and Volitional Value theories will be developed below. They are, as above indicated, inseparable from a history and classification of theories respecting the measure of value and the objects hoped for in deciding upon a standard measure of value.

1. A Single Standard. Beginning with John Locke and continuing to the present time the urgent necessity of all plans for a standard of value has been that of obtaining a fixed, definite, single, national or international standard instead of such divergent standards as gold, silver, ["corn" deleted on manuscript] or paper money. This was the standpoint of Adam Smith, Ricardo, Malthus and the classical economists.

2. Cause and Measure of Value. It was on this account that they distinguished between real value and nominal value. Real value had to do with the causes or substance of value, either cost-value or esteem-value (utility) while nominal value was price in terms of money. The same point of view held regarding the value of money. The real value of money was either its cost-value (Ricardo, Marx et al) or its esteem-value (Malthus, Aftalion, Anderson) while its nominal value was its general purchasing power.

Thus there were two objections to the use of general purchasing power as a measure of the value of money.

1. It does not tell changes in real value (cause of value) either of money or of commodities (Ricardo, Malthus)
2. Impracticable. It would require averages of prices of commodities, wages etc. (Mill, Senior)
3. Creditor and Debtor. There was, however, another consideration that came into play on account of the great fall in prices during the first half of the nineteenth century, and the rise of prices from 1850 to 1873 and the fall from 1873 to 1896 (secular trends), namely the question of justice between creditor and debtor. This led to the development of tabular standards (Lowe 1822, Scrope 1833, Jevons), and a more careful study of index numbers reached the conclusion that, for different purposes different index numbers may be constructed, and all prices need not be mixed (e.g., wholesale prices, retail prices, securities, etc.).
4. Overemployment and Unemployment. Malthus was the first to bring out the cycles of prosperity and depression, and to point out what has latterly become the most important object of a stable standard of exchange value, namely overemployment and unemployment. This is not merely a question of creditor and debtor, it is a question of the inducements that lead business men to overexpand causing the inevitable collapse. Hence the shift is made from money to credit and Juglar was

the first (1856?) to fully develop an economic theory on this subject, though it had been correctly described by J.S. Mill in 1848 (followed by Laughlin as cited above). Juglar's contribution consisted in his distinction between predisposing and precipitating causes, the predisposing being the over-expansion of credit (Laughlin's abnormal profit).

Hence, classified according to standards of Value, the first stage wanted a uniform standard of exchange value, regardless of the price level. The second wanted a constant standard of emobodied value and belittled the fluctuation of prices. The third wanted justice between creditors and debtors and wished to stabilize the exchange value of money, assuming that volume of credit fluctuated with volume of money (Fisher). The fourth wanted to smooth out the business cycles by acting directly or indirectly on the banking system (Fisher, Sprague, Cassel).

NOTES

1. Cp. Kocourek, Pound.
2. Continental jurists have been more logically relentless. Cp. Kelsen, Allgemeine Staatslehre (1925). Von Clausewitz also finds it impossible to separate his analytical military science from its functional relation to public policy and the will to war of the nation and the soldiers. von Clausewitz, War (tr. 1911)
3. [No content is provided for this note.]
4. See his Legal Analysis and Terminology, 29 Yale Law Jour (1919).
5. Corbin, Legal Analysis, etc.
6. Pollock, F., Law and Command, Law Mag. and Rev. 189 (1872).
7. Cp. Loria, Achille, Economic Foundation of Society (tr.). [No location is indicated in the text for this note.]
8. For example, compulsory arbitration in Australia and Commercial Arbitration in New York after 1923.
9. [No content indicated.]
10. Maitland, Justice and Police, 69, Holdsworth, Hist. of English Law, 3d ed. 65 (1922).
11. Proceedings, Amer. Bar Assn. 1890, also primarily Justice Holmes.
12. J. L. Laughlin, Principles of Money, 93, 95, 104 (1911).
13. Ibid, 105, 110.

THE CORRESPONDENCE BETWEEN CLARENCE E. AYRES AND WALDO EMERSON HAISLEY

Prepared by Warren J. Samuels

INTRODUCTION

Published here for the first time is the correspondence of Clarence E. Ayres, one of the leading institutionalists of the post-World War II period, and W.E. Haisley, an undergraduate student of Ayres's[1] and for many years a physicist at the University of North Carolina at Chapel Hill. Copies of part of the correspondence were given to me by Haisley in 1973, the year after Ayres's death; the remainder were provided in 1994 by the Center for American History at the University of Texas and are published here with the permission of the Center.

Ayres (1891-1972) is well-known to historians of economics and, of course, to institutionalists. Waldo Emerson "Rip" Haisley was born in Taft, Texas, October 6, 1914. He received the A.B. from Texas in 1936, the M.A. from Columbia in 1940, and the Ph.D. in physics from the University of North

Reasearch in the History of Economic Thought and Methodology,
Archival Supplement 5, pages 121-220.
Copyright © 1996 by JAI Press Inc.
All rights of reproduction in any form reserved.
ISBN: 1-55938-094-2

Carolina in 1952. After teaching at Brown and Lawrence College, he taught at North Carolina starting in 1960. He considered his principal fields to be cosmic rays and the history and philosophy of physics. He died July 6, 1994. The letters are *not* presented in their entirety. Personal and incidental materials are omitted except as deemed pertinent to intellect and career. These omissions, generally entire paragraphs, are *not* indicated. Double-spaced ellipses are used, however, to indicate omissions internal to or directly accompanying quoted materials; single-spaced ellipses are in the original letters. The texts printed here include changes of wording made by hand by the author of a typed letter. Only minor stylistic and typographical corrections or amendments have been introduced by the editor. (In his letter of February 18, 1969, Ayres attributes his worsening typing to his increasing loss of his sense of touch and muscular control in his left hand, for an as-yet unknown reason. In his letter of April 29, 1970, after surgery, he identifies it as due to two squeezed cervical vertebrae.) Except for these corrections, materials added by the editor are indicated by square brackets (in a few instances where Haisley or Ayres used square brackets these have been changed to parentheses, although twice in one letter they are retained with an indication having done so). Because of Haisley's interest in the problem, and their discussion, of how to address his former professor and intellectual hero, salutations are included; however, words preceding name (complimentary close) at the conclusion (signature block) of a letter, not always present but typically "Yours" or a variation thereon, are omitted. Locations of writing are given as found. Significant periods of time without correspondence are present; whether any correspondence is missing is uncertain, although, because of the availability of both the Haisley and the Ayres collections, each with an incomplete set of letters by both writers, presumably there are no, or very few, missing letters.

   The reader who is an economist may find some of the discussions strange and uncomfortable. Haisley and Ayres often discuss very serious and very deep issues in philosophy, issues which economics largely ignores or begs as an intellectual discipline; indeed, these are among their most interesting letters. (In his letter of June 30, 1971, Ayres queries, "I don't know whether all this is economics or philosophy, and I don't care. Should I?" See also Ayres to Haisley, ca. July 1, 1969.) Both were trained in philosophy and in economics, and while Haisley (with some pain) left economics for physics and Ayres became and remained an economist, an institutional economist, neither ceased to believe that certain important issues of philosophy were relevant to their work.

   The list of topics is wide-ranging, including, with some overlap: musical technology, the institution of salutations in letters (which has led me to include them, insofar as I can), the work of Alexander Meiklejohn in relation to the instrumentalism of John Dewey, positivism and instrumentalism, the systemically-specific social-meaning laden nature of words and the conduct of inquiry, the social myths of science and the absorption into science of other social myths, the role of hypocrisy in human affairs, ontological and epistemological aspects of knowledge, the misuse and limits of mathematics in both physics and economics, the relation of science and theology, dependence on religion, the role of the system of belief in the status quo, the predominance of ceremonial/institutional thinking, Ayres's conventional view regarding technological unemployment, human nature, the consequences of industrialism, the economics of the arts, science, and technology, parapsychology, the nature of science, science and philosophy, the psychology of academia, what Ronald Coase more recently has denigrated as "blackboard economics," values and valuation, the consequences of reading Veblen, superstition and medievalism, the practice versus the theory of science, the progress of the study of the history of science (and of physics), philosophical realism, the relation of biographical idiosyncracy to scientific advance, the work of Thomas Kuhn and Michael Polanyi, and so on.

The correspondence is useful for identifying the views Haisley and Ayres had of themselves and the world, their "own personal philosophy of living" as Haisley put it (November 29, 1942). Present is a sense of the force of Ayres's intellectual influence on his students. The reader also glimpses Haisley's travails in finding both himself and a career, and (to a much lesser extent) those of Ayres in finding himself an object of witch hunting.

Interesting twists and nuances abound: Ayres's denigration of neoclassical economics and economists is coupled with both his lament at being neglected and his chagrin at being treated in kind. Haisley writes that he finds open-endedness "a little disturbing" (June 17, 1968). He indicates displeasure at what he perceives to be nihilism, moral or epistemological, and therefore a threat to social integration and coherence of direction in science. Whereas Ayres finds the relevant position more congenial.

One of the highlights of this collection is the letter from Ayres to Alexander Meiklejohn (March 23, 1943) a copy of which accompanied Ayres's letter to Haisley of February 23, 1967, in conjunction with which it must be read, and is printed after it here. One of the highlights is Ayres's treatment of the nature of discourse in economics and in politics.

Some correspondence from 1968, concerning a manuscript of Haisley's, is not reproduced here because most of the discussion involves personal comments about various people, especially physicists. Here one reads perceptions which would convince the reader, if one needed convincing, that conflicts over turf and prestige and over epistemology and ontology (as well as the use of mathematics, treated in included letters) in economics also exist in other fields, including that object of economists' envy, physics. Questions of method, of definition of scope of subject, of ego and ambition, of who is and who is not beyond the pale, and so on, abound.

In Ayres's letter of June 15, 1944, he explains to Haisley that certain topics concerning ceremonialism were omitted from the *Theory of Economic Progress* so as not to carry the reader too far from the main theme. In his letter of August 23, 1944, he states his view that music can provide an emotional basis for the multiplication of technology ("a multiplier of the technological process") so as "to release the pressure that otherwise builds up to erupt as ceremonialism." To the historian of economic thought the former point is suggestive of how vagaries of authorial design can convey misleading perceptions (for example, of scope and content) to readers. The latter point, in light of the former, suggests that had Ayres dealt more with ceremonialism in the book, he *might* have identified arrangements otherwise deemed ceremonial as performing that emotional catharsis function; *or* at least made clearer the totality of the model into which the technology-institutions (ceremony) distinction fit. The latter possibility is underscored in Ayres's letter of February 3, 1949 (as well as elsewhere), wherein he refers to trying to fit institutionalism into a "larger frame of reference" (but where he also refers to such as "stuffing," at least insofar as applies to a textbook on which he was working. Particularly impressive, however, is the extent to which both correspondents subscribed to, indeed believed in, the technology-ceremony dichotomy.

Pervading the correspondence are discussions, largely, though not entirely, by Haisley, of technology in everyday life, in music, and in the practice of physics, in part giving expression to Ayres's emphasis on the ubiquity and importance of technology.

The correspondence of greatest interest to historians of economic thought and institutionalists concerns the interpretation of Ayres's instrumentalism and the manner in which it is to be held, and therefore the nature and content of his institutional economics. A close and open-minded reading of many of the letters will indicate a number of topics on which Ayres takes positions and specifies the domain of relevance and meaningfulness of what he had to say, which positions and specifications are not, or not necessarily, always those subsequently adopted by the Ayres's disciples. These letters will contribute to the exploration of what Ayres meant but likely will not resolve the issues, although they may help to more completely focus the issues, or at least identify the larger set of issues in which the controversial questions arise. The problem, of course, is the hermeneutic-circle one: positions can be defined in terms of issues, but the definition of issues can be influenced by the positions taken on the issues, with no final criterion available to permit conclusive choice as to definition of issue and thereby of position.

Ayres's discussions of instrumentalism and ceremonialism are not entirely dispositive of the controversies which have ensued with regard to the so-called "Veblenian dichotomy." But they suggest, at least to this writer, that Ayres had in mind by ceremonialism not a set of precise a priori identifications, such that something either was or was not ceremonial in nature, but a *possible* characterization or identification given the circumstances. Certain ideas derivative of cultural practice, perception, and belief *could* be deemed functional of established power positions, but they also *could* be instrumentally useful in knowing what was going on and/or working out pragmatic solutions to problems. For example, some definitions of capital may function to legitimize certain practices and structures, but they may also be analytically useful for someone who is not taken in by the conventional ceremonial metaphysics. In other words, there is neither no closed category nor unique specifications of the ceremonial. Moreover, the category of the ceremonial applies especially to some questions we can ask, and not solely the statements which form possible answers.

Ayres's discussion of ceremonialism also throws light on the social function of the antipathy which Haisley and others have for "nihilism" and "relativism." This function is at least that of setting minds at rest, of psychic balm.

Considering the technology/institutions dichotomy more broadly, the category of the technological appears here to refer to an existential, empirical, instrumental, and pragmatic-utilitarian perspective; and the institutional (or ceremonial) to refer to that of grandiose teleology, metaphysical idealism, wishful thinking, and lines of reasoning singularly functional for maintaining the status quo (or selected elements of it), all typified by superstition (once called medievalism). One finds mention of the empirical importance of the incidence of the machine process, or the logic of industrialization. Concern over what is perceived to be relativism and nihilism, again, is deemed by Haisley to be as wrongheaded as superstition. Haisley stresses the importance but also the incompleteness of instrumentalism for understanding the human condition, but without thereby resorting to superstition. Surely Ayres appreciated the necessity of normative choices as perceptively as he understood neoclassicism's effective, albeit selective, reification of the status quo of property relations in order to generate determinate solutions. The problem has to do with the ontological and epistemological character of the normative choices. The Deweyian problem of the quest for certainty pervades many letters and is explicit at least once. The technology/institutions dichotomy is clearly a tool of analysis for Ayres, not a closed system. One overriding point, however, certainly is the importance of the technological process of socialization and life.

The foregoing comments notwithstanding, the correspondence speaks for itself and each reader will find that it speaks to particular issues of interest to him- or herself.

Methodologists will be interested in the wide-ranging and deep exchanges between Ayres and Haisley on the complex and intertwined issues of (1) nihilism and relativism, (2) philosophical realism, (3) epistemology and the nature of science, (4) instrumentalism, and (5) the ceremonial treatment of technology, institutions, and instrumentalism. Indeed, much of the correspondence between April 28, 1968 to the end of the collection deals at length with these questions, the stage being set, as it were, by earlier discussions.

I refrain from all personal substantive comments but one: In Ayres's letter to Haisley of July 23, 1944, he refers to Friedrich von Wieser as "a beautiful example of unadulterated marginal utility theory." This is not correct. Wieser was a perceptive analyst of power (in conjunction with utility) and the role of institutions in economic affairs. Had mainstream economists followed Wieser (of course, they did not, but that is another story), institutionalists would have had much less to complain about.

Finally, apropos of Ayres's remarks (letters of December 1, 1936 and August 23, 1944) concerning listening to music in general and the provision of classical music by radio in particular, I note first that I transcribed these materials onto my word processor (during the summer of 1994) often while listening to classical music through both the radio and compact disks. The aesthetic world has improved since the advent of radio, with the same impact identified by Ayres. And second, I quote Ayres's statement (April 17, 1972) that "The 'Hallelujah Chorus' (which is one of the greatest pieces of music ever written) may well survive Christian theology, if it hasn't already done so," commenting only that the work has not survived monarchism, as U.S. audiences invariably stand during the chorus, a practice started by a king.

N.B. Among the publications mentioned in the correspondence are:

Haisley, Waldo E. 1969. "The Instrumentalist Interpretation of Science." *Soundings* 52 (Spring): 60-83.

Schwartz, J. 1962. "The Pernicious Influence of Mathematics on Science." In E. Nagel, P. Suppes, and A. Tarski (eds.), *Logic, Methodology, and Philosophy of Science* (pp. 356-360). Proceedings of the 1960 International Congress. Stanford, CA: Stanford University Press.

Palacios, March 2, 1935

Dr. Ayres:

On my last visit to Austin I found it expedient to exploit as much of your time as I could avail myself of. This letter may be regarded as a further exploitation,—it is at least a useless but more or less ungovernable overflow of youthful exuberance. Finding it impossible to restrain myself completely, I am choosing this as the most harmless immediate outlet—although I hope to harness the bulk for effort on papers for economics 369. I hope, however, that some of my observations will be of interest and will in some measure compensate you for time thus idly spent.

By virtue of four months in economics 369, your article in the January International Journal of Ethics, and the intellectual fodder which I gleaned from our recent conversations, (pardon mixed metaphor) I am beginning to see the light. It has come over me in a sudden burst, much like the insight observed by Köhler in his problem-solving apes, and it is such a simple thing that I find it amazing I haven't tied the strings together before. I suppose it was stumbling over the obvious in an attempt to make things difficult and esoteric that kept me confused. The haziness I mentioned concerning your course has vanished; puzzling points I find dropping neatly into place; and I am acutely conscious of what you were driving at in various sessions which at the time I considered vague in import. The light of day has spread from economics to any number of fields: psychology, sociology, neurology, ethics, and even personal conduct. Solution of long-pondered points has become child's play, like the last stages of putting together a jig-saw puzzle, and instead of being forced to weigh the merits of various outlooks, theories, etc., in hopeless confusion, I can see where many of them are not inconsistent, can even spin off a number of new theories myself. I am at last prepared, I think, to work in real earnest on the task of separating in classical economic theory the scientific from the theological elements. [See Haisley to Ayres, June 4, 1944, regarding further enlightenment upon reading Ayres's newly published *Theory of Economic Progress.*]

Naturally, all this has been quite exciting, and I'm telling you about it simply to get it off my chest. There is no one immediately available to whom I can spout off, and of all correspondents and potential correspondents you are in the best position to understand what I am talking about with a minimum of preliminary explanation on my part. You may not believe it, but my excitement has kept my brain racing on two nights until about one o'clock, leaping over the hurdles of wealth, exploitation, technology, instrumental logic, etc. This, then, is a somewhat roundabout means of carrying out the spirit of doctor's orders. By unburdening myself I'm hoping to attain to a greater measure of calm and prevent a recurrence of the insomnia. Were it not for that I should probably be content to restrain my impatience.

Postscript on our talk of Sat., Feb. 23, regarding "the brutality of youngsters": I denied the accusation at the time, you will remember, but brushed away all attempts at analysis in order to proceed with the narration. Later, after a slight amount of "prayer and meditation," I came to the following conclusion, which I trust will clear me of brutality charges.

In probing and tapping at the moral and religious beliefs of the individual in question, I am doing what I practice in some degree with everyone whom I can draw into reflective conversation. I am continually analyzing situations and people, watching their reactions to ideas, etc.; so much is this the case that a friend of mine recently tried to taunt me with the appellation, "Analyst!" Mrs. S- happens to afford the best opportunity I have of studying an intelligent individual in the extremely rigid grip of Methodist morality and theology. (My sister, by the way, affords an equally good opportunity for studying institutional forces under the sanction of philosophy, that borderland "between the time when people have lived with religion and the time they are able to live without it.") The incident I mentioned was, I think, a very good illustration of the working of theological crystallizations in the face of subtle insinuations. It shows quite well the hardness and toughness of the theological shell that such a character as Mr. Barrett, portrayed so vividly by Charles Laughton, can fail to force Mrs. S- to reflect deeply.

In a sense there is the same juvenile brutality about it that makes a child continue to wind up a mechanical duck to "see it hop," but I think that to a certain extent it is educational and instructive, and it is certainly quite humanitarian. For even as the mechanical duck feels no pain, Mrs. S- comes off without injury. Her faith is too rock-ribbed to be disturbed, and she in unaware (thank God!) of the full import of my remarks, inasmuch as I once professed theological aspirations and she believes me to be an inquiring but passably devout Presbyterian. With her I sacrifice the solid ground of frankness for the more strategic position of the "unseen watcher." Your figure of "taunting and tormenting the cripple" is, as I remarked at the time, ill chosen.

All this being out of my system, I trust that I can procure for myself the blessings of a less active stream-of-consciousness. Thanks for bearing with me.

Sincerely,

W. E. Haisley

San Antonio, October 14, 1936

Esteemed sir:—

Bob Burns once told a story over the Gulf Hour about an uncle whose son grew to manhood without speaking, bringing great sorrow to the family. It so happened one day that as father and son worked together in the field, the latter broke his silence with the words, "Look out pa, there's a bull coming right at you." Overjoyed at his good fortune in thus being forearmed with such practical and well-timed information, and quite overcome by the fact that the dumb now spake, the old gentleman asked the boy why he had never before given tongue. Replied Abner, "Well, I don't know, pa, but somehow I just never did have nothin' to say."

In such terms only can I account for the fact that the copious and undoubtedly worrisome stacks of mail in your personal box have not since February been further overflowed by contributions from this quarter. Topics of conversation in such attempts at correspondence might have been either a recounting of sundry happenings within the D[epartment] of Eco[nomics], or miscellaneous assortments of brainstorm and inspiration from my own meager bag of intellectual tricks. Neither were forthcoming. Life within the cloistered walls of Garrison Hall last spring was strangely humdrum, and for my own part I consider it one of the most wasted five-month periods I have ever spent. I did a great deal of poking around, to no particular purpose, I encountered a multitude of flat ideas, in trying to untangle which I fell in the way of almost endless confusion, I suffered from a dearth of original ideas and a suspicion of ethereality toward those I had considered my own, and, from the standpoint of doing anything academically, socially, or personally constructive, became one of the most worthless mortals God ever withheld a thunderbolt from. Economic and politico-economic theory, as exemplified by forensic and expository passages in the press, magazines, textbooks (even Veblen!) became as so much drivel, so much inconsequential juggling of words, until I took to drowning my spare moments in chess, completed my required work in an uninspired, routine fashion, and decided, for the time being, at any rate, to forsake all things academic until (and unless) the staleness should wear off and the time should come when I might again yearn to tinker with an institution.

And so, my good fran', the present date finds me the veteran of three months' work at Stinson Field, San Antonio in the personal employ of one Frederick C. Harman, the proud possessor of a coat of tan and a high resistance (let us hope!) to cold germs. I have found it quite gratifying and soothing to grapple in close contact with oil cans and gas pumps, dirt and grease, windsocks and weather reports, airplanes and army trucks,[1] and a million and one other homely but reassuringly concrete objects in a land where people who have never heard of Adam Smith believe intrinsically in the righteousness and efficiency of capitalistic institutions, in R.O.T.C. units and the necessity of national defense, in the constitution and the supreme court. In a land far removed from the dusty smell of a library stack, where written material is confined to forms, invoices, and timetables, which my duties for the most part pass over lightly.

Outside of the social embarrassment of being a "flunky" (which is only on rare occasions acute) and the fact that my hours run from six to seven days a week on a pay check which could under no circumstances be considered fat, I am at present having a great deal of fun. I enjoy working hard, I enjoy being out in the open a great deal (one of the main motives in steering clear of office jobs), I enjoy the opportunity of learning any number of little tricks which I should have known years ago, and I am quite gratified by the attack and solution of technological problems which come up wherever there is a job to be done. Putting an aeroplane into a hangar, for instance, is a task of some nicety; installing a windsock on a long iron pipe at the edge of a large hangar, as I discovered today, presents a wealth of fascinating difficulties for the budding engineer. It is of the same stuff as this that more intricate problems are made. I have never before had so forcibly brought home to me the fundamental nature of what we have been calling technology. Naturally it would be exaggerating to magnify my own specific problems into any importance, but the fact that stands out is the multitude of such details confronting everyone connected with the running of an airport, details which must be worked out if the wheels are to keep turning. This is of course due to my previous lack of contact with actual productive employment. One is unfortunately apt to assume the attitude, when one remains in and around a university, that technology today is entirely a matter of big things, something cooped up within factory walls or the engineer's workshop or the mind of the "men who make the plans." It is indeed reassuring to be smothered with concrete evidence to the effect that human ingenuity is being exercised consistently and universally, that without its repeated use in daily activity the whole framework would be one blundering mess. A university is a poor place to learn that simple and obvious fact and an excellent place to forget it. No wonder institutional relationships dominate the thinking of so many of our professorial minds!

As you are doubtless by this time aware, I am once more attempting to follow the dangerous practice of tinkering with ideas, once more the enthusiastic and eager young man. Fortunately I am at present too occupied with details during the day to put much effort into such channels. During the last few days, however, I have done more reflection, philosophizing, and generalization than at any time since last March. If good fortune is with me, it may be only temporary. Otherwise I may be a college professor yet.

... What about Washington? Did you find the Consumers' Bureau an interesting piece of work, a dull interval, a hopeless tangle of politics? Are you as disillusioned concerning government machinery as are most idealistic people who come away from Washington? And so on.

N.B. Stinson Field, though not connected with the army, uses a White Truck which some absent-minded supply officer inconsiderately neglected to leave in France.

Rip Haisley

Austin, November 4, 1936
Dear Haisley:
... Did I never tell you about the time when I was for a few weeks a freight brakeman on the old Lakeshore and Michigan Southern Railway? It was an existence as completely satisfying as any I have known, intellectually interesting too, just as you say. You are certainly profoundly right about the technological details. [See letter of August 12, 1940]

The Consumer's Division was pure grief from beginning to end. The whole thing was blocked and its continued existence became shear farce. It gradually worked up to a climax in July when I slammed a threat of resignation on the secretary's desk which, as she plainly saw, was intended for publication and would have blown the whole show up. But it would have done no good. She was just as impudent as I was, as she admitted, virtually weeping on my shoulder; so I shrugged said shoulders and spent the rest of the summer on a long memorandum for the guidance of the second Roosevelt administration, which will no doubt be a greater success on that account.

C.E.A.

Stinson Field, San Antonio, November 23, 1936
Dear Dr.— (!!)

What is the trend brought about by the impact of twentieth century technology on the art of composition and reproduction of music? You are doubtless familiar with the subject, but in the December issue of <u>Coronet</u>, a magazine put on the market recently by the publishers of <u>Esquire</u>, is an article without which your education will certainly never be complete. It is "Music in 1955", by George Antheil, and if you fail to run it down and read it the next fortnight, I shall surely shoot you on sight at the earliest possible opportunity thereafter.

W. E. Haisley

Austin, December 1, 1936
Dear Haisley:

As you might guess, the impact of technology upon music is something in which I have a very special interest. Did we ever discuss it together? Are you just banking on my interest in technology? Consequently I went for the article you mentioned with real eagerness. But I found it disappointing. Isn't Antheil a composer? I have that impression and the article heightens it. In so far as he makes any point at all, it seems to be the hope that composers will get a break after machines have displaced performers since it seems unlikely that composing can ever be done by machines.

As a matter of fact machine technology has impacted upon musical composition from earliest times. Obviously composition waits upon the invention of instruments, systems of notation, and the like. One might say that the threshold of modern music is the invention of equal temperament tuning for pianos, organs, etc. As you doubtless know Bach was the great promoter of that system, composing especially to popularize it. If you know anything about music, you know that his two series of preludes and fugues entitled (for the system) "The Well Tempered Clavichord" contained preludes and fugues in every possible key, all capable of being played with one tuning under the new system. Before that time an instrument had to be specially tuned to the key in which it was to be played and modulations were confined to that key and those immediately related.

Doubtless the phonograph and radio will have their effect upon music and why not? But I think they are more likely to affect the institutions of musical distribution than music itself or even its performances and I am all for that too. The concert is a loathsome institution! (Did you ever read an essay by Carl Van Vechten entitled "Cordite for Concerts"? He wanted to blow them up.) I don't see why radio should be denounced for enabling me to sit at my fireside in Austin, Texas, listening to Casadesus play Weber and Cesar Franck. And as a matter of fact, quite apart from distance I would rather sit by my own fireside puffing a pipe than wedge in between two dodgers [written at top, connected by a line: "dowagers, not Brooklyn"] in Carnegie Hall. Wouldn't you? By the way, did you hear Casadesus on the Philharmonic program Sunday afternoon? He did a grand job.

In my opinion, phonograph records and radio have given a tremendous impetus to musical literacy. In my childhood the whole town turned out once a year when the Boston Symphony Orchestra played its annual concert in Springfield—that is, all the musical literates of the town, enough to fill a trolley car packed full! Once a year! Nowadays fine orchestras can be heard over the radio several times a week and dozens of people in this little town have portfolios of complete symphonies played by the world's best orchestras. What's wrong with that?

Most of the bleating against the "mechanization" of music has been done by tenth rate hacks who have lost their jobs. But like most cases of technological unemployment, the machines have given more expert employment to other people somewhere else. You are too young to remember what ordinary movie or even theater orchestras were like. Well, I assure you the music reproduced by the talkies is incomparably superior. [Added at bottom, connected by a line: "Much of it especially composed for the particular film. Chance for a movie Mozart here!] As a matter of fact, I think mechanical distribution has greatly improved musicianship everywhere by exposing it to high standards of comparison.

All this is shooting in the dark. Perhaps it is only what you have known and thought all along, but if I seem to talk loud it is because of a faint suggestion to the contrary which your letter seemed to convey. If you really are contrariwise, we certainly will have to argue it out.

C.E.A.

San Antonio, December 8, 1936
Dear CEA:

Oh Mortal Man, how doth thy soul delight in argumentation! Really, my dear Watson, you excel yourself. How you contrived to stay clear of the legislative halls must indeed remain a Major Mystery. Your propensity for finding an opponent and an issue on the shadiest pretext is startling at times.

At the next possible opportunity I must reclaim my last letter, of which I unfortunately made no copy, in order to search therein for the alleged "faint suggestion to the contrary," which, though I cannot recall it specifically, may well have sprung from the tendency I share with the rest of your students to give your intellectual ear an occasional tweak, good naturedly and without serious intent. Of such an impish gesture I was unaware, however, and it must have been totally unconscious.

Doubtless I gave too high a recommendation to the article in question, which certainly made no pretense on its own part of being ambitious or profound.

What struck me about it was the clarity with which its point of view ties in with Ayresianismus. Here, appearing in a popular magazine, was an article remarkably free from the fetishes usually clustered around any treatise on art. May I name a few popular cobwebs dealt ashcan sweeps by the Antheil broom?

1. The arts are a thing of "creative genius" alone, and are something above and beyond such trivialities as the instruments employed by the artists. ("...sheer mechanical genius produced Bach's pipe organ and later the modern machine-like pianoforte." "Music is an art involving not only the human soul but the most abstract of celestial mathematics as well, and it adapts itself...easily to man's engines." "One can safely credit the new pedal alone for the tremendous tonal revolution of Chopin.")

2. Increasing mechanization is the death of all true Art. ("Those who spoof against the machine and the machine-made music of the future, spoof, I fear, against the Wall of Inevitability." "I, for one, believe that the purge and the revolution of the *oncoming* (?! italics mine) mechanical age will be a healthy one...." "...the handwriting already on the wall is in a good clear honest hand, reminding one of the writing of automobile mechanics.")

3. Enjoyment of the art involved in good music consists of hearing and seeing "great" musicians play and having gooseflesh therefrom. ("Is there not...a much greater thrill to be discovered by humanity at large in music per se, and not for the sake of some great virtuoso's rendition?" "...a great deal of unnecessary fuss has been made over the performing reproducing artist." "Music will be music—and not gossip.")

Such clarifications are of course elementary to you and me, but to the public they are points which need to be driven home repeatedly, and I should say the article could stand on its own merits from this angle alone. I must confess, however, that a good deal of what he says concerning the mechanized trend in composition is news to me, and that I was highly interested in his predictions which, though daring, are quite plausible. In the delight of the moment I dashed off a letter to you, the contents of which you already know.

... [Now working in the construction industry] I am learning a good deal outside which would be difficult to learn in a library, and while I am again yearning for a University Career I do not wish to come back to school too soon. I have noticed that the most vigorous academic personalities and intellects belong to the men who have "been around" a bit.

W. E. (Rip) Haisley

Taft, Texas, February 26, 1937
Señor:
... I am at present working in the Cage Lumber Yard of Taft, taking a peek at life through a different lens and becoming more familiar with the technology of merchandising lumber, cement, lime, pipe, plate glass, and miscellaneous

hardware, as well as the institutional framework so closely associated with the name of Cage in South Texas.

W. E. Haisley

Taft, April 16, 1937
Dear and Esteemed sir:
You will doubtless wonder why the delay, since the nature of your last letter to me [March 5, 1937, suggesting that Haisley apply for a half-time instructorship in economics at the University of Texas] warranted an early reply....

The issue is (was!), of course, whether to forsake, for the present, the tempting, fertile and challenging fields of economics in particular and social science in general for the equally tempting, equally fertile and also highly challenging field (should I say sheltering pinions?) of natural science,—hereafter designated NS—with consideration to its industrial, as well as academic ramifications. The decision has in each case of reconsideration been in the affirmative. Main drawbacks to this course have been and remain: the permanent loss of personal contact with the development of a system of ideas that have perpetually intrigued me and that I have found highly stimulating; the friendship of a man whom I place second to none in the list of those I know, and whose ideas and opinions have been a source of more help to me than I can readily set down—which friendship will now be subjected to the double hindrance of spatial separation and divergence of interest, although, I hope, by no means done away with; the difficulty of avoiding the feelings of a general who is defeated and retreating, of rationalizing them into those of the general whose retreat serves a major strategic purpose.

Main arguments for course taken: I have always been somewhat more apt at things mathematical and at such NS as I have studied, than at things literary and philosophical. The difference has been slight but quite definite. Whether this reflects a "natural" variation of aptitude or an inferiority of intellect, supposing the problems of the economist to be more complex than those of the chemist, I cannot say. (Footnote: I am quite aware of the mediocrity of my own mental powers, although I have always been pugnaciously inclined toward those problems and complexities tending to bear out the fact.) It may be my opinion on this difference is merely the oft-recurring illusion of extra-pastoral greenness. But in view of the fact that I did so completely lose my footing during the ignominious spring term of 1936, I am willing to gamble on it. The considerations that originally moved me to pick the social sciences are irrelevant to the present (recent!) issue.

(2) During the past eight months I have had more contact with the technological pursuits than at any time previously. I have dabbled with homecraft of all sorts, including masonry, cabinet-making, etc.; of pursuits of

like nature at Stinson Field intimated in a previous letter. Nor are walls of lumber, brick, mortar, lime, pipe, plate glass, and miscellaneous hardware by any means devoid of similar pursuits, which may [be] defined loosely as work done manually with things more tangible than words. I have found a good deal of satisfaction from this sort of thing; it is, moreover, to be found in abundance in the NS—you might term it instrumental craftsmanship as found there.

As to the relative merits of the two fields, I need not go into detail or even present an argument, as such considerations in one's choice of work are apt to be more purely rationalization and self-justification than any other. What determines one's own choice is more a matter of personal preference and ability than any high-flung, idealistic conception of service to society at large.

I confess a good deal of disquietude in making this change, as I have indicated, and am conscious of a number of charges I may make against myself—of giving up too soon and being too easily discouraged, of wasting several years in the allotted three-score-and-ten (less discount for probable life expectancy) in trying and proving. On the other hand, as long as I am able to choose and experiment (financially, I mean), which in the absence of Acts of God I will be, I see no reason why the change is not fully worth the chance, and that the soundness of my own estimation of my abilities is not worth a gamble. It may be that I shall return to economics—in fact, those pastures, having receded somewhat, appear even now to be greener. But at any rate I am off for the NS, for better or for worse, and request your blessing and opinion, which need not necessarily coincide. Should you feel inclined to give me either or both some time before long, please do so, as I have need of them, and will promise to be less tardy in replying a written appreciation of same.

Number of interesting books suggest themselves for me to tell you to read or make note of. Among them are The School of Femininity, by Margaret Lawrence, which I am now reading and enjoying thoroughly, and Man the Unknown, by Alexis Carrell, which I abandoned after a chapter or two and do not care for, though it seems to be attracting a good deal of attention and is a sine qua non in my sister's library. With her I have held a number of spirited arguments over its merits, which seem to be based mainly on the fact that Carrell, who has been practically everything from a medicine man to a physicist, knows first hand the whole panorama of modern scientific thought and development. He is highly popular with ministers (not the diplomatic variety!) and dealers in the new and true religion. His thesis is that we have highly overdeveloped our knowledge of material phenomena and machines at the expense of our knowledge concerning man himself (where have I heard that tune before!). This he couples with a "genius" theory of innovation and a "group of great brains" account of progress. If Newton, says he, had turned from his study of the physical world and set instead upon the nature of man, how much better would we have been, how much more balanced our knowledge. In explanation of the fact that material innovation and investigation has taken precedence in science, Carrell cites the great complexity of human nature and wags his head profoundly as he ascribes to the human mind the peculiar trait of being better able to understand simple things than complex ones, a truism if I ever saw one. He also cites the greater longevity of experience and development in an individual, the fact that as an experiment a human life takes too long a period of years for any one man to study, said student being limited mortally in his study by a lifetime of similar duration. To remedy this he proposes an institute of "great minds," which shall perpetuate itself by handing down to younger geniuses the partial pickings harvested [by] the older geniuses. This he postulates as the sine qua non for saving our civilization from the inevitable decay and collapse into which industrialization is leading us. He even hints that we may have to give up said industrialization in favor of some less urban existence. The body of his work is devoted to a great body of fact dealing with the facts we now know, biological, physiological, psychological, about man. Whether they are relevant to what he thinks should be found out I cannot tell, as I did not go through them, nor do I know what he wants to find out, except that he is intensely anxious to see man as a "whole," to view him synthetically, whatever that means. What Shakespearean play comes to your mind? Or perhaps you are familiar with the man's work and hold another opinion? I dare you to do so and be consistent! But enough of this, or I shall work myself up into a two-inch coating of lather and catch cold.

Another book I might call to your attention, if it has not already fallen under your scrutiny, is The Return to Religion, by Henry C. Link. Although I have read nothing more than a condensation of same, I believe it to be, from what I have heard, a most worthy contribution, making some excellent observations and deserving a much better title....

Have been listening with great delight to CBS Sunday Afternoon symphony broadcasts of late when the opportunity presented itself. Remember with great pleasure one occasion upon which Deems Taylor laid on rather heavily in rebuking the symphony-listening public for their shortcomings. It was on the occasion of a rendition of a "Symphony in One Movement," by a currently up-and-coming American composer (whose name I have most-ironically forgotten). His theme was on the reasons for the non-development of great American talent in composition, his explanation based on the difficulty a newly-composed symphony has in finding its way into the permanent repertoire of an orchestra. This he brought in turn to the fact that what the listening public craved was not new music but familiar music, that they were saying today, "Give me my Beethoven and Brahms, and Mozart, and you can have all your modern stuff," just as they were saying one hundred and fifty years ago, "Give me my Bach, etc., and you can have all your Beethoven, Brahms, and Mozart." This, coupled with the fact that a composer in America is expected to be well-to-do, an assumption not shared in Europe, was the substance of his argument. He put it in the second person and minced no words. If you didn't hear it you should have. (Trust you will read nothing serious into my apparent peremptory comments.)

Rip Haisley

Austin, May 4, 1937

Dear Haisley:

Your interest in a scientific career sounds very exciting. I hope that as it develops you will keep in touch with me and shoot me a lot of new stuff on the nature and significance of technology.

What you say about Carrell is particularly amusing. I confess I haven't read the book but I have heard a lot about it, all highly disgusting! You win all the bets on that point.

I wonder if you would be interested in an article by a physicist who feels that any one who is sincerely interested in science must on that account hitch his wagon to socialism since capitalism restricts production (and therefore science) and is obliged increasingly to sustain itself by suppressing freedom of thought (and therefore science). Any how I think I will send it to you.

Yes, we also have found Deems Taylor's comments interesting and to the point. One thing I like most in him is his candid admission that nine-tenth's of the product of any generation is tripe.

C.E. Ayres

Taft, May 22, 1937

Retel—

You are more than kind, especially in forwarding the book, which I am returning currently. Have made a cursory examination of most of the essays contained therein, a more thorough study of the one you recommended and a population treatise entitled "The Invention of Sterility." More of that later.

"Frustration" was aptly chosen for the whole book. Have had Huxleyan (Alduous variety) nightmares for six weeks, and challenge any thinking person to read hither and yon throughout the book and avoid feelings of profound apprehension for the future of mankind. Especially gloomy was the outlook in "Science and Industry" and the paper on population. Turning from the last page of the title essay one hears sounds of distant thunder, beholds a great Darkness, and from somewhere comes the voice of Veblen, in deep, sonorous tones. "Business enterprise ... stands to lose in the end whether the one or the other of the two divergent cultural tendencies wins, because it is incompatible with the ascendence of either."

Prof. Blackett is to be commended for his emphasis on the connection between science and industry, scientists and the trend of current events, political and economic. Also for the sophisticated manner in which he brushes aside the "stupidity theory" of history (which, fallacious as it obviously is, enjoys at the present time a great popularity). Again for sundry comments showing a good deal of insight. Believe he is all wet, or at least on a tangent, when he attempts to account for the combination movement and the introduction of machinery as a phase of class interest and interaction (i.e., the forcing of machine methods upon the workers by the big "industrialists," who presumably sprang full-grown from the head of Jupiter, their inability to force same on the middle class, because "the attempt to rationalize trade is against the interest of the great part of the middle classes, those that are engaged in small shopkeeping—???—). When he speaks of the "economic forces inherent in Capitalism that have caused *combination and the introduction of machinery* (italics mine), he betrays lack of comprehension, or so it seems to me.

Regarding his conclusion, that a definite cleavage is inevitable, I should like to satisfy myself on a number of points. Is rationalization actually losing ground today in Fascist countries? Is curtailment of output the rule there except insofar as it is an inevitable corollary of intense nationalism? i.e., are internal prices being held rigid by the monopolists themselves. These two questions bespeak considerable lack of information on my part concerning the details of economic life as carried on currently in Germany and Italy. Can you recommend an authoritative reference on the subject?

I should like to know further what Blackett means by "complete Socialism", and whether the gloomy tone of his article, as well as of the entire book, is more characteristic of current British comment than it is of current American writing on the subject. Certainly it seems so, and it may well be that we of U.S.O.N.A. and the western hemisphere may take hope for a liberal future, though hell, high water, and other extremes continue to rage throughout Europe.

I am sending you a May copy of the <u>Scientific American,</u> recommend that you read therein an article by Charles F. Kettering on "Research and Industry," which comes out big and strong for more and better achievements in technology, emphasizing the need and opportunity for same, and containing incidentally some interesting footnotes on the Diesel engine and current difficulties in financing research laboratories and research projects. Significant sentence: "I think," says Kettering, "we have become too expert bookkeepers."

Would like your reaction to the aforementioned article "The Invention of Sterility." I find it extremely convincing, am unable to shake his logic or question his statistics. Can you? He attaches minor importance to a scientific technique of contraception (which he affirms, to my surprise, has for over two centuries been available), attaches major importance to the increased mobility of today (also a technological function, though he fails to recognize its derivation), and the elimination of child labor. Only serious challenge one can make to his thesis is against his tacit assumption that the reproduction rate will remain less than unity once the effects of a declining population begin to be felt.

W.E.H.

Kerrville, Texas, June 1, 1937
Dear Herr Doktor:
    I note with dismay that Rhine, McDougall, and crew are gaining an increased degree of recognition with regard to "Parapsychology," having launched a magazine on the subject and been well-wished by the Scientific American, written up by Time (April 26). Am torn between the impulse to tear my hair and shout "Why doesn't somebody do something?" and the ha'nting suspicion that there may be something to what the boys have done. Have read, somewhere or other, fairly complete reports of the ESP experiments, which have been performed under conditions which baffle any attempt to explain them away (subjects removed from each other and correlations made by telegraph, etc., etc.), at least on my part. Has the Psy. Dept. at U.T. made any attempt to check the experiments, as I understand other universities have? Have you any inclination to modify your stand on the subject? If not, are you seriously bothered by Rhine's results?

Rip Haisley

11 June 1937
Dear Haisley:
    ... Kettering has the right idea about the fertility of research, of course. But of course the contrary opinions he is knocking down are loose-packed straw-men. Nobody who has any direct knowledge of the state of science and engineering holds such views.
    Your "h'nting suspicion" is a credit to your youth and sincerity. But you remember my old dictum, that the most difficult thing youth has to learn is that the world is as foolish and corrupt as in fact, alas, it is. You would be justified in reasoning thus. Anything that McDougall has any connection with is discredited in advance. The fact that a McDougall influenced movement may gather momentum, even considerable momentum, is not surprising. Look at the Brit. Soc. for Psychical Research. The Scientific American has suffered from this taint for many years. I don't know the personal commitments that account for this, but the fact is imposing. E.g., it was the Sci. Am. that offered a $10,000 prize for any authentic spirit-raising evidently with the intent to raise and pay since they were on the point of paying off to "Margery" and were only stopped by the stubborn exposing-crusade of Houdini persisted in even after he had been forced off the committee of award (if I remember aright) by disagreement with (among others) the editorial representative of Sci. Am.

Somebody in that outfit hopes desperately to find his dear departed in the Great Beyond and is not above using the mag. to provide himself with satisfaction that he will.

"Why doesn't somebody do something?" Well, few people have the persistence of Houdini and Joseph Jastrow in so negative a crusade. The attitude of most people is one of weary disgust and hope that something will happen to discredit the absurdity without their having to take time to smash such utter silliness. Like zoologists and the Loch Ness "monster." That is the feeling of the psychology people here—and my own. We know why such hopes spring eternal. There is nothing we can do to prevent that. Are you aware that Voliva still proclaims the flatness of the earth? Does that arouse your crusading zeal?

I think all this must be a reaction to the ME part of your encampment! The encampment part sounds grand, especially the function of the Protector of the Weak. [In his letters of May 22 and June 1, Haisley writes of his month stay at the Methodist Encampment in Kerrville and of his "role of male protector of family" in regard to his sister, nieces and maid, in the absence of his brother-in-law.]

[signature missing]

[no location given], 18 June 1937
Hail, 1912!
... If any remember me as Dean Meiklejohn's philosophic protege, they will not be surprised to learn that his is the closest friendship I retain from college days. [Letter written by Ayres on occasion of the twenty-fifth reunion of his Brown University graduating class.]

As you see, I am now ranked as an economist. But don't let that fool you. Maurice Clark once told me of lunching downtown with a friend and a group of his business associates who were invited after some little conversation to guess what his department is. Their guesses were all different agreeing only in this, that he couldn't be an economist since he professed to know so little about such things. On a smaller scale I am that kind of economist. Still spinning theories and no nearer to making a fortune (or losing my shirt) on the market than twenty five years ago.

I have never had a brokerage account and probably never shall; own no property, "have" nothing, and probably never shall. Nevertheless, while millions starve not quite unresistingly I live in virtually perfect security and ease, have everything I want. [See in this connection Ayres to Alexander Meiklejohn, March 23, 1943, accompanying Ayres to Haisley, February 23, 1967, end of fourth paragraph from the end.]

Perhaps I should say by way of "Hail and Farewell" that I have been and am quite ridiculously happy. In spite of certain crises such as we have all been through, I have had a really glorious time. I am doing just what I want to do, and I still cherish the illusion that what I am doing amounts to something. "What about Communism?" Well, I don't see barricades ahead for us. John Lewis? Ho, hum. But if they do come, I am as good a candidate for garroting by communists as a reactionary as by fascists for a red. But in either case I shall have got it in the neck after a swell time.

[no signature on copy]

San Antonio, July 2 [1937]
Dear Dr. Ayres:

I came away from our last meeting rather rueful and highly confused. It is very difficult indeed to escape the conclusion that I have, in abandoning my academic aims, betrayed the confidence you have always placed in me and my work, and your suggestions regarding the possibility of an instructorship at TU next year, necessitating a clear-cut choice on my part, brought home the point more than ever.

I don't think I can elaborate very much on the reasons I gave you at the time. Since I left Austin fourteen months ago with an incomplete thesis in my brief case, things have gone badly with me, so far as serious intellectual interests are concerned, and I seem somehow to have lacked the spark that makes people conceive important projects and push them on toward a successful conclusion. About the only tangible results of this year's residence at Columbia have been passing my foreign language exams (no great achievement, certainly) and completing the thesis, after a drastic revision of its title, plus thirty more hours of course attendance credit on the records of Columbia University. Measuring my own progress against the general average of other graduate students I saw around me, I can't say the results stack up very high.

It may be, as you say, that filling an instructorship, and thus putting the whole thing on a professional basis, might snap me out of it. But this is the third time I've gone sour on the academic milieu, and I can't help feeling that something more fundamental must be at fault than any change of tactics can remedy. Maybe that something is completely with me, and maybe it's with the combination. But the best plan of action I can dig out of the situation is to act on the latter assumption and seek salvation elsewhere. May Heaven have mercy on my soul!

I hope you won't consider it mere idle rhetoric when I say that I am deeply grateful for the support you have always given me whenever and wherever I needed it, and that I still hope to repay you in some way or other for your confidence and encouragement. One of the worst pills I have had to swallow in making the choice is the knowledge that in making it this way I am probably disappointing you.

But at least I hope you won't be among those who feel I am throwing my life away by not pursuing further a career in economics. And if you're still

of a mind to be visited and written to by me, from time to time, I shall continue
to pester you with letters and pop-in calls (when I'm in Austin). It was very
nice chatting with you and Mrs. Ayres again, and I now feel quite free to say
that the opportunity to make your acquaintance and absorb your ideology was
the thing about my college career that I will remember longest and value most.
You are as swell a person as you are able a thinker, which is saying right much.

Rip Haisley

San Antonio, August 15 [1937]
  Dear Dr. Ayres:
  Thanks for your "Go thou in peace." Believe me, it meant a great deal.

Rip

Columbia University, New York City [undated; see next letter, Haisley to
Ayres, dated "11, 7, 37" for indication that this letter was written in October
1937, per reference to salutations and to Wolf book, plus reference to this letter
said to have been written two weeks earlier; see also Ayres to Haisley,
November 8, 1937 regarding recency of Haisley to Ayres, dated "ll, 7, 37"]
  Dear Ayres:
  From among the usual salutations we employ in the ordinary letter I am
always at a loss to choose when addressing your esteemed presence. "Dear Mr.
Ayres" sounds stilted, as does "Honoured sir," "Esteemed teacher," etc., and
between these and the slightly-too-familiar connotations of "Dear Ayres" I am
always at something of a loss to choose. The only possible compromise that
suggests itself is "Dear doctor," which smacks too much of the M.D., so I shall
ask you to supply the necessary middle-word or expression by conventional-
izing the above expression. Please note for future reference.
  ... I trust ...[a]lso that proposed curriculum revisions in economics have
gone through with great success and that your lectures in the new introductory
course are giving you the widespread reputation on the campus which you
would have had long ago had more students been exposed to you (pardon
this obvious pat on the back, the temptation to make which I could not resist,
inasmuch as the profundity of the impression you have made on the few people
I have met in the "run of the campus"—out of the department—who do react
to the name Ayres, coupled with the numerical paucity of same, have often
puzzled me). I might also add that I have been following the Reader's Guide,
and will continue to await the appearance of the next article.
  My own plans have unfolded very smoothly. Having tentatively settled on
chemical engineering as a degree-goal, I am now taking qualitative analysis,
physics (which I have never before formally studied), calculus, engineering
drafting, and solid geometry, the lack of emphasis on which in Texas secondary

schools I find is a source of wonder to academic people up here, where it is a prerequisite to college admission. As I anticipated, I find the work interesting and absorbing, discover I am still able to untangle mathematical problems, etc. If things continue as I have them outlined, and granted that seven years is the usual period of preparation for a professional degree, I shall have lost about one year by making the shift.

One disconcerting development has occurred. I find that the ghost of economics has not been effectually laid to rest but is continually bobbing up and touching me on the shoulder. For one thing, my present contact with the "natural" sciences has brought out all the more clearly the instrumental nature of scientific inquiry, my renewed study of mathematics has showed more adequately how it, too, is purely instrumental (abstraction, of course) and partakes of the nature of technological development by being the cumulative putting together of "tools of inquiry." For instance, there is a parallel to the oft-recorded phenomena of simultaneous-independent discovery in other fields which we have so often remarked in discuss[ing] science and technology) in he fact that both Newton and Leibnitz are credited with the discovery of the mathematical tool differential calculus. Even more significant is the fact that both discoveries came within half a century after the publication by Descartes of La Geometrie, in which he in turn had brought analytical geometry into existence by crystallizing the developments implicit in the combination of algebra and geometry, etc., etc., etc. In all the natural science work I have observed so far there is a frank acceptance of the instrumental nature of their work, and a delightful sense of freedom from philosophical complications. Or so I find it. The question of course arises, try though one may to forget about it, "Why can't economics be the same way?" Does the answer lie in the fact that mathematical rigidity cannot be attained in the social sciences? Well, the fact is that neither can it be attained in chemistry and physics. If you try to apply a mathematical rigidity to the constants of his formulas, your physicist or chemist will shrug his shoulders and say that in actual experiment other factors introduce a variation, or that the mathematical equation holds true, "other things being equal." Precision is always possible on a small enough scale or in an abstract enough medium, which amounts to the same thing. Thus the economist who offers the young shoe-shine a quarter to run an errand for him and observes the result (supposing economists were to engage wholesale in such rather inane activities) is being just as precise and experimental as is the physicist who drops two weights off a table or a cliff. People who are in business are always and forever conducting experiments in the reactions of their customers to this or that situation and acting in accordance with what they have learned, just as the engineer uses experimentally-ascertained facts to bring about certain results. And so on.

The parallel further enlarges itself when one considers the concatenation of interests beginning in the most abstract sections of the natural sciences on the one hand and ending up in the most highly practical end of engineering on the other. On the one hand, there is emphasis on the examination and understanding of the materials of the physical sciences; on the other, there is emphasis on using these materials to practical purposes. To be sure, the divergence of interest is apparent all along the line, and "men of science" are sometimes inclined to thumb their noses at the engineers, and vice versa, but there is very little of the bitterness that marks the mutual aloofness between the department of economics and the business school. It is possible, moreover to conceive that an understanding of economic activity and "sound business judgment," the antithesis in this case, may mutually reinforce each other and that the department of economics is losing just as much by the spirit of moral indignation which dominates its attitude toward business men and the business school as the latter is losing by its general contempt for "impractical" economists.

You can see the train of thought suggested and its possibilities for ramification. None of this is essentially startling, except that it has brought back into focus for me a picture which I have not seen clearly since around December-January, 1935-6. And of course it puts me once more on the wrong side of the fence, if allowed to continue. For just as truly as my scrambling to get into chemistry and physics was a "flight" from the social sciences, so with the returning belief that I could actually keep my feet on the slippery floor of eco[nomics] comes a cessation of the necessity for making the flight so headlong and precipitous.

This raises the question of whether I would not, in economics, go into another spin, and of course that cannot be easily answered. I have finally come around to admitting that most of the difficulties I encountered in the spring of '36 were my own fault, and that they derived from a combination of allowing myself to have ideas faster than I could assimilate them and of committing myself to the logically-absorbing but energy-consuming complications involved in the problem of converting (at the expense of other considerations involved the Riley, the Stocking, and the Allen points of view and terminology into the terminology of institutions and technology. Perhaps a second time I should have learned a few lessons and would be able to proceed on firmer ground (Hope you don't object to a variety of metaphors all dragged into the same discussion.)

So you see, once more I'm in something of a quandary, which seems to be my perpetual state of mind. On the one hand, I am firmly resolved not to humor myself and further accentuate the habit of vacillation which I seem to be acquiring by giving in to my impulse to return to the pastures of economics. On the other, I am keenly regretful that I was not able to feel this way six months ago, and it seems a great pity to scrap the background I have in social science, like so much lost motion. The logical solution seems to be in a synthesis of the divergent trends, but as yet I cannot see what that would be.

I hope you aren't irked by my repeated lengthy discussions of what are essentially my own private problems. I find I still have need from time to time of unburdening myself on paper to some one, and I know of no one who is as well versed in the background of the ups and downs of my academic ambitions as are you. So don't consider these ebullitions as appeals for advice (although any comment you might make would be gratefully received). I have always found that the emotional necessity of telling some one your troubles seems satisfied whether you get an answer or not, as long as you are assured of an understanding ear.

Went to the national business show last Thursday night and stood amazed before the variety of electric typewriters, calculators, index-filers, cash registers, etc., which are on the market today. Discounting the fact that some of them are not in actual operation throughout the country, and are mainly "dog" there remains a rather high residue of mechanically induced efficiency which the balance of them impose on the conduct of business affairs generally. I was once more impressed with the fact that the combination movement, about which we talk so much, brings with it the accompanying problems of interchange of information (business correspondence), keeping of accounts, and cataloguing of relevant data on a mass scale, the solution of which has depended on <u>mechanical</u> or <u>essentially technological</u> developments in this field. Especially has this been true of the structures of our more impressive financial institutions. Where they are not concerned with the handling and safe-keeping of money itself, they are concerned almost exclusively with the filing cabinet, the calculating machine, and the typewriter. Witness the existence of "recording sections," correspondence divisions, etc. With this phenomenon you are, of course, most familiar. Why hasn't some one interested in technology given some attention to the effect, in business organization, of the typewriter, the adding machine, the filing cabinet, and the technique of writing known as shorthand? (Question rhetorical. We both know the answer.)

You probably have the book on your shelves by now, since it bears so closely on your subject, but just in case it had slipped your attention, may I call attention to a work entitled "A History of Science, Technology and Philosophy in the Sixteenth and Seventeenth Centuries," by Wolf (New York, '35). I ran across it yesterday morning in the Science Reading Room here, and was rather impressed by its scholarly proportions as well as the fact that it contains a pretty clear conception of the relation between scientific instruments and the progress of science, although the author is also inclined to give some weight to the "new spirit of freedom" of post-Renaissance days, which spirit of freedom was of course an immediate factor in the situation. He has a separate chapter on the development of such scientific instruments as the telescope, the microscope, the barometer, the thermometer, the air-pump, the pendulum clock, etc., and such statements as these are particularly striking,

"It was only by slow degrees that the growth of natural knowledge and the invention of mechanical contrivances for doing wonderful things by 'natural' magic helped to rid the world of the mysterious powers of darkness which haunted the Middle Ages."

"Galilei's experiments were also handicapped by the lack of a suitable instrument for measuring short intervals of time."

The book also contains, toward the last, a chapter on the development of economic thought, which I did not get time to read. It devotes a section to the development of the practical arts (building, etc.) and should indeed be a windfall if authentic.

Also call your attention, if you have any more than a casual interest in the subject, to an article in the current Scientific Monthly on the Rhine controversy, concerning which a good deal of a stink seems to be arising in psychological circles around here, judging from the comments of an acquaintance I have made in the psychology department. This particular article is written by a professor of math at McGill University, attacking the validity of Rhine's results along the lines of probability, and pointing to the fact that we have as yet had no definite tangible results given out, no figures to be analyzed by psychologists at large. By the way, have you ever heard of "brain waves" (cathode ray oscilloscope phenomena in field of psychology)?

Went yesterday to the Radio City Museum of Science and Industry, which is one of the best, from the standpoint of teaching things, that I've ever been in. Particularly interesting was the demonstration of "Polaroid," of which we have read for some time but which is now on the market commercially. I had no idea its ramifications were so wide in scope. Besides the elimination of headlight glare, which it was nominally developed to effect, its uses touch on illuminated advertising, on the analysis of stress in glass models of engineering designs, on photography, on the elimination of sun-glare in daytime without corresponding darkening of the landscape. Particularly striking was a demonstration of three-dimensional projection in motion pictures, effected by polaroid glasses and closely resembling the old style stereoscope in principle. Two images are projected on the screen, differing in that they are shot from slightly different angles of the same object. The right lens rejects the view which would in three-dimensional vision be seen by the left eye, and vice versa. The result is most striking.

Rip

New York City, 11, 7, 37 [see previous letter regarding dating]
Sir:-

Another experiment in salutations. I hear it used quite frequently up here in addressing the professors. Perhaps it, better than anything else, epitomizes the higher degree of classroom formality you find here.

Just as a footnote to the letter I wrote you two weeks ago, let me add a word or two about this book by Wolf I spoke of. I gathered from an acquaintance who is a history graduate here that it is quite well-known (although the historians view it as somewhat too sanguine in conclusions for the evidence available), so that you probably have it on your shelf. I did not recall seeing it there two years ago, and since it came out in 1935 thought it possible you might have missed it. Pray do not impute to me the attitude of superciliousness which is frequently taken toward alma mater by graduates who come East.

All the same, the book is significant and certainly should be thoughtfully scanned by any one interested in the history of science and technology. One passage I thought so striking that I was moved to copy it, and (in case you aren't familiar with it) went so far as to make a carbon, which I enclose [not present]. I find also, in reading his chapter on the development of mathematics, that my effusive semi-conclusions regarding Newton-Leibnitz developments following Descartes were most superficial, since the development of the calculus was at time of invention not nearly so closely related organically to analytic geometry as I supposed.

Moreover my idea about the simultaneity of Newton's and Leibnitz's discoveries is rather overturned by the controversy which has raged in mathematical circles over this very thing (and in which I notice Wolf, by the way, has a definitely pro-Newton bias, which is understandable, international affairs being what they are). Found most interesting the facts (quite familiar to you, I know) that the most revolutionary developments in the development of mathematics in Europe were the introduction of Arabic numerals and the development generally of the symbols of mathematics, many of which today we regard as quite elementary. Quite astonishing the difference our exponential notation makes in the ease with which one may understand logarithms, and also quite a credit to Napier that he was able to do something with the concept in the absence of such a notation.

Rip Haisley

Austin, November 8, 1937

Dear Haisley:

How came you to omit from your list of possible salutations, "Honored Master"? Or possibly "Maestro"—though that seems to be reserved for musicians.... what you say interests me very much, especially your points on the technical character of mathematics and on the techniques of managerial organization. I try to bear down hard on both, though of course not as much as I should like. Don't you dare abandon me when so much needs to be done. I have always wished, for example, that every orthodox economist could be made to take a trip through just such an exhibit as you saw. Yes, I have Wolf on my reserve list for 369. Try me again.

C.E.A.

New York, November 20 [1937]

--------------: (I give up!)

...I am herewith classing my "excursion" into the natural sciences as definitely that and nothing more. Think I can justify both the excursion and the decision to return to economics on practical as well as sentimental grounds, although there has been a good deal of time and effort put forth tangentially, I suppose. Have also succeeded in convincing myself (from the sort of a stride I have hit this fall) that I will be able, barring unforeseen disturbances, to keep my balance better, progress more slowly, get a better visual grip on more of the focal points of economics....I see no very good reason why I should not go into the graduate school the second semester with the greatest of ease.

Will discuss the matter with Goodrich....[In Ayres to Haisley, November 8, 1937, Ayres suggests that Haisley call on Carter Goodrich, Winfield Riefler, and Joseph Dorfman. Goodrich and Dorfman were at Columbia, Riefler at the Institute for Advanced Studies, Princeton. Goodrich and Riefler had been at Amherst with Ayres. Haisley reports on his meeting with Goodrich in Haisley to Ayres, November 28, 1937.] (Please note for all future reference as a convention between us that when I drop a title in any letter to you I do not imply any lack of respect! I confess to being a bit oversensitive on the subject and am becoming somewhat irked at my lack of success in striking a fine balance between my dislike of appearing pedantically formal and my fear of appearing too familiar, a fear which is, of course, heightened by the sense of formal appellation so prevalent up here. It is always a problem for a younger person to know how properly to address or refer to an older man. In the case of these letters the convention I suggest seems to be at least one obvious way out.)

On re-reading the passage in Wolf I can see that he does indeed, as you point out, miss the instrumental nexus, which is after all the crux of the whole situation. That it is rather close to the surface in what he has to say is undeniable, however, even if he does emphasize the aspect of divergent interest ("creative instinct" versus practical necessity) as his point of departure....

                                                                                        Haisley

New York City, December 11, [1937]

[no salutation]

...Perhaps I've committed the unpardonable social sin of becoming a bore, although I hope not. At any rate, I apologize for making you bear the brunt of my "outlets"....

Wish you could have been here today to go to the exhibit of the chemical industries (have forgotten precise name and auspices) at the Grand Central Palace. You would have revelled in it, as it was, although pointed a good bit in the direction of chemistry, nothing more or less than an exhibit of technology. I found it more exciting than the auto show, although it was a bit less intelligible, as I confess most of the stuff on exhibition was quite novel as far as I was concerned. There were all sorts of machines for mixing, centrifuging, drying, conveying, etc., exhibitions involving the prominent display of superior points of various and sundry metals and chemicals (I remember especially Alcoa and U.S. Steel), and a number of precision instruments, including torsion balance, calibrated glassware essential to chemistry, the microscope, and a pH meter which, according to the glib assurance of the attendant, measures pH from the e.m.f. of the pH electrode. I left, resolving to find out at earliest opportunity exactly what a pH electrode is, as Zanetti, teaching qualitative analysis, has omitted it from his discussion of pH, and I should certainly be discomfited if, at some future gathering of men-interested-in-science at which I happened to be inappropriately present the conversation were to turn on pH electrodes and leave me utterly unable to follow.

The exhibit was aimed primarily at industry itself. The cards to be filled out required that you state specifically what your connection was with the chemical industry, and it was apparent that the general public, which was coming in in spite of everything, was not a little in the hair of the exhibitors. This is of course quite out of keeping with the current trend of good-will cultivation, and I was rather surprised to see it in the chemical industry, which doesn't seem inclined to miss opportunities to impress on John Q. what a noble service the heads of its institutions are rendering to humanity. Children under 19 were not admitted, it presumably being subversive to the morals of the high-school-age American Boy to gaze upon sights indicative of the remarkable properties of stainless steel.

I left the exhibit with the firm conviction that if I had continued firm in my intentions to be a natural scientist and were to spend a good twenty years of study I could still go to such a collection of technological impedimenta and come away bewildered.

While we're on the subject of excursions I must ask you whether you've ever been through South Hall, Columbia's library building, since its completion in 1934....it is a book-lover's paradise if ever there was one. It is an amazingly massive nine-story structure, and most of the thirty-odd department libraries are located somewhere in it. I have always tried to go poking around on bookshelves when I got the chance, but if one goes poking around here one must do so in terms of something greater than bookshelves, or one never finishes making the rounds. In fact, time can profitably be spent just in going from room to room (as you look them up on the bulletin of library information), spending only a very short while in each place. In that respect it's like the Metropolitan Museum of Art, in which I think a good two or three days could be spent in getting oriented without ever looking at an individual exhibit.

...[Carter Goodrich and I] went over the catalogue together and found that, although there are the usual complications of entering the season at mid-year, a course of study can be worked out which will be something more than a makeshift. It will include courses under Clark, Dorfman (The development of American economic thought), Wolman (problems of labor), and Goodrich himself, who will not be here next year and whose course in economic history I want to get first-hand, although to do so will involve missing the first half. Think I'll go on into the integral calculus, too, as I have found the differential quite interesting and the subject seems to be a useful tool in such a statistical subject as economics (or perhaps you disagree!).

Although my main energies this month are (I hope) consolidated on organizing and throwing into perspective the things I have learned/am learning from natural science and the natural scientists, I have still been thinking along the lines of technology and institutions, and I wish I might go into a lengthy dissertation on discoveries made. Time forbids, however, and necessitates only a brief comment. Which is probably just as well, since you are probably aware of the relationships I have seen, and I doubt whether I have uncovered anything especially new. Indeed, I frequently find myself harking back to some statement you made in or out of class and feeling that for the first time I really begin to understand what you were driving at.

Specifically, my posing of problems along this line has taken the course of personal efficiency and how to get the most distance in a given amount of time. As you are probably aware, my tendency to be overenthusiastic is most conducive to inefficiency. In boom cycles it prevents a sound evaluation of ideas and precludes to some extent their control. Always, too, there follow depression cycles, during which I can't get up much steam.

Solving the difficulty has involved an analysis of work, and to what extent it is dependent on effort, to what extent it is independent of effort. For certainly one's ability to put out is a function of his emotional tone, and the whole problem of working efficiently may perhaps be posed in terms of getting the right tone— of getting excited enough without getting too excited. If effort is to be a criterion of how much one may accomplish, then one must keep said tone high.

...I heard Eric Knight make a statement last Wednesday night (in a lecture before a film-study group on the movies as creative art forms) that brought into sharp relief the other part of the picture. It was that genuine artists who accomplish much are often notable for the apparent effortlessness of their activity.... It would seem that the use of skill is interfered with by the use of effort, and that skill is apt to get one much farther in the long run than effort. It remains only to show how skill itself is an integral phase of the technological relationships of the external, material, world (function of timing, balance, leverage, etc.), and we have the whole business tying in very prettily with technology and institutions.

There are other related questions—how to start from a state of rest and build up with gradual acceleration instead of leaping at one's work with full tempo; how to increase efficiency in memory and understanding by following trains of thought (put forward by others) passively until they finish, thus avoiding the mental irritation produced by conflicting trains of thought that occur when one tries to criticize as one follows. I needn't go into them here. All this of course represents conclusions made concerning the way to get things done, and not actual achievement—but I think I've gained a good deal of proficiency in the latter respect, too, although such proficiency doesn't come at once, I know. I'm able to handle a time schedule of my own making much better than I used to be, and I'm less easily diverted from a course I've set down. Which sounds like bragging, and which probably is, but Heaven knows one must brag to some one some time. So excuse it, please.

I see an article in the New York Times this morning which I should send you except for the fact that I want to keep it. It concerns experiments made by Davis and Shaw at Indiana University done by oscillograph in measuring the muscular accompaniment of brainwork. It certainly lends tremendous support to the idea that muscular activity and cerebral activity (the physical and the mental) are never divorced, that it is impossible to have one without the other. On second thought, I believe I will send you the article and ask you to send it back next time you write. I suppose you'll come back with the fact that you were already aware of the experiments, at which I shall be greatly disgusted, but which is to be expected. Just wait, though. Some day I'll catch you!

Haisley

Austin, December 17, 1937
Dear Haisley:

Your salutation troubles have provided me with several chuckles. I wonder if it would make you feel any better if I could convince you that the difficulty is a matter of age discrepancy, complicated of course by institutional sanctions. I mean it arises quite generally between people who are a generation apart and is by no means a special difficulty of the academic profession. Only the other day at a committee meeting Dr. Battle was chuckling over a letter he had received from the president of the University of North Carolina, whom he regards as a close personal friend and calls by his first name. The younger man, however, finds it emotionally (institutionally!) impossible to address Battle by his first name and so resolves the difficulty by calling him "Mr. Will," to Battle's great amusement. Incidentally, our community's habit of calling each other by first names but "Doctoring" the elders, like "Dr." Battle and "Dr." Miller, is another instance. In addressing Alexander Meiklejohn I resolve the embarrassment by using a half-jocular, half-affectionate title. I always call him "Prexy" though he calls me "Clarence."

I am awfully glad to hear that you have worked out a plan with Carter Goodrich's help that will get the wheels rolling right away—and a good one, too, I think. I don't need to comment on your work with Carter and Joe [Dorfman], but I am especially glad that you are going to get in touch with

Maurice Clark so soon. He is a giant and no mistake. When you get in touch with him please give him my regards.

C.E.A.

New York City, December 22 [1937]

Dear Mr. C-:

Your remarks on the salutational difficulties were quite to the point and provided me with the tentative term above, which seems to be less objectionable than anything I have thought of so far. It should do, at any rate, until something more spontaneous springs up of its own accord. I think the problem, as you outlined it, is somewhat further complicated in this case by a tendency on my part (of which I think you are aware) to deify you as a "great mind," while at the same time I have been fighting against it by trying to get to know you as a person. Hope it doesn't disquiet you when I say that I am gradually getting away from the "great mind" obsession by realizing how insignificant in the social set-up, how utterly dependent on civilization as a whole, are the efforts of any one individual (including my own projected efforts!). At any rate, the problem still has its hangovers, and addressing God by his first name has, I believe, been a ticklish proposition since ancient times.

I have another article to recommend, although I am becoming increasingly cautious about such recommendations. I have even wondered whether I should not make a resolution and hold my tongue religiously. I think I have been influenced too much in the past by the desire to make a stir—to beat on my chest and say, "look what I found," and am still no doubt influenced by that sort of thing, in which I suppose there isn't a great deal of point. It is really difficult for a younger person, whose fundamental tendency is to believe that none of his personal discoveries have ever been made before, to sense which things will appeal to the seasoned veteran and which things are old stuff. Just as truly, I think, older people are apt to impute to youngsters their own grasp of the situation at large and fail to realize fully that the enthusiasms of the "children" are a direct outgrowth of the fact that they "hain't been around yet." So I hesitate to keep on recommending at this stage of the game for fear that you will grow indifferent to the cry of "wolf!" (no pun intended).

But I'll venture forth once again. I ran into this article last night when I was diverted by it (happily no doubt) from an article by Stuart Chase I had casually intended to read—I believe Chase has now taken up the cause of purging economics from its confusion in the use of words; do you still shudder when you read him or read of him? The sidetrack-article was entitled "The Age of Schizophrenia" and was written by a self-styled amateur (Leslie C. Barber) who has taken up the study of psychology in the aftermath of a nervous breakdown—I think he has a book out, of which this is a portion. He poses the problem of maladjustments in terms of its social setting and is very emphatic about the dichotomy between intellectual habits and emotional habits. The former, for some reason he doesn't quite clarify (he manages to talk all around and about technology without hitting it on the head), tend to progress, to ramify without limit. The latter tend to fixate, even though one is intellectually aware of their stupidity. He is quite clear-sighted about the problem, I think, although he is perhaps over-optimistic in hoping that its solution may come mainly through applied psychiatry. It is one of those articles that reassures one by showing him that other people see substantially the same things that he does. I think you'd enjoy it.

What do you think of the current international situation? It looks to me very much as if we are on the spot. I have been trying of late to think the thing through, for the idea of war, I must confess, makes my blood run cold. I have never been a particularly warlike animal, and the thought of bullets, bombs, and bayonets gives me much anxiety, as does the thought of how much worse a shape we would be in after a war than we were after the last one. All the fundamental factors are emerging, too, including the "cause," which seems to be the preservation of democratic peoples from the menace of fascism. Do you join me in believing it possible that people are yet far from ready to fight and that it will take some time to get them to the fighting pitch? We both know that "incidents" by themselves do not make wars. If only people could be prevented from stampeding!

I am reminded of your contention that if we could just stave off things for five or ten years it would make a hell of a big difference. It in turn suggests a remark made by T.Z. Koo at an address he made here some time ago concerning the Eastern situation. He stated that China was trying to build up a modern civilization, had been trying to since the chaos ensuing after 1911, and that what she most wanted was to be left alone—to develop in peace. Just a few more years, he seemed to feel, would have meant much.

Maybe that's the way the dinosaurs felt about it.

I believe that if we could let the Fascists alone—and if they really are as intent on turning back the clock as people seem to believe—that eventually they would defeat themselves by their own stupidity, although I am still inclined to wonder whether they are succeeding in their attempts to stop the march of industrial progress. If anything is beyond question in the history of civilizations it is the superiority which a highly developed technology gives to its people in the struggle for power over technologies which are less highly developed. Not entirely in the military sense, of course.

I think I could find most comforting at the present stage a survey of your evidence to the effect that the continuity of technology was not seriously interrupted by the institutional breakdown accompanying the decline of the Roman Empire. What historical authorities do you usually cite to support your point? I did not take your course in the economic history of Europe, and I cannot remember from your articles whether you came down strong on specific references at this sector.

Enjoyed talking to your sister last Saturday night, although everyone was
a bit tired and none of us really got warmed up. She was of the opinion, as
was her husband, that this country must eventually go Fascist. We debated
the point of technology and institutions in its relation to the matter of
permissive vs. causal relationships, and I think I held your ground....

Rip Haisley

New York City, December 31, 1937
Dear Mr. C:-
...I confess, though, that I have chafed a good deal under the necessity of
completing the courses in chemistry and physics, which have occupied during
the past month and a half a position all out of proportion to their significance
as far as I am concerned. But such is the inflexibility of institutional forms.
...although I am far from free, I confess, from an emotional attachment
to personal success, ...I am sincerely interested in the battle you are fighting.
It is becoming increasingly plain to me, as time goes on, that it is a battle that
is being fought on many fronts, which are closely linked with your own, and
I can see very clearly, I think, that the distinction between technology and
institutions is one whose use in explicit form (I think most people sense it in
a vague sort of way) is clearly justified. It is every bit as justified as a sign
in a cave at the juncture of divergent passages, saying "This way leads
somewhere," and "This way leads to blind alleys." ...

Rip Haisley

February 18, 1938
Secretary
Columbia University
New York, New York
Dear Sir:
This letter is written in behalf on Mr. W. E. Haisley, at present a graduate
student in economics at Columbia and a candidate for a graduate scholarship
for the ensuing year. [Haisley has requested this letter from Ayres in his letter
of December 31, 1937.]
I have known Mr. Haisley intimately for a number of years. He was a
member of my classes as an undergraduate and as a first year graduate student
in economics in this department, and an assistant to Professor Riley. The
relationship became sufficiently personal so that it has been followed by a more
or less continuous correspondence. I feel partly responsible for Haisley's having
gone into economics here and for his having returned to it at Columbia.
Haisley's academic record speaks for itself. What I am more concerned about
is the quality of his mind and personality and even his personal circumstances.

He had what is sometimes called a "gentle" bringing up, that is, his people are moderately well-to-do and unusually well educated, cultivated people. He has lived in an atmosphere of books and ideas of intellectual interest and active self-expression all his life. Consequently it is not surprising that he is an unusually thoughtful, imaginative boy, unusually earnest in his pursuit of ideas that interest him, and unusually well-equipped for intellectual pursuit. I hesitate to make a remark of disparagement of other types of students but it will bring out my meaning more clearly if I say bluntly that Haisley is not a "careerist." He is not the kind of boy who is primarily interested in a good degree, good connections and a good start on an academic career. He doesn't need to be. He can afford to take his time, to travel, to study abroad, and to wait for the finger of fortune to beckon him when, as and if it does.

As a staunch friend of the proletariat I dislike to admit that a youngster with these perquisites has such an advantage over others as I nevertheless know he has. It seems to me that a post-Ph.D. distinction is coming to be recognized between the mere grubbers and the lucky ones who by virtue of personal advantages or one of the big traveling fellowships have been able to take a sort of post-Ph.D. degree. It is to be expected that the higher positions in the greater universities will be filled increasingly by recruits from this group.

Haisley has all the advantages that qualify a man for this higher stratum. It would not surprise me at all if he never returns to Texas except as a visitor!

In short, on the theory that them that has gits, and help should always be given first to those who need it least, Haisley should be at the top of your list.

C. E. Ayres

Professor of Economics

February 23, 1938

Dear Haisley:

Just a note to let you know that I have written as strong a letter as I could to the Secretary in your behalf....

Let me know how the scholarship comes out and don't stop the flow of clippings and comments. I very much enjoy all your messages. Have you seen my <u>Problem of Economic Order</u> yet and what do you think of the job Farrar and Rinehart did with it?

C. E. Ayres

New York City, March 7, 1938

Esteemed sir:—

...Riley, by the way, advises me to push mathematics and statistics, as the statistician seems to be a person in some demand, and as he also felt that my own temperamental characteristics are better suited to technical work than to controversial subjects. I have indeed been thinking quite seriously on the issue of fact vs. generality, with slight leanings toward the former of late, although it seems to me that the chicanery and conjury of figures is more monstrous than that which is done with words, since it leads to so much more forcible an illusion of precision. Particularly do some of the meanings which are imputed to national-income figures give me nightmares. Whatever can be said against the school-of-business people, I feel that they are inclined to be a heck of a lot more realistic in their approach.

...the Problem of Economic Order came to light. I was of course tickled to pieces and made all haste to secure a copy, since when I have been pondering over it at leisure. I think you have been quite successful in covering a good deal of territory quite well in a small space. Is this part of the idea of "The Professor's Contribution to the Course," which you have been developing? If so, it impresses me as being quite adequate. If I remember correctly, you had very much this same thing in typewritten form in connection with the same idea two years ago. With much trepidation I suggest that a money man might be disposed to quarrel with the price-of-gold approach to the value of money—but then a money man would probably not be too sympathetic anyhow.

I have been poking around with the idea of warming up the wire hash and making something respectable out of it for a master's thesis. Have been torn somewhat between the desire to push forward with the gospel of technology and the advisability of introducing the pecuniary aspect strongly enough to assure potential readers that I am writing economics and not a combination of engineering and sociology. I've found some interesting material on the subject, though, and the sources seem to be quite voluminous. They include the copies, since its inception in 1926, of Wire and Wire Drawing, a trade periodical which is quite voluble, and sundry works in the engineering library devoted to the subject. It seems to be much better covered than I thought, although one reason I didn't get any further than I did was that I didn't fully realize that wire is regarded by many as a portion of the iron and steel industry. For instance, V.S. Clark, in his History of Manufactures in the U.S., treats of the development of the wire industry under the heading of "iron and steel forms." And, indeed, the drawing of a metal through a die can be regarded as primarily a technique of metal-work rather than a technique-whose-aim-is-to-produce-wire, and as such it is closely akin to rolling, welding, founding, hammering, etc. By the way, do you remember the book called "Outspinning the Spider" which we tried so hard to get? There is a copy in the engineering library here, so I finally got a chance to have a peek inside. It is just what you'd expect—quite dithyrambic and utterly unreliable. States the theme of "how little does the common man appreciate what is being done for him by the makers of wire" in a way that makes it quite trite and repulsive. Otherwise it is an extolment of the virtues of John A. Roebling and a description of the beatific state of laboring men at Roebling, N.J., which is interesting if true. Damned if I don't go there some time just to see if the sb was lying. One thing seems certain—the suspension bridge was very closely associated with the commercial and industrial development of wire rope, for obvious technological reasons. By the way, did you know that the first application of machine methods to nails was in a slitting process, which was not driven out by the wire-cutting process until somewhere in the eighties? (Don't quote me on the decade.)

Also, I suppose you have noted carefully the book on technological trends brought out under William F. Ogburn by the National Resources Committee last year.

The only thing I can't reconcile myself to about sticking to wire is that it seems to take one a good distance afield from Texas. In some ways it seems more to the point to take something like sulfur (since oil is pretty well crowded) and work on it both from the standpoint of industrial organization and control and from the standpoint of technological development. What do you think? Perhaps it is stupid of me to keep Texas as a base-line to which I intend eventually to return somehow or other, but the idea becomes more irresistible the longer I am away. By the way, I haven't explored sulfur at all. Do you know of anyone who has done any work on it in the department?

...Winfield Riefler...says he wants to see some Veblenian sail into automobiles, which are of course technology rampant, as we know....

By the way, I attended a meeting of the Economics Club last Wednesday night, at which I struck up a conversation with a chap by the name of Lichtenstein. We came around to the subject of mutual interests, and I happened to remark that I had been a little too thoroughly inoculated with the institutional approach to appreciate the subtler beauties of the Marshallian approach or the mathematical analysis of supply-demand schedules. Apparently I had put a very unholy hand on the veil of the temple, for I immediately became the object of the utmost solicitude. That an economist could grow to manhood without a thorough comprehension of marginal utility seemed to this individual to reflect a benighted state which was horrible almost beyond belief. Tchk, tchk!

...I enclose a bit of doggerel, ...which, while not a product of current difficulties, reflects the state of mind I get in not infrequently.

Rip Haisley

> Twinkle, twinkle
> Upon matriculation
> Our hero's expectation
> Of higher education
>   Was eager, bold, and wide;
> But after much reflection
> In this or that direction

He yearned on retrospection
To toss it all aside.

The academic litter
Had set his brain a-jitter
His ideas all a-twitter
    His intellect agog;
In seeking the illusion
Of harmony and fusion
He could not quell confusion
    Or rise above the fog.

The patterns and the schisms
Reflected by the prisms
Of multi-morphic-isms
    And scattered all around
Were still, for all his sorting
And logical contorting,
The meaningless cavorting
    Of shadows on the ground.

And when, with temples burning,
He left the Halls of Learning,
His sanity, returning,
    Became his only law;
He lost for good his leaning
To grand attempts at gleaning
A Universal Meaning
    From everything he saw.

We join him and the preachers
In shouting from the bleachers
At young and giddy creatures
    Who run with eager feet
That joys of digging ditches,
Pursuing solid riches,
And scratching-where-it-itches
    Are very hard to beat.

New York City, March 15, 1938
Esteemed sir:
    I have just attended a dinner given by the economics club, at which a lecture was given by Dr. Haberler on the theory of international trade. The comments of Dr. Haberler were punctuated and illustrated by a series of charts which he drew on a blackboard with much earnestness and gravity. Such things as "indifference curves," "heroic assumptions," and other figments of "pure theory" figured prominently in the discussion. So far as I was concerned it was about as edifying as the comments a South Sea Oyster might make on the poem about the Jabberwock. From the perplexed expressions I observed

on the faces about me it was equally obscure to others. There are two possible reactions to such a fact. One is that one's confusion is due to intellectual shortcomings, and this is undoubtedly true to a certain extent. The other is that this sort of thing is as rigorous and consistent within itself as a game of chess, with about as much relation to anything which is not chess. In the light of such a suspicion, the fact that in this day and age a man can grow into a position of academic prominence on the basis of such lucubrations, so that a large group of students are compelled by considerations of decorum to listen with respectful frowns to such a demonstration, is nothing short of monstrous! But Dr. Haberler insists that these formulations can be carried forward and made the basis of policy, with no more serious obstacles than, as he expressed it, some "slight complications." I suppose one can expect this sort of thing from a Harvard economist of mathematical predilection, yet to see it actually in operation leaves me gasping.

There was also a most exasperating discussion of the issue of whether the economics club should affiliate with an organization which is currently on the campus for the avowed purpose of expressing sentiment in favor of democracy and intellectual freedom, with the idea of "combatting" all encroachments against these most worthy ideals wherever they crop up. I don't know when I have listened to a discussion which was more futile or devoid, with a few exceptions, of anything approaching a tenable argument. If I may say so, it was a God Damn mess, and would provide among other things, an excellent source of material for a book entitled, "The Asses have it; or Children, Let Us Bray." One piece of reasoning might, I think, interest you. The organization in question is presumed to be "combatting" the enemies of democracy, etc., by "peaceful" means, included in which is the sending of money to Spain. It was proclaimed with much satisfaction that the purposes were not militant, since they did not propose the actual use of the bayonet. With similar reasoning one might also suppose that in an actual war, the causes for which the war is said to be fought are prosecuted by "peaceful means" by all except the actual combatants. This should be quite a useful notion in the current problems of casuistry in international law.

It might interest you also to hear of an encounter I had with one Oxenfelt, who is from the University of Pennsylvania, is a student and disciple of Raymond Bye, and who told me with great condescension that said Bye is one of the "foremost minds in economic theory in America today." Said Oxenfelt is committed to a policy of the very positive statement of very positive opinions, a very persistent use of the "knowing smile" and supercilious sarcasm, and the general practice of intellectual browbeating at every opportunity, all of which seem to imply that he is himself a very gifted person and knows a great deal more than a great number of other people, including J. M. Clark and Wesley Mitchell. He also professes to see nothing whatsoever in Veblen. Much to my surprise, he is not squelched by anyone among the graduate students, who so far as I can see exhibit a very commendable tolerance toward him and who seem to have no disposition whatsoever to exterminate him. I might say that I am unable to share in this attitude.

Rip Haisley

March 19, 1938
Dear Haisley:
    Your account of the session with von Haberler amused me very much for several reasons: (1) Only a few days ago a young chap we have here this year as an instructor gave the departmental seminar a lesson in neo-classical free-hand drawing which has been the subject of amused discussion ever since; (2) Only a few days ago I had a long conversation with a Harvard man who is much disturbed over the state of economics in his alma mater and thinks he may be in a position to do something about it, in the course of which von Haberler came in for an overhauling, along with others of his ilk; (3) Another long letter from Marion Levy contains the same gripe.
    However, I don't see that you fellows have any grounds for gripe whatever. It's your world and you know it. Those boys are on the run. That is why there are becoming greater extremists than ever in the asseveration of their doctrines. Just look! The present season has produced, in addition to Thurman Arnold's best selling opus, first and best, my sister's article in the current International Journal of Ethics, "What Shall We Do with Economic Science?"; Barbara Wootton's Lament for Economics (Farrar and Rinehart); and a reprint by Random House of Hogben's Retreat from Reason, a retreat which seems to be led by neo-classical economists. With all that support, you should whine! By the way, see Lament for Economics, page 272: "... the very welcome news that The Economic Intelligence Service of the League of Nations is to test out current theories of the trade cycle (as presented in Professor Haberler's recent masterly summary) by reference back to historical data. Since it is clear that some of the more practical minded economists are already alive to the need for thus tossing their theories over to the buffetings of experience, it isn't necessary to enlarge further upon this particular aspect of the subject."
    Your feeling about the absence of any family atmosphere at Columbia is more important. But that, too, is general. It is the curse of "great universities." But it has a corresponding advantage. You thereby enjoy a very special freedom to do as you damn please.

C.E.A.

May 1939
To Teachers Appointment Committee
    I have known Mr. Haisley for several years first as an undergraduate, later as a graduate student and assistant in this department and still later as a

graduate student at Columbia[.] I have been in active correspondence with him. I consider him one of the best, a man of genuinely inquiring mind, with a capacity for getting excited over ideas and infecting other people with his excitement. He is, I feel sure, one of the small group from whom the important economists of the next generation are now being recruited.

He did excellent work as an assistant, and I feel very confident that he will make a fine teacher. Whoever employs him now won't be able to keep him very long. He is going places. But anyone who has the good sense to prefer young men who are going places will get a prize in Haisley.

CEA

[In the Ayres Papers at the University of Texas at this point is included the following, with the name "Haisley" marked in handwriting in the upper left corner:]

The Way of the Transgressor
or
Justice Just as She Is

It wasn't that he wanted to be fickle,
That his nature was unconstant or unkind;
    And it wasn't that he didn't give a nickle [sic]
When a maiden couldn't get him off her mind;
    It was not because he was so sure to make 'em
That he shied away at making one a wife;
        It was only that our James
        Had a knack for playing games
And a sensible philosophy of life.

It wasn't that Matilda was immoral
Or that she wasn't sweet and undefiled;
    Her purity was worthy of a laurel,
And her innocence was that of any child;
    It was only that this loving little cherub,
Who was courted by that rather artful boy,
        Was a simple country lass
        Who didn't know a pass
From the tender touch that marks the real McCoy.

And it wasn't that her father was a terror,
Or a Tory with reactionary views,
    For he didn't storm and Shout about her error
When Matilda came to him and broke the news.
    But the wisest and most tolerant of parents,
Though he close his eyes and count to ninety-nine,
        May get madder than he ought of
        At the right distasteful thought of
Illegitimate descendants in his line.

It was no resolve to make a new beginning
Nor a rediscovered clarity of sight;
And it plainly was not consciousness of sinning,
That made our hero Jimmy see the light.
Matilda's father's methods of persuasion
Were simple but were carried out with vim;
It was not that he was older;
'Twas the shotgun on his shoulder
That made a true believer out of Jim.
It isn't that there's genuine instruction

In this rather oft-repeated little tale;
We are not antagonistic to seduction,
Though we know it's apt to land a man in jail.
So you see that it was not to draw a moral
That we added on another stanza more;
The poem seemed to need it,
But you do not have to read it
If you're sure you understand the other four.

Austin, August 12, 1940
Dear Rip:
... I must have told you some time about the spell I served as a freight
brakeman and how completely satisfying I found that way of life. I found I
could easily look forward to a lifetime of it. [See November 4, 1936.] ...

Clarence

San Antonio, November 7, 1941
Dear Mr. Ayres:
...As an old convert who has never lost the core of his convictions, I have
continued to cherish the hope that one of these springs will bring off the press
an Ayres bible, which can be used as an intellectual weapon to brandish over
the heads of the unenlightened as well as a touchstone for one's own reflection....
...A year of work with a bank has proved of some value as a stabilizer,
but has not, as might be expected, produced any profound results in intellectual
growth or stimulation, except as any new job gives one a peep at the big, wide
world from a different angle and perspective. I have, it is true, spent some time
learning a smattering of commercial law and analysis of financial statements
in two A.I.B. night-school courses, and acquired a speaking and reading
knowledge of Spanish by taking some private lessons, not to mention the
perusal of an occasional book on banking or economics from the library, but
I am afraid that my truly ambitious reading has been <u>nil</u>, and that my current
reading has consisted of nothing heavier than <u>Harpers</u> and <u>Time</u>, which two
magazines have been practically my sole sustenance.

Not that the former is entirely devoid of significant reading. I would recommend to your attention particularly an article in the May number of this year, by Paul Schuster Taylor (of the U. of Cal.) entitled "Good-Bye to the Homestead Farm," which sets forth very pleasantly and clearly the thesis that (1) The size of the farm-operating unit is steadily increasing, (2) This trend is traceable directly to the development of farm machinery, and (3) The bulk of our farm labor displacement problem (as, for instance, that of the "okies") is directly traceable to this development. No foe of technology, the unpleasant social effects of which he so clearly traces, Professor Taylor ends on the note, "The real question is not: Are we for or against more farm machines? It is: How can we distribute the benefits that more machines in agriculture can confer?" (N.B. doubtless this is giving up the problem in a grand manner, but it seems like an excellent way to end a magazine article.)

I note, on the other hand, with some concern, a "trend" (?) which seems to be running strongly in recent thought (if Harpers is a representative example). There is a growing tendency to speak of our recent "neglect of values, ends, and objectives," so prevalent in thinking people, runs the thesis, ten to fifteen years ago, and to state with some authority that we will attain smooth going only when we set some big bugs on the problem of deciding just what our goals and (above all!) our values should be. This sort of talk may be futile and refutable, but it is occurring in sufficiently large quantities to make one feel like tearing one's hair. Take, to give some examples, a recent article by President Hutchins in Harpers, the dicta of a certain biology professor on last Sunday's U. of C. Round-Table of the Air, or Lewis Mumford's latest booklet, "Faith for Living," a series of reflections full of illuminating insights all adding up to the very mistaken conclusion that modern Western Civilization has betrayed itself by denying "Value," can only raise itself again by seeking new ad-valorem polarity. Do I mistake myself? Is this a trend, or only a literary rash that breaks out again and again periodically? Maybe you can tell me.

I have not yet regretted my decision not to teach school, for although I am not resigned to being a bank teller for more than an indefinite temporary period, I believe I would be temperamentally more suited to that existence than to the life of an instructor of economics. Still, I do miss the academic atmosphere and viewpoints in many ways.

Rip Haisley

[On the stationery of the Panama Limited, of the Illinois Central System, dated "Mississippi, 19 November 1941," Haisley, who had recently visited Clarence and Gwen Ayres, addressed a hand-written note, "Dear Clarence"—a significant change in salutation practice. The note treats their recent visit and touring.]

San Antonio, December 29, 1941
Dear Dr. Clarence:

I'm enclosing some articles from Harpers Magazine, for your perusal with the request that, if you aren't completely irritated at me for forcing them on you (and thus goaded into tearing them up), you drop them back to me whenever you've given them a gander. I've taken to saving such things in my own files, since library magazine files are not so readily available now as formerly.

The article on the Chicago school is not particularly significant, but it is another straw in the same wind I wrote you about last month. It is the old slugfest between theologian and scientist, reproduced in its 1940 version, and what I would particularly like to know is whether, in the perspective of your own years in the world of ideas, you do not find that the tide of academic opinion has ebbed recently in favor of value-hunters. I have had neither the years of observation nor the constancy of exposure to place too much reliance on my own judgments, but I do repeatedly fancy that the hue-and-cry is becoming louder (witness, for instance, another article in the January issue entitled, "The Anti-Industrial Revolution," by some talented jackass named Roy Helton), and a considerable portion of it seems to spring in some not quite evident way from the vicinity of Robert Maynard Hutchins. I probably should not find it disquieting, in view of the fact that technological progress does not wait on the approbation of university professors, yet I can't help viewing it a bit gloomily. The various converging viewpoints by which you and other intelligent followers of John Dewey approach the logical and spiritual problems involved have always seemed to me so thoroughly useful and workable that it is disheartening to see them so grossly mishandled by friend and foe alike. For it seems to me that at least some of the charges of sterility and insufficiency levelled against the partisans of "pragmatism" (or whatever you choose to call it) have been well founded, and, what is worse, that the deficiencies have been due to the failure of these partisans to develop, or to clarify the implications of their point of view.

The other articles are the first three of a series which has been running recently in Harpers. I found them significant and meaty, although I hesitate (remembering past experience) to predict that you will find them so to the same extent that I did. Do you know Nicholson? His articles are enough like the ones you used to have us write in "economic forces" to have been written for that course under your tutelage. (Also, I believe there was a series of such articles done, with slightly different emphasis, for the Consumers Bureau, but these seem closer to the focal point of the "technologist's" interest than were the "price study" articles.) Such articles seem to me to be a tremendously effective way of showing the all-pervasiveness of technological advance, as distinct from such narrower things as the mythical "Industrial Revolution" or "Advent of the Machine." Was the idea original with you? If so, how did you happen to think of it? If not, where did it come from? And where do you suppose Nicholson got it?

Rip

Austin, December 31, 1941
Dear Rip:
...I am quite touched that you should still be interested in the product of my labors. Well might you wonder when the mountain will bring forth! As a matter of fact two, or rather three, circumstances have combined to bring me to the definite decision to take decisive steps. One is the maturing of the positive, affirmative value-theory aspect of "institutionalism" which has been going on with the assistance of a new course, "Value and Welfare," instituted for the purpose two years ago. Another is my increasing and now decisive exasperation with the effort to get things done in the midst of the interruptions of the academic routine. And the third, incidental but important, is the fact that the children are now all grown up and permanently located in homes, or at least perches, of their own, so that for the first time in many years I am privileged to make plans for myself (and Mrs. Ayres).

The price study series you refer to was organized and edited by Walton Hamilton, my old friend and initiator into institutionalism, which explains that. Surely you identified him. But I don't know Nicholson at all. However, the second paragraph of the Plywood article contains the answer to your question. Wharton School to the contrary notwithstanding, the guy's read Veblen, and the inevitable has happened.

Which brings us to the current backsliding. Or is it? To some extent I think it is. A war of nerves has been going on for some years now which has as an almost inevitable accompaniment a certain amount of emotional-relief finding. It happened in World War I. But that is a short-run thing. WWI was followed by a sharp reaction against all the nonsense that had been talked in high academic places in the war years. There is also a longer secular trend which is more significant. After all, the social sciences have thought themselves out of old sanctions without as yet establishing any very definite or general scientific "scheme of values." And they are going to have to. That is what Mumford is groping at. Definitely it's groping. Some of his blind gestures are most disconcertingly reminiscent. But what he is reaching for is findable. The technological principle contains the key to the riddle, and sooner or later this will be realized by all and sundry, after the fashion of Nicholson's Veblenizing. And that is how Adler and Hutchins will get it in the neck. They have done a neat job at Chicago.... But it won't stay put. On the contrary, the more completely Hutchins has committed Chicago to medievalism the quicker and more certain and decisive the reaction will be. The general post-war reaction might well be touched off right there. For the truth is, those birds haven't solved their own problem, as even Adler admits; and we know they can't. And that will finish them. A new period of fruitfulness in the social sciences, with some such positive principle as we have been working on providing the solvent of the relativism-nihilism of the past generation, and all this pieced-together Thomism will tumble into an ideological rubbish heap. Have courage! It won't be long now!

Clarence

San Antonio, April 15, 1942
Dear Clarence:
    Your last letter was as cheering as December's reports from the Russian front—it is always so heartening to know that your batteries are still blasting away from the same position. I hope that war developments have not altered your plans to go ahead this summer and bring it all to a head. Personally, I am convinced that the most critical times that lie ahead of us will be post-war conditions, when a science of social dynamics will be more sorely needed than ever before. Go to it!
    Wish I could come to Austin and lure you into a bull session. I have wanted for a long time to discuss with you exactly what kind of structural alterations and additions you have been incorporating into the edifice through the past several years....By your last comment concerning the "maturing of the positive, affirmative value-theory aspect of 'institutionalism'," and that concerning the "positive principle" which is to provide the "solvent of the relativism-nihilism of the past generation," (in which relativism-nihilism you apparently shared to some extent), I deduce that these new alterations have been to a good degree completed, and that you are probably arrived at a vantage point from which you could give a very interesting account of the transition.
    I would enjoy talking with you also because there are numerous points of confusion which I have never been able to clear up to my own satisfaction, and which I believe you may now be in a better position to shed light on than you were five years ago. If I read your meanings correctly, you are, among other things, trying to effect a juncture between the technological principle and the two guides to human action, individual ethics and public policy, the idea being that since we have learned to act sensibly regarding inanimate objects (to a marked degree) we may eventually learn to handle ourselves, individually and collectively, with the same amount of skill and success. If this is so, I want to know more about how you are going about it. If not, then what is in the bag?
    I have been quite apprehensive of late about the military situation. I am quite prepared to admit that the world, even though it lapses into barbarism, will again become civilized, but the consequences to us of this generation of such a cataclysm as now seems possible are difficult to face without a shudder. The enmity and hatred that this war stirs up may easily last for a century, with

us on one end of the log and the bear (not meaning Russia) on the other, and it is difficult to see how much real progress can be made during such a period toward the kind of world I am hoping technology will bring us to. The cheering side of it, of course, is that the war is cutting lots of knots (both technological and institutional) which might have taken much longer to cut in peacetime, just as the last one did. For the present, I suppose, all we can do is bite our nails and get on with it.

Whatever happens, I shall be most interested to watch Japan's archaic institutional structure do battle with her twentieth century technology. I still cannot find it inconceivable that her technology might find itself tethered to a set of institutional and geographical facts too rigid to be broken through, and even though I'll put my money on the levelling influences of developing industrialization to win out, I'll keep my fingers crossed. This century has upset the dope-bucket too many times to leave one much room for confident prophecy.

My current magazine reading consists of Time and Harpers still. I cannot share your aversion for the latter hunk of pulp. The bias of management may be reprehensible to all bold spirits, but the signs of the times and the drift of the current are discernible there as elsewhere (as witness the Nicholson article), and there is a devil of a lot of thought-provoking material between the covers. As to Time, has it occurred to you that a liberal education in modern technology is to be found by reading the "public relations" ads which a lot of the big companies are putting out? (Of course, I know it is also one of your stand-bys.)

Rip

San Antonio, April 22, 1942

Dear Clarence:

I don't know whether I made my point about Harpers last week or not, but at any rate, I am sending an article under separate cover which I just read in it, and which illustrates why I think the magazine is worth reading.

The article should speak for itself, but lest you parry with the remark that, after all, it doesn't say anything which a student at the end of sophomore economics would regard as particularly startling, this is what seems significant about it to me:

The article is animated by a certain spirit of conservatism throughout, and pays lip service to the cherished institutions of free private enterprise; in fact, it speaks in one place of state socialism as a consummation devoutly to be shunned. And yet it contains a large number of basic assumptions which no conservative would have been expected to make fifteen years ago (correct me if I'm wrong!). It reads, for instance, except for a certain smugness that at times verges on fatuousness, like some articles I've read of yours. And I think it is equally significant when an idea or nexus of ideas arrives at the stage of general public apprehension and acceptance as when it first comes onto the intellectual horizon. So I am as much impressed when a Harvard professor accepts and develops a new idea as I would have been when an unorthodox pioneer first wrote it. And I am convinced that Harpers is a better place from which to observe the shifts in the focal center of our general climate of opinion than would another periodical be which was more advanced but less representative of the reading tastes and acceptance of the public.

At any rate, you'll have to admit that the article is a far cry from an exposition of a "natural" equilibrium in our economic order. Witness, for instance, the sentence, "there can no longer be any reasonable doubt that fiscal policy can actually bring about substantially full employment and utilization of resources." And again, "Clearly fiscal policy is now and will continue to be a powerful factor in the functioning of the modern free enterprise economy." And again, "We must know what we are doing. We must apply the skill and understanding necessary to make our financial mechanism not the masters, but the servants of our society."

Incidentally, I should be very interested in knowing what you think of the work of J.M. Keynes, whom Hansen seems to run parallel to, or to follow. I don't recall discussing him with you, but would be quite interested in knowing just where, in your estimation, he fits into the picture. He can hardly be called an institutionalist and yet I have felt that he has made some important contributions toward the synthesis of a body of economic theory which will be free from theological animus and adequate to the purpose of giving a comprehensive explanation of the workings of economic systems. What about it?

Rip

State College, PA, June 11, 1942
Dear Dr. Ayres....
...to tell you that in spite of much I am still writing on the thesis.

Since we are teaching a third semester with only a ten-day break, and have no vacations, one's own work proceeds slowly. Nevertheless, there is yet an expectation that I shall finish it by August. The vast amount of almost necessarily aimless reading remains depressing to this inveterately lazy person.

Rumors come of academic trouble in your department. Is this again the dirty hand of the Regents, or is there more than meets the eye in the case? Since I am not in contact with anyone there, the rumors are of the vaguest. We have no such trouble here, since almost everyone is as conservative as any group of Regents. They even vote Republican.

Wjg

Lexington, KY, August 2, 1942
Dear Clarence:-
In case you're interested, the June Harpers has another article by our friend Mr. Nicholson. This one is on automobiles and should be right up your alley. Some representative statements:

"The chief invention contributed by the United States (to automobile design) was Charles Kettering's self-starter.... For the most part American automobile makers have been satisfied with refining the principle of the engine and chassis that the Europeans gave them. The genius of the Americans was shown, not in design, but in production."

"Was the automobile (in the twenties) a necessity or a luxury? For thousands of people circumstances of employment were making it a necessity; the industry—except for Ford—was trying to combine both ideas."

"The ideal of medium-priced luxury was now established (after Model T quit)...from now on the selling argument was pitched on power and swank...."

"The manufacturers, early in the twenties, brought in the stylists, who of course were not engineers at all.... At first their designs were repudiated by the engineers as impossible. But the pressure of competition was acute and eventually the engineers gave way...until, at length, they were all but pushed aside."

"It was in the midst of the great style wave—in 1927—that Model T quit."

"By July, 1941, the daily average traffic volume (at the junction of Routes 21, 25, and 29 near the Newark, New Jersey, airport) was 100,000 cars. The average value of the cars was $197.00 [and] more than half of them belonged to families with less than $30 a week to live on."

"The era might be over but the necessity for cars was not. When the luxury cars are taken away and the middle-priced cars that are used mostly for recreation and the cars that are used mostly for convenience..., it will still be found that there is an irreducible minimum—and a big one—necessary to operate the country during a war."

There's also an article by Douglas Haskell on Housing developments which you might like to look at.

Don't be surprised at the new address. I have become meshed in with the civilian training program (in radio and related equipment) carried on by the Signal Corps....

My nomination for one of the more clear-sighted, straight-thinking men the spotlight has shone on of late: Elmer Davis. Agree?

Rip Haisley

October 23, 1942
Dear Rip:

I have enjoyed all your plugs for Harpers, agreeing in every case. As a matter of fact we devoted one of the meetings of our social science club (Faculty) to a discussion of Hansen's views on the debt. And as regards Elmer Davis, don't tell me you have forgotten that he is an old friend of mine. Don't you remember how I used to plug his novel "Giant Killer" for its institutional analysis? I can't really claim him as an intimate friend. I have corresponded with him and spent a day with him at his place in the Pennsylvania Hills in

1930. But I do most enthusiastically agree with you that he is a swell guy and an ideal appointee for his present office. And if you didn't read "Giant Killer" when I assigned it, go and do so forthwith and be ashamed that you never heard of Elmer Davis before he became a newscast analyzer.

What are you doing up there besides the hush-hush stuff? ...

C. E. Ayres

Lexington, KY, November 29, 1942

Dear Clarence:

I have hardly had time lately to keep up with the latest Harpers gems; hence no plugs. In the light of your feelings about Elmer Davis, I might, however, clinch my position by pointing out that for an extended period he was one of their regular condtributors.

Shamefacedly I confess that your plugs for "Giant Killer" were either before or after my day or were not pushed with sufficient aggressiveness on your part to make a deep impression on my youthful mind. I can remember no reference you ever made to the book, nor do I find it in the bibliography you gave us in the fall of '35. However, I shall secure a copy of it and go through it, with an enjoyment which will be no less keen for having been deferred.

From a practical standpoint, I have had occasion to regret the amount of time I spent in pursuit of a professional economist's status. It was a painful and futile period, and it was far from panning out as, even now, I wish it had. I believe I can see now where, if I had it all to do over again, I could avoid some of the misconceptions and unfortunate emotional tangles that finally threw me for such a complete loss, but maybe even that is an illusion.

But weighing the disappointment, frustration, and wasted time in the balance sheet against the residue, I still wouldn't trade my two courses under Clarence Ayres for a six-year course in electrical engineering, complete with a $15,000-a-year research job thrown in at the end. The ideas and insight I acquired by listening to your lectures and participating in your discussions, classroom and private, become more and more valuable to me as time goes on, and I see no reason why they should not continue to do so. I have used them in pounding out my own personal philosophy of living, I have used them in orientating my thinking during these chaotic and changing times, I have used them in analyzing the behavior and motives of the people with whom I have been thrown, I have used them in the analysis of every new job I have ever undertaken, I have used them in trying to make a more efficient social animal of myself. The more I see of the wide, wide world and the people and things in it, the more convinced I become of the essential soundness of "institutionalist" thinking.

These ideas are "in the air" now, and I would probably have been exposed to them anyway. But I think you have made a real positive contribution to them, and I doubt in any event whether a man exists on any campus who can present them with as much punch as you, or as clearly. I have certainly never run into any. And I know that my experience has been paralleled by that of numerous others who took your courses.

[no signature evident]

February 12, 1943
Dear Rip:
　The manuscript [for *The Theory of Economic Progress*] was finally sent off a week ago Tuesday so I am hoping it won't be long now. You are quite right about business machines and I have only just indicated the technological character of the administrative process with bare mention of the incidence of the machine process upon office work. [In his letter to Ayres dated January 29, 1943, accompanied by a newspaper clipping, Haisley brings to his attention the use by the army of keypunched record-keeping techniques employing machines produced by I.B.M.] Why don't you go after it? A full length study would be most interesting and who is better qualified than you to make it?

C. E. Ayres

Lexington, KY, April 5, 1943
Dear Clarence:
　After some deliberation, consideration of future prospects, etc., I have finally decided to make a pass at the Navy! Much as I shudder at submitting to the idiosyncrasies of "Intelligence, Military," it is probable that such will be the eventual outcome anyway, and a Naval Reserve Commission seems preferable to becoming an enlisted man in the army. I have hopes that I'll be able to remain in the same field (radio, electronics, & related hush-hush) I'm in now; otherwise I may not take the commission. [At this time Haisley was a civilian instructor, cleared by the F.B.I., at the Lexington Signal Depot. This letter requests a letter of reference.]

Rip

Lexington, KY [undated]
Dear Clarence:
　Thanks very much for the l.o.r. I can only say that it was of a caliber which one comes to expect of anything you turn out of a typewriter, and that I feel as unworthy of it as I feel grateful to its writer.
　I have been reading over some of the points of etiquette expected of naval officers, and am unable to repress numerous shudders. I was rather amazed, for instance, to learn that a military officer is not supposed to carry any bundles or luggage in public, or to smoke in public. I can only hope that the bulk of

these points are winked at in actual practice, although from what I have heard
& seen about the military I'm afraid many of them (equally senseless) are not.
There are altogether too many people in the services (as in other walks of life)
who eat that kind of stuff up. Shades of the old fraternity days! [Haisley to
Ayres, dated July 10, 1943, relates his commission as an ensign. Earlier, Haisley
was unable to accept an attractive offer from the Johns Hopkins Research
Laboratory, because the Lexington Signal Depot would not release him,
writing to Ayres on May 10, 1943 that "It was quite a long story, tinged with
high-handedness and skullduggery...." A postscript in the former letter says:
"Look in the July Fortune for an article entitled "Electronics: A Lever on
Industry," for a good description of the field I'm in. It is a continual source
of amazement to me to reflect on the technological bombshell which Mr.
DeForest's invention, so innocuous in appearance and apparently (at first) so
limited in application, has turned out to be. It is a good example of
technological evolution, too."]

                                                                    Rip Haisley

Austin, February 3, 1944
Dear Rip:
    ...I can tell you that The Theory of Economic Progress is coming out
presumably in March—University of North Carolina Press. It is now in the
galley proof stage and meantime I am all steamed up over a project for
present[ing] the consequences of the theory to the lay reader under the title,
After Capitalism. Like it?
    Are you still working on R— — — —? The current issue of Time quotes
no less an authority than Hitler as having attributed German defeat in the battle
of the Atlantic to one Allied invention. Since radar is older and is more
connected with this reference, we are all wondering if Paul Boner's laboratory
at Harvard really turned the trick. Some day I suppose you boys will tell us
all about your adventures and meantime we will live in mystery.

                                                                    C. E. Ayres

Cambridge, MA, June 4, 1944
Dear Clarence:
    [Writing about his acquisition and complete reading of a copy of The Theory
of Economic Progress, that "Certainly it was a treat worth waiting for."]...it
is indeed a sledge hammer blow in the forging process out of which the true
economics will eventually emerge (or should I say "is at length emerging?").
I can add little to Alexander Meiklejohn's statement on the back cover except
hearty agreement and the fervent hope that...[it's consequences] will be as far
reaching as is consonant with its merits.

For my own part, I found much that was reminiscent of old stamping grounds, but there was also much more that was relatively unexplored territory, as far as I was concerned, and many misconceptions and confused areas cleared up for me in the process of reading. Particularly valuable was the opportunity of getting a chance to go through the whole elaboration in an orderly and consecutive manner. I hit your course on the Background of Economic Thought when I was a junior at U.T., and I must confess that many of the continuities between the "theory of price theory" and the actualities of economic analysis (including the analysis of pecuniary data) have been pretty muddled in my own thinking since that time. They are clearer now than ever before and I am sure will be more so after I have had time for further reflection on the first four chapters.

And I had the course on "Economic motives," when it went by that name, and so was fairly well steeped in the theory of technology and institutions, but I had had nothing on the history of modern industrial civilization (Ayres' version) except what I had picked up from your written articles and gleaned from those office bull sessions. As to the strategy of progress, the cogency of the arguments there has also come home to me in a way in which it never had before. It was not from any single chapter, however, that I got the real lift, so much as it was the "stick-together-ativeness" of the whole set of ideas, which I think is apparent from a reading of the book as it never was from a series of lecture-discussions or the perusal of individual articles.

I suppose critical comment is rather presumptuous, but I cannot resist the temptation. The section on the classical background seemed very well done indeed, and I thought the chapters on technology and industrial evolution were masterpieces, but the picture of the institutional power system(s) as a feature of society, with its hierarchy of status, its complement of mores, and its elaboration of make-believe and fairy tale, seemed less clearly etched in than it deserved to be (less clearly, for instance, than it appears in some of the best passages of Holier Than Thou). Possibly I will not feel this to be true on second reading (the first reading of these chapters was late at night and probably without a sufficient number of interspersed periods of reflection). Possibly you desired to soft-pedal the asperity with which you used to handle institutions, in view of the fact that it is easy for a reader to confuse a direct attack on institutional organization and interpret it as an attack on social organization as such (I think some of your less critical students made that mistake), just as it is likewise easy for a sophomoric reader to jump from the statement that sentimentally motivated activities are apt to be technologically fatuous to the conclusion that one should try insofar as possible to repress completely one's "gut storms." (I once fell into this pit myself, I must confess.) But it seems to me that a stronger formulation is in order of ceremonial behavior patterns as well as further examination of the extent to which they are "inevitable" concomitants of social organization (i.e., what evidence can be marshalled to

174 WARREN J. SAMUELS

support the thesis that the cripple will eventually be able to throw away his crutches?).

The theory of value was very well presented. I was particularly struck by the figure which likens price judgments to motion picture frames. It could be elaborated on, I think, particularly as most economists would still be apt to argue the point. They are, of course, quite prone to think of the market as a continuous stream of purchases, so that the essential discontinuity of these purchases (from the standpoint of the individuals making them) is apt to be overlooked.

As to the strategy of progress, I am once more confident, after reading it, that "aught good can come out of economics." It certainly gives one confidence in the scientific validity of under-consumptionism. If I had been less thoroughly despondent during the period I spent at Columbia I should probably have been aware of the continuity of the work of J.M. Keynes with that of such economists as yourself. As matters stood, I am afraid I was pretty completely lost on this point as on many others.

As has always been the case whenever I have come freshly into contact with your formulations of twentieth century instrumentalism, I have done a great deal of self-probing and re-examination of my own policies, aims, and ambitions during the past week. It will always be one of my major regrets that I fumbled the ball so thoroughly during the years when I had the best chance to make a success of my academic career. And even though my intellectual progress has been that of a going concern in the field of electronics, as it never was except at intermittent intervals in the field of economics, I have occasionally been haunted during the past two years by the idea that some day I might take up the banner again, and that this time, with a little more actual experience with the ways of the "wide, wide world" behind me, I might be able to make a go of it. It is not that I am dissatisfied with my present field, which is exciting, stimulating, intellectually satisfying, and possessed of a bright future. But there is always the intriguing thought of economics lying in the background, like a crossword puzzle laid aside half-finished, and the insistent thought in the back of my mind has been that maybe I was just on the verge of getting my sea legs when I left the bank two years ago to go to Kentucky.

It would require a considerable amount of fortitude to leave at the end of this war what seems like a damned good vessel and return to what was always, for me at least, a leaky and unmanageable ship, and it may be that I will not be able to bring myself to do it. Certainly I shall not be content to make such a move without first making a thorough analysis of the factors which sent me on the rocks before and some sound reason (besides my own stirrings and aspirations which I had in the past no less than currently) for believing that I could make a go of it this time. But the tug on me was very strong as I read The Theory of Economic Progress. And while there is a pretty sharp discontinuity between the levels of generalization with which I have been working and those of economics, there ought to be a pretty good amount of carry over as far as the techniques of instructing are concerned.

I realize that some of the men with whom I came into contact have reason by now to be fairly skeptical both of my potential competence as an economist and of my tenacity of purpose. George Stocking, for instance....

I have been in Cambridge since the first of February, and was engaged in completing my training in radar up until last Wednesday, at which time my status changed from that of "temporary duty under instruction" to that of instructing. All the work with actual equipment (or gear, as we call it in the Navy) has been at M.I.T., for which Harvard, Princeton, and Bowdoin (where I was) are feeder schools. Instructing at M.I.T. bids fair to be quite interesting, although it seems a bit early to pass any judgments as yet.

Rip Haisley

Austin June 15, 1944
Dear Rip:

It is awfully nice of you to write me such a swell letter about my book. I am delighted that you like it. You strengthen my back to receive the blows of the reviewers—the chief of which, I'm afraid, will be total neglect.... A writer is indeed at the mercy of people who discuss his book without reading it—something anybody can do with the greatest ease and complete impunity.

You are right in thinking that I was deliberately holding down my discussion of ceremonialism. It wasn't that I meant to pull the punches—as a matter of quietism—but that I feared lest the fascination of that aspect of the problem carry me, and the reader, too far from the main theme. The problem was to say what couldn't be left out, and not one word more! If this resulted in chapters too little, I'm sorry. Some day perhaps the omission can be repaired.

Your situation there at MIT is most enviable. Congratulations! And don't let Boston get you down. After all, those people are in the terrible situation of all has-beens, and correspondingly on the defensive. What can they do to maintain the illusion that Boston is the cultural center (Hub!) of our civilization? Be gentle with them. Don't disturb their dream of former grandeur!

Clarence

Cambridge, July 23, 1944
Dear Clarence:

...And I trust that, in the post-war world which seems to be looming on the horizon you may get a fairer treatment at the hands of the reviewers, once we recover from our current preoccupation with the war. I was quite disappointed to learn that The Theory of Economic Progress had made so little splash. The NR review may have been uninformed, and it is understandably irritating to anyone to have his ideas misconstrued and misinterpreted, but the "thunders of silence" are far more serious, to my mind, since a book can do good in proportion to the extent to which it is scattered near and far, for all and sundry to read.... the lack of proper publicity may constitute quite an impediment to the library circulation of any book in the field of economics....

...I also dug out the Problem of Economic Order and re-read it with the realization that I had missed the boat on many of the most cogent points in it back in 1937, and in particular had fallen very short in comprehension of the concrete manner in which classical price theory entrenched our belief in the creative efficacy of capital funds (I think I saw the point pretty well that the so-called "laws of the market" did not constitute an effective guarantee to stable equilibrium in economic progress, but who doesn't, these days). More than ever before, I can now understand the continuity between what you are doing and that social process which is represented by the thinking of economists today all over the world (including many writers who still open their textbooks with glib generalizations about scarcity and the satisfaction of human wants). In the old days the chasm looked pretty broad, which I suppose reflects the fact that I too often accepted your ideas and arguments because I had become convinced you knew what you were driving at rather than because I myself understood the sense in which they applied. And it is only by the complete assimilation of such a set of ideas that one can use them instrumentally, free from the connotations of crusading emotion which very often lead one to read a book with stubborn opposition to every idea presented rather than as the basis upon which to do some constructive analytical thinking. I recall that, in a seminar at Columbia, devoted in part to the examination of the work of economic thinkers, past and present, I was assigned the job of reporting on von Wieser, who was of course a beautiful example of unadulterated marginal utility theory. It was a chance to make some real progress in understanding the sets of ideas of which marginal utility consists and into which it fits, and I believe that today I would find it very stimulating. But at the time I regarded the whole set of ideas with fear because I couldn't cope with them, being unable to separate the strands of truly scientific thinking, which gave many of the specific arguments force and plausibility, from the classical framework which I of course did not believe but which I was unable to refute with confidence because I did not fully comprehend its significance. This in turn derived from the fact that I had never fully understood the ideas developed in "The Problem of Economic Order."

I certainly wish I knew whether my newly-regained self-confidence is an illusion! I venture to think it is not, and yet I have been disappointed so many times in the past that I hesitate in making any concrete decisions just yet as to what I should do about it after the war. I find myself feeling like a jungle explorer who stands on a mountaintop looking down and wonders whether the perspective he has gained from his present detached position will prove adequate in coping with the maze of intricate trails he will find below.

...I think part of my trouble]at Columbia] lay in setting my sights too high, in trying to do too much, in trying to "stay at the head of the class," so to speak, rather than striking a level of achievement consistent with my abilities and making what plodding progress I could at my own level. A great deal of emphasis is placed, in all universities, on the attainment of a "high level of creative achievement," and I know that I had a strong tendency to set for myself some fairly high standards and then to grow progressively disgusted with myself for not living up to them.

In this respect I have achieved a good deal in the way of wisdom during the past four years, and I have seen it work out that by doing small, unimportant, routine (but not necessarily uninteresting) tasks one fills in the gaps between the more significant periods of more obvious progress. And I have developed the conviction that, although I may never become a first-rate thinker or scholar, I may nevertheless become a useful member of some academic community, and have had repeated proof that genuine intellectual progress is well worth while, no matter at what level it takes place.

So maybe I'll go back to Columbia for another year and take my orals after all. Are they really as bad as everyone makes out?

So much for the economics. During the past week I have become interested in fitting some sort of a theory of aesthetics into my general scheme of thinking, and have used some of the ideas in TOEP as a point of departure. I know very little about painting, sculpture, architecture, or the like, but my musical education, although of much too rudimentary a nature to be adequate for the purpose, is at least sufficient to give me a basis for trying to understand the developments of modern music, from Bach to Shostakovich....The Victor [Book of the Symphony] contains some interesting and relevant information, but there is so much malarkey mixed in with same that I am not finding it very useful as far as understanding the work of individual composers. The write-up of Bach, for instance, is full of "oh's & ah's," with never a clue as to the fact that "he added to the contrapuntal intricacies of his day a harmonic richness which music had never known before" or, which is even more to the point, a clue to the nature of these additions, from the standpoint of theories of harmony. And when you come on the other hand to modern composers like Stravinsky and Debussy there is no clue as to what were the developments in harmony (I'm ignoring rhythmical patterns for the moment) of which their technical achievements consisted. Nor have I found any satisfactory discussion as to what significance, if any, there is in the modern trend toward "programme music," a trend which I find disquieting since the "programme" idea seems to suggest that the piece of music is unintelligible as such, requiring some extraneous ideological pattern to give it meaning.

Naturally, I have neither the time nor the inclination right at present to plunge neck deep into a study of the history and theory of music. Yet there must be a few good clear elementary references one might pick up on the theory of harmony and/or on the history of music which would make the developmental pattern more obvious to me. Since you are a music fan, I thought you might be able to call off two or three I could look over.

Then there is a broader problem, distinct from an understanding of the lines along which musical ideas and patterns have developed, which I find rather puzzling. You have always pointed out that developments in the "fine" arts and technology are continuous with each other, just as developments in science and industry complement and reinforce each other. But there seems to me to be a difference. The scientist and the production engineer rely on each other's work to a striking degree. The development of a method of phase modulation involving archimedes spirals and cathode ray tubes is contingent on the existence of cathode ray tubes, for which we are, at least in part, indebted to the fund of high vacuum techniques, glass blowing, means for generating high accelerating potentials, and the like, accumulated by modern industry (with the able assistance of other related scientific developments). But such a development is in turn of potential significance for industry itself, and might at any time be made use of in the design of commercial PM transmitters (it hasn't to date, of course).

In the field of music, on the other hand, the continuity seems to be a one way street. Modern music owes much to technological developments in the arts of instrument making, which are in turn continuous with the development of all the industrial arts. But I cannot for the life of me see that all the creations of the modern composers, throughout the last two hundred and forty years, have added materially to scientific knowledge or industrial progress. This may be ignorance on my part, but if this is a true state of affairs, then the principle of continuity does to some degree break down when applied to music, or else music must be evaluated at a considerably lower level from that to which we have ordinarily elevated it.

It may be argued that an interest in music, by giving a man a side-interest, stabilizes his personality and makes him more productive industrially. So, for that matter, however, does a side-interest in handball, which also contributes to his physical well-being. So also does an interest in such dramatic arts as the motion picture, which are educational as well as entertaining and so contribute to the (technological) effectiveness of the citizen so educated. So also does an interest in chess, but that does not elevate the works of Dr. Tarrasch to the same social value level as those of Veblen, even though each may be an equally significant intellectual stride forward in its particular field.

As to the "music while you work" programs, they are all very well, but can it be argued that musical progress has evolved "better and better" forms of music to accompany factory production? It will be generally agreed that Beethoven is more advanced music (i.e., more complex) than Strauss. Does it follow from that that Beethoven is superior to Strauss for purposes of providing a pleasing musical background for workers, even supposing the workers to have had a musical education? Is Stravinsky superior to Bach as a technique for accomplishing any result, in the same sense in which an automobile provides faster transportation than the buggy it supplanted?

It is possible to argue that musical interests are continuous with the other interests which form the continuum of individual experience on the one level or social culture on the higher level, and that they are inevitable in an animal which has a sense of pitch, a sense of rhythm, and an ear for harmony. But part of the force of the technological argument rests on the fact that it is itself (as a network of tools, ideas, instruments, and the like) a sort of closed system, continuous with, dependent on, and contributory to the life process, but not at all identical with it. And it does seem something of a defect if one has to admit that progress in the field of music is dependent on but not contributory to general technological progress. Either one's position as a music fan or one's position as a proponent of technological value judgments must suffer. As a parallel, one might like to argue that the development of chess analysis is in some way tied up to the development of mathematical analysis, particularly since many mathematicians have also been chess players. But if the ideological content of chess is examined it is found to have damned little relation to anything except more chess. It, too, is self-developing in a sense, but it can hardly be put on a par with geometry and calculus when evaluated by the technological principle. Perhaps, then, musical progress is neither so valuable nor so important as literary progress. Can you refute me? I hope so, certainly.

We are quite interested in the political developments this year. I have my tongue in my cheek regarding T. Dewey. I hope he may turn out to be more of a liberal than I think he is, but I'm afraid my hopes are largely based on the fact that a man's actions in office don't always agree with his implied intentions when campaigning. What do you think of Truman? Is his earlier connection with the Pendergast machine a mere political coincidence? Is he truly the open-minded liberal some of my friends around here think he is? Was all the machine support given him at Chicago based on common dislike for Wallace?

Rip

Cloudcroft, NM, August 23, 1944
Dear Rip:
Your letter has given me courage to complete AFTER CAPITALISM. [In Haisley to Ayres, June 4, 1944, Haisley wrote, "As to After Capitalism, may it be a worthy successor to the Theory of Economic Progress, as I know it will be."] For it is DONE! And I'm well pleased with it, though I may live to regret ever having thought of such a thing. My colleagues can defend TOEP [*The Theory of Economic Progress*] on the ground that it is a work of

scholarship, but I'm afraid they won't have that out with AC. And some of them won't want any out—but out!

Your thunders of silence have given way to even louder reverberations of disapproval, at least in the case of the Saturday Review of Literature. Did you see what Hazlitt did there? Gwen insists that it's a grudge job—that I must have committed mayhem on him at some time in the distant past. Maybe. I had that experience with a sociologist at Univ. of Washington. He came into my seminar there and denounced me to my students with a virulence that was quite inexplicable to me at the time; and it was more than a year later, back in Austin, that I discovered an old review in which I had flayed him! But I can't recall a Hazlitt episode....

I was much interested in your discussion of music. With regard to the technical development of music itself the case is pretty clear, I think. Do you know Robert Haven Schauffler's books on Beethoven and Brahms? (B.—The Man Who Freed Music, and The Unknown Brahms....) He is very good at showing just what it was that his subjects accomplished, with lots of short excerpts of the actual music to clinch the points. The works of Sir Donald Tovey are excellent, too, more scholarly but less readable. It is impossible in my opinion to make a quantitative judgment of any one work of art. Beethoven would be judged by all to be far greater, in his total achievement, than Debussy, for two obvious reasons: (1) his total output is far greater, and (2) the developmental process which is spanned by his work is obviously tremendous—Tovey says (Encyc. Brit. article) it is the greatest span covered by any artist in any art. Play a Haydn record and a Wagner record and consider that B.'s earliest compositions were almost indistinguishable from the former, his latest from the latter.

Judged in terms of this process, Debussy is obviously farther along the same path than Wagner, and is therefore much farther along than B. My conviction is that B. himself would recognize this. Thus E. M. Forster's Passage to India is obviously farther along than Stern or Richardson. But he is a man of one book. His total contribution to literature, and therefore his total achievement, is far inferior to Richardson's.

What is the process, in music? It has many strands, of course. But one obvious one is the development of the possibilities afforded by the diatonic scale (itself, perhaps, a mathematical, or physical fact) for key-movement, or tonal fluidity. I mean, first you have composition limited strictly to one key. Then a flirtation with the corresponding minor key; then with the most closely related keys; then with others less closely related, etc., etc. Until with modern music you reach a situation in which more than one tonality is suggested simultaneously, etc., etc. And the same progression can be made out along other strands....

I agree with you that musical developments don't work straight into other technical fields, and that music is like chess in that regard. In others, also. My conviction is that its contribution to total activity is as an instrument of emotional catharsis. (Yes, Aristotle had something big by the tail.) Schauffler quotes on a fly-leaf a pronouncement Beethoven once made to the effect that people who understand his music are thereby saved from the gut-storms that afflict the rest of the race. And that is very important indeed. In order for our technological energies to be released there must be some emotional safety valve to release the pressure that otherwise builds up to erupt as ceremonialism. This release could be no less important than the effect of adequate diet, heated houses, and comfortable beds as a multiplier of the technological process. Thus "music while you work" has a very broad figurative meaning, which I meant to imply, or at least provide for the possible development of, though I thought best not to try to develop it in TOEP.

Music also has a hobby value which it shares with chess and all such things. While there is no direct "transfer of training," there is a relief of preoccupation. This is in part emotional. I get the impression that chess may have saved you from a much more violent reaction than you actually suffered at Columbia insofar as it saved you from the brooding you might otherwise have done. It is also true, I think, that a mind (or intellectual habits) develops an appetite for exercise, very much as habitual physical activity does.

All this would be very offensive to art-worshippers of the Dr. Battle type. But I think we have got to deflate our ceremonial aggrandizement of the arts simultaneously with our appreciation of their technological function. The latter provides ample ground for recognition of the arts as among the highest creative activities of man—not higher than scientific discovery, I think, but also not lower. It certainly provides ample ground for recognition of the actual differences that validate a judgment that music is superior to chess on the same continuum on which the value of chess in established, & good music superior to bad music. (On this point old Oscar Ameringer had the right answer, I think: "classical music," he said, "is music which the more you hear it the better you like it"—in contrast to the stuff that wears out fast.) And if this removes all ground for worshipping the arts, so much the better! The actual values of the arts aren't established either by the pope or by Andrew Mellon.

Clarence

Austin, January 16, 1945
Dear Rip:
    ...[In *The Divine Right of Capital*] I attack capitalism, and so perhaps outrage the conservative, but as a dogma and not as a conspiracy, and so perhaps outrage Marxists even more.

What you found in Meikeljohn's article is just what I would have expected. (I haven't seen it, and rather hang back.) Didn't we ever discuss him? He is an anomaly, suspended even more vacuously than I between heaven and hell— Dewey and the metaphysics of the "SPIRIT." He is too honest and intelligent to brook the latter, and somehow or other he has got himself set against the former, and that leaves him with no friends. My theory is that many years ago when he was in the camp of metaphysical idealism he got Dewey identified as his arch opponent. His native good sense working in the medium of his educational experiences weaned him away from that [line drawn indicating that by "that" is meant metaphysical idealism], so that the present upshot of his own constructive thinking is entirely consonant with Dewey's, though couched in somewhat different language. But he can't acknowledge this by reversing his earlier and unfortunately explicit antagonism. Thus he continually affirms in one chapter and denies in the next. This is most completely explicit in his last book, EDUCATION BETWEEN TWO WORLDS. Parts I, II, & IV are, I think, the essence of instrumentalism, while Part III is a frontal attack on Dewey. A completely confused and wrong-headed one in which he reproaches Dewey for not doing the very things he does best and for doing what he has never done.

C.E.A.

Austin, May 29, 1946
Dear Rip:
  So far as I know the phrase "limited capitalism" is my own. I used it in the original MS. of AFTER CAPITALISM on the analogy of "limited monarchy," and in the same connection I also used the phrase "divine right..." which Paul Brooks, of Houghton Mifflin, later suggested as the title of the book....
  Glad to hear that everything is all set for Chapel Hill. I think you'll enjoy it there....
  Yes, all Hell has been popping around here. A special meeting of the Gen'l Fac. is to be held this afternoon which may give our masters something to think about. Sure hope so.

Clarence

Austin, February 3, 1949
Dear Rip:
  I'm afraid I'm deep in the rut. I haven't founded any new religion, or even added much to institutionalism. I did do a piece last year, of which I'm sending you a reprint herewith (though you may have seen it: I think Cary has one), that does try to fit institutionalism into a larger frame of reference. Tell me some time how it strikes you. I hope to develop it as stuffing for the "textbook."...

Clarence

Austin, February 13, 1950
Dear Rip:
   I have read the David Hawkins piece... with interest. He has made interesting use of the Bohr "Correspondence Principle." Interesting how we in the social sciences reach into the physical sciences for figures of speech. "Actual prices gravitate about normal price," etc.... That the new incorporates the old isn't really a new discovery, I suppose. And of course they do so in more than one way. Also through technology men not only build new working relations with nature (a form of discourse which always disturbs me a bit, with its suggestion of man standing outside nature). More significantly, they build new relations with each other, or at all events extend previously existing team-relationships to areas where previously the relationships have been those of institutionalized status. Hawkins is groping; but he certainly is groping our way.
   Gwen and I were terribly sorry to hear (for the first time) that you lost your baby. But you are both young. I hope you will still have a family. (I think families can be technologically sound arrangements, too!)
                                                                                          Clarence

Chapel Hill, March 20, 1951
Dear Clarence:
   This morning's mail brought a copy of Friday's DAILY TEXAN, mailed by my niece, and containing the miserable story of Marshall Bell's, and the legislature's recent action. I am reminded, as I often am nowadays, of the old question, "After all, is the human race really worth saving?" The way in which the student body and the Daily Texan (and, I trust, the faculty) has rallied to your cause leads me to hope that there is still enough virtue left in Texas to keep it from sinking to the level of Marshall Bell. I trust you will be able to weather the storm and be the stronger for it! Certainly your cause is one which ought to provoke violent defense from many quarters which are usually silent nowadays.
   I read "Ordeal by Slander" last summer, and it gave me a good deal of hope to see what could be accomplished, even under circumstances as diabolical as the Lattimore affair. Surely institutional stupidity and cupidity doesn't always triumph!
   I guess you know we have had a lot of similar trouble in our department here, and particularly since the Freistadt affair. Three excellent men, two of them very able theoretical physicists, have been pilloried locally, to the point where they would surely be unable to get security clearance, although any suspicious of actual disloyalty in any of the three cases is utterly preposterous.
   I am writing to the few people I know now who might be of any help in this business. I feel pitifully inadequate to be of any real help to you. I only hope the new editor of the DT is as sympathetic as this one.

Bell's comments on "undermining confidence of people to go into business for themselves" is one of the most damnably ridiculous things about this whole affair.

Rip

April 2, 1951
Dear Rip:
...The Administration's official reply to the House was delivered this morning informing it there is nothing to investigate and was received in silence. So I guess the incident is over.

C. E. Ayres

Cloudcroft, June 26, 1952
Dear Rip:
Interesting that you should be going to Brown. Did you recall that I am a Brown graduate? My class held its fortieth reunion this month! I have never been back for any such low-grade ceremonial.

I'm afraid you will find *The Industrial Economy* another version of the same book I have written two or three times already. In some respects, though, I feel that it is the most satisfactory version to date.

Clarence

Austin, May 12, 1964
Dear Rip:
I am much interested in your course on the history of physics. It's just beginning to be understood, isn't it? Early this spring our history department sponsored a series of six lectures by imported scholars on the history of science. The opening lectures by Derek Price of Yale discussed the problem in a fashion that made me hug myself with glee. He said in effect that nobody understands science less than scientists; and the reason is that the history of science is cluttered with myths—chiefly those invented by the scientists themselves about their own work. A scientist confronts a conundrum. He doesn't know what to do about it. He casts about, gets nowhere. Fiddles and stumbles—and eventually stumbles on a solution. Then he sets down the problem and its solution as a series of theorems each of which leads directly to the following one so that the whole series gives the impression of inexorable logic. But that isn't at all what actually happened.

Claggett of Wisconsin gave a beautiful lecture on the work of a group of schoolmen who got working on falling bodies at Oxford in the fourteenth century and managed to work out all the theorems Galileo later claimed were entirely new and original! How wonderful it is that science somehow manages to transcend the scientists! I was reminded of Lord Acton's conviction that the Church must enjoy divine grace, since otherwise no human institution could have survived the scoundrels who operated it.

Clarence

Cambridge, MA, February 17, 1967

Dear Clarence:

Wednesday I had lunch with Bob Cohen.... He was a great admirer of Alexander Meiklejohn, and quite impressed by the power of EDUCATION BETWEEN TWO WORLDS. We were wondering whether you know of any good reply in print to the attack on pragmatism contained in that book—you remember, perhaps, that you had introduced me to it right after the war, and so I thought you might. He had read Sidney Hook's reply (or was it a review?), but didn't think it was very effective.

I was wondering, too, whether you could recall the answers to a couple of questions that keep recurring in my own thoughts nowadays. (1) Back in 1934, you described in our seminar a piece of work done by a scholar who had learned Greek in order to satisfy himself that Aristotle's work in biology was perfectly respectable science if interpreted and evaluated in the context of the instrumentation available at the time. Do you remember who this was and what the publication facts were? (2) You used to be fond of the quotation that "philosophy is what people believe between the time when they have depended on religion and the time when they have learned to live without it." This isn't exact but is as close as I can come. Do you remember the exact quotation, who said it, and where? I've always assumed it was Cornford (perhaps in FROM RELIGION TO PHILOSOPHY), but wasn't able to run it down the other day when I tried.

... Last semester I audited a seminar in epistemology, listening to the patter of the philosophers about sense-data and all that, but didn't push very hard— I was mostly trying to get to the point where I could speak and understand the language a little better. I find I can usually understand philosophers pretty well but can't speak cogently to them in their own dialects. Moreover, I tend to get impatient with the tediousness of the analytical minutiae, which is doubtless a commentary on me rather than on them—I've really come to have rather much respect for their way of going about things and disdainful of the contempt which is practically universal among my scientific colleagues, many of whom accept history of science, which is becoming quite well accepted,— even fashionable. Actually I'd like to have stayed with Max Wartowsky and the epistemology—he was getting on to the mind-body problem this semester and planning to study things like Dewey's NATURE AND EXPERIENCE; however I checked out because I felt I couldn't do justice to the 19th Cent. H.S. (a small seminar course at Hvd, in which I've become a "participating auditor") and to the paper I'm trying to finish up, unless I did.

One of the greatest things around here is the Boston Colloquium for the Philosophy of Science....

Rip

Austin, February 23, 1967

Dear Rip:

No, I don't know of any answer to Hook's attack on Meiklejohn which appeared in print....

You might be interested to know that Helen told me at the time that she had pleaded with Prexy to leave out Book III (the attack on Dewey). But of course Prexy wouldn't. I say "of course" because, as he once told me, he considered the refutation of Dewey his mission in life. My guess is that personal circumstances entered into this commitment, so contrary to his mature character and mind.

When Meiklejohn was an undergraduate at Brown (class of 1893), James Seth was teaching there. He left Brown for Cornell just about the time Meiklejohn graduated, and I have always thought that was the principal reason M. went to Cornell for his graduate work and degree. M. was always intensely loyal, and I always felt that personal loyalty to Seth (who returned to Scotland and won considerable eminence as a neo-Hegelian "idealist") played a significant part in M.'s life-long aversion to the critics of that tradition.

There was also some sort of personal bitterness in his antagonism to "pragmatism," and I have always suspected that F.C.S. Schiller had something to do with that. Schiller was also a degree candidate at Cornell when M. was; and Prexy once told me a wild tale of being called into conference by the head of the department (Creighton?) and given a prodigious list of major works in philosophy for which Ph.D. candidates would be held totally responsible on the final examination. He said that for the first time in his life he went into total training for this ordeal, scheduling and rationing all his time, preparing a detailed calendar, etc. He even obtained from a doctor a prescription for a sustaining drug (something like Benzedrine, I suppose) with strict instructions on its use, etc., etc. And he said that he realized clearly at the time that the intent of this maneuver was to fail Schiller—which it did. (Schiller returned to England without the degree.) This ordeal was validated by M.'s passing. Question: Did he rationalize this academic assassination by life-long hatred of what Schiller stood for? Note his persistent identification of Dewey as a "pragmatist," despite Dewey's abandonment of that term.

As regards the attack on Dewey in Book III: it is the work of a writer who is determined not to understand what he is attacking. On the third page of Book III (p. 125 of the book) I find that I underlined the word "merely" and put an exclamation mark in the margin of this sentence purporting to summarize Dewey's position:

All the activities of the mind, such as discovering, experimenting, doubting, theorizing, verifying, valuing, are, like those of the contracting of the muscles or the circulating of the blood, merely organic responses to specific stimulations.

Dewey once said that the most dangerous word in the language is "merely," and this passage surely bears him out. The strange thing is that M. never, anywhere, invokes anything even faintly suggestive of other-than-natural substances or processes, "parapsychological," or anything of the kind. And if he were asked pointblank, "Do you understand such a proposition of Dewey's to exclude, e.g., language behavior, cultural considerations, etc., etc., as having no more to do with discovering, experimenting, theorizing, etc., than they do with the circulation of the blood?" surely he couldn't give an affirmative answer. He is just determined to misunderstand Dewey; and that is the sort of project (as I keep telling students) anyone with sufficient determination can surely succeed. A strangely contradictory personality.

Hook I can understand. Taking M.'s misrepresentation of Dewey as his cue, he reads subtle neo-Hegelian meanings into everything M. says, a natural human failing. But is Alexander Meiklejohn subject to "natural human failings"? One reading of Books I, II, and IV shouts a denial! Nevertheless, there stands Book III, as egregious a job of misrepresentation as I have ever seen. How human is the best of us!

With regard to "the scholar who learned (or relearned his schoolboy) Greek" and verified Aristotle's science, I think either you or I telescoped two incidents. My guess is that the former was Warner Fite, who refurbished (I think) his Greek to read Plato in the original and verify his hunch that the popular blending of Socrates and Christ was sadly mistaken and a product of bad (Bowdlerizing) translations (especially Dr. Jowett's). Fite wrote a book on the subject. Thomas Huxley (so I learned in my Huxley excursion) reviewed Aristotle's account of the human skull, undertaking an examination of the skull with instruments accessible to Aristotle, and decided that Aristotle's account was a valid one, given those limitations. (You remember that Huxley contested with Sir Richard Owen on the comparative anatomy of the skull, inventing the "cephalic index" in the process.)

I don't place the aphorism about religious belief, though it sounds like something I might have cited.

Clarence

Austin, March 23, 1943

[In longhand at top of page: "First part of a letter from C. E. Ayres to Alexander Meiklejohn." And in a different hand: "Attached to letter (Feb. 23, 1967) C. E. Ayres to W.E.H.)." The letter is reproduced in its entirety.]

Dear Prexy:

I was delighted to get a letter from you. When I mailed my note I thought it would probably have to be forwarded, but I felt sure that your home postman would be able to handle that. I'm sorry the occasion of your writing should be such a foul review, but I'm glad of the chance to write you at some length about the book, a thing I probably would have been too slothful to do otherwise.

Before your letter came I had heard reports of the Hook review but hadn't bothered to read it. But at your prompting I went and did so straightaway. Hook certainly missed your meaning completely and therefore completely misrepresented your position. As you say, explaining why he did so doesn't correct the error. But one can't otherwise identify his crime. If, as I think, it was your discussion of Dewey that threw him that, should have been the main object of his attack. For him virtually to ignore that certainly is bad analytical practice quite apart from the fact that, on this assumption, what he did do therefore seems to be a flanking attack—an attempt to discredit a critic whose criticism he hasn't met. I don't mean to say that his resulting misrepresentation of your position is dishonest. But it is so far from the truth as to raise a serious question of the competence of a critic who, for whatever reason, can make so egregious an error. I confess it shot a scare into me. I have just finished a review article of Schumpeter in which I did my very best to demolish his position and discredit him, and I find myself wondering how much misunderstanding and misrepresentation may have figured in my treatment! His only reference to Veblen is a sarcasm, and I ignored it in my piece. But I really don't think it was that which put me off, and I do think I addressed myself to a criticism of the position he really occupies. I certainly hope so! But Hook didn't. There's no doubt about it.

As a matter of fact, your book is grand. I read it with delight mounting to enthusiasm as I got deeper into it, and I finished with the conviction not only that it is the best thing, far and away, that you have done but that it is really a great book. Whatever its immediate reception may be—and that is affected so largely by immediate circumstances, the war and all—I am convinced that serious students will return to it and that it will stand permanently as one of the major contributions to the thinking of our day and our descendants.

In developing your way of thinking you have made extraordinarily effective use of Comenius, Locke, and Arnold. Objection might certainly be made, perhaps in each case, that your treatment isn't adequate to a complete understanding and just estimate of the entire work and influence of any one of them; but it seems to me that it doesn't pretend to be and shouldn't be expected. For modern civilization generally it is doubtless true that Comenius was a whole lot less important and Locke a whole lot more than your treatment might suggest to a wholly innocent reader, but that isn't the point. As I understand it you have meant to point the contrast between different conceptions of conduct and education. This you do most effectively. Your characterizations, "I am a Christian, therefore..." and "I am a Christian, but..." state your issue with vivid clarity. And it is true that Locke's whole intellectual position, and for that matter the whole cultural phase of which he was the spokesman, were equivocal: Christian, <u>but</u> naturalistic; naturalistic, <u>but</u> teleological—and so on. His rejection of divine right and counter-establishment of property on exactly the same ground is a case in point.

You are very right indeed, I think, in saying that this dilemma permeates the whole Protestant-capitalist culture. I see it in the very concept of capital, which is surely one of the intellectual (i.e., conceptual) and institutional foundation piers of modern western civilization. Duplicity is the very essence of the idea. To conceive the economic life of modern times in terms of capital is to think simultaneously of two distinct things, the physical equipment of industry and funds of money-claims, and to think of these two distinct phenomena as identical, as one and the same thing. The whole thought process of our time has been permeated by a sort of duplicity. To be sure, "duplicity" is a strong word. In common speech it implies conscious and intentional deception or double-dealing, whereas the condition we are discussing is one of self-deception. But "consciousness" and intent are always matters of degree, never clear and definite except as the rules of law more or less arbitrarily make them so with regard to specific acts; and the truth is that our civilization has deceived itself pretty systematically and in a fashion that has resulted in double-dealing on an immense—societal—scale. I hope you won't think I am buttering you if I say straight out that I don't know any discussion of this tremendously important aspect of our problem that is clearer, more effective, more telling, than yours. On this account alone <u>Education Between Two Worlds</u> would take its place on the (pathetically short) list of books I want every student of mine to read.

But what arouses my greatest enthusiasm is your triumphant resolution of the dilemma. The use you make of Rousseau in this connection is most effective. No doubt it is true in this case also that yours is not a complete portrait and that you are more concerned with showing what might be made of Rousseau's ideas than with judging them as he left them. But again that can all be taken for granted. I agree with you very strongly that Rousseau did have hold of something much bigger than he was, much more important for us and for the future than his contemporaries or even he himself fully understood. Indeed, your characterization of his predilection for opposites and zest for going to extremes is suffused with your own unique charm. For sheer pleasure it is the most delightful part of the book. But of course it is more than that. It is the point of departure for your own constructive statement, and as you use it, a most effective one. I don't see how Sidney Hook could have read it and still have said the things he did. At every point you seem to me to have realized fully the danger of the very misinterpretation (of Rousseau and of yourself) into which he fell, to have pointed it out quite explicitly, and to have proceeded in a direction precisely opposite to the one in which Hook somehow supposed you to be moving.

To say that this danger is a matter of terminology is to make it sound trivial. It is that, but "in a big way"! The trouble is that we use innocent-sounding terms (how common this is in economics) with ostensibly clear and modest definitions but nevertheless manage to smuggle into the discussion by sheer association, unnoticed and uncriticized, an immense quantity of suggested meaning all the more dangerous because its extent is quite indefinite. Rousseau's terminology is of course notorious in this regard. But the fact that it is easy to go wrong in using words such as "contract" and "will" in phrases such as "social contract" and "general will" certainly doesn't close the possibility that important truths underlie those phrases. I agree with you strongly that such is indeed the case, and my enthusiasm reaches a climax at the very point at which, perhaps, terminological vulnerability is greatest. I mean the point indicated by such words as "brotherhood and "agreement." I think I understand what you mean. Certainly I agree with the greatest enthusiasm with what I take it that you mean. There is a passage in Schumpeter's book in which he is most disgustingly plausible in his ridicule of the idea of brotherhood, arguing at the same time with devilish ingenuity and complete misunderstanding that "the will of the people" is nonsense. (Chapter XXI, "The Classical Doctrine of Democracy." [*Capitalism, Socialism and Democracy*]) But as I tried to say in my article, he just fails to see the biggest and plainest and most significant thing in modern civilization, to wit, common knowledge and understanding. I would not argue that you should avoid using the words you do use because people may misunderstand them in spite of anything you say. What words should you use? I use others myself, but I certainly can't boast that I have found a way to prevent readers from misunderstanding, or non-understanding, my vocabulary!

Furthermore I agree with you that the two "insights" which you identify with Socrates and Jesus and symbolize in the imperatives, "Be intelligent!" and "Be kind!" are indeed one; that in the sense in which I understand you to use these terms reasonableness is kindness and vice versa. And this seems to me to be the master-insight of the book, the culmination of the way of thinking about society and education which you are setting forth. I have sometimes tried to use the conception, "teamwork," as one which contains both the criterion of "reasonableness" and that of "kindness" or friendliness or, in the functional sense, brotherhood. I would certainly agree with you that in this sense Jesus and Socrates symbolize the same thing (or way), and doubtless you would allow that "great spiritual leaders" generally have done so and that such insight is by no means limited to the Western world.

I have reserved any mention of Book III to this point for two reasons. One is the extraordinary unity which the book attains when Part III is disregarded.

Book II flows directly into Book IV, which builds on it most effectively; whereas the effect of Book III, quite apart from one's opinion of it, is to break that continuity. But my other and more compelling reason for postponing discussion of this part is that what you say here seems to me directly contrary to everything else.

Your constructive analysis seems to me one hundred percent consonant with Dewey's thinking. I can see nothing in Book IV (and this of course carries I and II as well) that might not have been said by Dewey—if he had your gift of lucidity! What you are saying here is precisely what Dewey has been saying (or trying to say) in many different ways over a period of many years. This is what he is getting at. I wish I could convince you that in saying this I'm not trying to score a cheap debating trick. If I am wrong—if your assertion of a fundamental difference between your way of thinking and his must be taken as correct—it means that my failure to understand you, or him, or both, is dismally complete.

What I ought to do to validate my understanding of you both is to put your whole argument into his language, and his into yours; and with the help of my students I shall certainly do so. But that would be too big a task even for such a letter as this has grown to be, and so I'll have to forego that demonstration for the present. But there is something else I might just have a shot at doing here and now. I wonder if you realize how defective your criticism of Dewey is as a matter of logical form? What you do is to cite Dewey's statement of a problem. You accept that statement and acknowledge the importance of the problem, for example, the problem of "the relation of an individual to the larger group." Then you deny that he has any solution of the problem. Now that's where you're wrong. I read Chapter 10 to an advanced class, and when I got to this point they gasped with astonishment and indignation. Why, said they, that's the one thing he has done nothing else but! However, that isn't my present point. My point is that your assertion is a denial—a denial that something or other exists. Such an assertion can be made only on the basis [of] a complete survey of the field, in this case of Dewey's entire work. But you make no such survey even by indication. On the contrary, you ignore the very works in which as a matter of common knowledge he has done his fundamental thinking, in particular his logic. Your primary concern is with values, but you don't even mention his 1939 <u>Theory of Valuation</u>. And for an argument which takes the form "...to those questions Dewey gives no answer" (P. 193) omission is fatal. In effect you condemn Dewey for not having done all his fundamental thinking in <u>The Public and Its Problems</u>, as of course he didn't. Why should he?

I'm scolding you! But for your own good—and mine! For the good of all of us. <u>Education Between Two Worlds</u> is far and away your best book, and a great book; but it is only a beginning. What fills me with enthusiasm for it is the knowledge that you have arrived at this grand statement altogether independently of Dewey or any other contemporary influence. But having arrived at the same place, what a glorious discovery awaits you! How much more compelling your argument is when it is seen to be another route to a land which others also have discovered. Perhaps yours is a better route. At all events your arrival fills in blank spaces on the map.

What you ought to do now is to discover Dewey! Let's do it together! You discover Dewey, and I'll discover you—as I feel I have come nearer doing in this book than ever before. We're both still young and vigorous and free. For I am about to be purged. Three Regents whom Pappy O'Daniel appointed to the University Board are out to "clean up" the place, and according to rumor my name is on their list along with three other members of my department and of course Rainey. The compliment is undeserved. All that they know about me is that I publicly condemned O'Daniel's "transactions tax," and a few other tidbits of that sort. But I really may soon be "at liberty." It doesn't matter. The Theory of Economic Progress is finished, and it's time to move. And what I yearn to do next is to tackle the logic of the social sciences. Let's do it together! You on your hillside in California and I on our mountain top in New Mexico. (Thank God, we own it!)

Yes, I like Scottie Buchanan very much. Our association has been curiously spasmodic. For instance, with little preliminary contact and none thereafter we once shared a cottage, with Miriam and Gwen, on a Long Island beach. The last time I saw him was in Chicago in 1936. We talked all one afternoon and evening, far into the night. He is one of the few people I seem to be able to communicate with instantaneously and with the sense of full understanding on both sides. Not that I understand his associates or his doings with them— except when he is talking. He makes me understand his part in it, and what it looks like from his point of observation. I wish I saw him often. Seven years is too long.

Last week I hoped to see Kenneth. (Yours. Mine is in the army. Air corps, technical training detachment, learning to service Pratt & Whitney engines, etc.) I flew to New York for an Industrial Committee meeting. An earlier one to which I was appointed was attended by Kenneth, but I was prioritized out of my plane seat and failed to arrive; and this time when I insisted on having a priority Kenneth wasn't there. Harry Weiss told me you had served as chairman on earlier committees, and with your usual distinction.

Don't let Helen wear herself out trying to realize reasonableness in government! The planning of post-war education sounds exciting, enough to justify postponement of the logic of the social sciences. There is a point where reasonableness will be needed. I do hope you can give it to them.

[no signature on copy]

Austin, October 31, 1967

Dear Rip:

Since you see the <u>Graduate Journal</u>, I presume that you saw the long article in the most recent issue (Spring, 1967!): "Science and Culture in the Nineteenth Century," by Stephen G. Brush. If so, I should be interested to hear what you thought of it.

It's a fascinating essay, and I am appalled to read that it is to be buried in a book on "the history of statistical mechanics"! The man is prodigiously learned, and has focussed the whole of nineteenth-century culture on this article. But will it stand up? Are "romanticism" and "realism" as distinct and shapely as he makes them?

More important: are these leitmotifs as important for the development of science as Brush seems to imply? Suppose that in "disproving" the geological "theory" of uniformity by citing the physical doctrine of "entropy" Lord Kelvin <u>was</u> motivated by a "romantic" distaste for evolution, and suppose he <u>did</u> consider this his most important contribution to human knowledge and understanding. What of it? He was wrong in opposing uniformity and evolution, and he was wrong in thinking that his most important job. Does any of this affect what we know to be the value of his work in thermodynamics?

I am quite willing to suppose that the romantic notions scientists entertain even about what they think they are doing are affected by the prevailing climate of opinion. But does this affect what scientists are really doing? Was the discovery of the phenomenon of radioactivity and of the heating of the earth by the decay of radioactive elements either advanced or retarded by such "romantic" nonsense?

Derek Price says that no one has misled mankind with regard to the nature of science and the reality of what scientists are actually doing so much as scientists. I wonder if "romantic" and "realistic" climates of opinion aren't virtually irrelevant to science and the technological process generally.

I'd be interested to hear Haisley on this subject.

Clarence

Chapel Hill, November 13, 1967

Dear Clarence:

It was delightfully "past-reviving" to get your last letter, most especially the invitation to comment on Steve Brush's article in the GRADUATE JOURNAL. It was, as a matter of fact, from him that I learned of that periodical's existence last spring when I read a preprint of the paper while I was a participant in a seminar he directed on the history of nineteenth-century physical science.... He is, incidentally, a perfectly competent theoretical physicist, though he has been seduced, like Tom Kuhn—one of his more inspiring undergraduate teachers at Harvard in the early '50's—into ideological history. I don't think I've ever known a more omnivorous reader, nor a more skillful collector of bibliographical minutiae!

Now as to the substantive comments on his essay. Kuhn, who obviously had a lot to do with the formative period of Brush's ideas, has been very fashionable recently, as a topic of conversation among science historians and the scientific public generally. Perhaps you have seen his THE STRUCTURE OF SCIENTIFIC REVOLUTIONS; if not, you should by all means have a look at it; it is eminently readable and quite well grounded (Kuhn did his Ph.D. in physics under Van Vleck at Harvard, who still finds regrettable Kuhn's loss to the discipline—he is now officially a historian at Princeton). The tendencies and viewpoints which you find suspect in Brush you would find stated with more force and explicitness in Kuhn.

As I read Tom Kuhn, his central idea is essentially the application of cultural relativism (or "mores nihilism," if you prefer) to the sociology of science, except that cultural fault lines dividing different ideological-technical complexes are temporal rather than geographic. Each interval of what he calls "normal science" intervening between major scientific revolutions is characterized by a complex of "paradigms," established under the intellectual stresses of the immediately preceding revolution, which guide and channel research during that period and retain their sway until they break down under progressively acute stresses. Kuhn maintains that the "normal science" of a particular period, as embodied primarily in its scientific textbooks, is essentially incommensurable with that of previous periods, and rather cautiously questions whether the whole concept of cumulative, progressive development in science has any general validity.

In the sense that these ideas represent an attempt to work free of the naive formulations of cumulative empiricism which controlled science history up to the turn of the century (roughly, Duhem's work represents the breakaway point, though it has ben carried much further since then) I find Kuhn's work (and Brush's) both fresh and rather exciting, since the "thematic" aspects of scientific development are clearly (to me) necessary to any adequate understanding of its growth. The suggestions of epistemological nihilism are of course unpalatable and, I believe, surely wrong. In spite of all our traumatic upsets of the past two-hundred years (and they have certainly been most considerable) surely no one in his senses can take seriously the notion that we do not know vastly more about the physical universe (or the sociological continuum, for that matter) than did the Greeks. On what precisely this knowledge rests, and in what exactly is the nature of its convergence is still for me a fascinating and largely unresolved question. Though I am of course thoroughly convinced that science does achieve a progressively certain and stable dependability, and that the empirical and instrumental nexus contributes substantially to that processs (often in ways which mere scholars, because of their literary and documentary biases, tend to ignore), I have also become convinced that instrumentalism cannot be the whole story and have been forced to abandon a number of the preconceptions with which I entered the study of physical science twenty years ago.

Rip

Austin, February 7, 1968
Dear Rip:
...It is my feeling that a revolution in the history of science is getting under way and that you are just in time for it. I was much amused by Stephen Brush's careful distinction of science from the Culture which I spell with a capital, as a preliminary to describing science as responsive to the winds of "romanticism" etc. Technology still occupies what Balchin identifies as "the small back room"! Well....

Clarence

Austin, April 28, 1968
Dear Rip:
You and I are divided by some pretty basic (though not, I think, irrecoverable) ideological differences; and I think communication could best be effected if I begin with them.

As you know, the Veblenian distinction of technology from "ceremonialism" (myth, mores, etc.) is basic to all my thinking. (And I find the same distinction at the basis of Dewey's "instrumentalism.") Thus I would argue that "real," "true," etc., have two sets of meanings. One relevant to "tool" operations, and the other to mystical (and "untrue," in the tool sense) operations. Thus when one says a given proposition is "true," one means one or the other of two things: a) that it squares with tool operations (including throwing something in the water to see if it will float), or b) ceremonial operations and ideologies. Thus the question whether a given scientific discovery is true may (and often does) have two meanings: a) whether it squares with other scientific (tool) operations and b) whether it squares with tribal beliefs, arouses veneration and awe, is suitable for worship, etc., etc.

The logical positivists seem to me to have pulled their punch in this regard. Instead of saying (as Dewey seems to me to do) that the question whether scientific knowledge is "really true" is a nonsense question, it says "We can never know." This, to my mind (backed up by Dewey!) is nonsense—just as the moral agnosticism of the same people is nonsense, and for the same reason. We have two choices: either to say that the proposition "Sticks float" is true— and that is what we mean by truth; or to say that "truth" is beyond all human "understanding" and is a matter of belly reaction, tribal conditioning, etc., etc., in which case nothing is "true."

Thus I would agree that the passages you cite on p. 41 do indeed represent apostasy to "thoroughgoing positivism;" but not from instrumentalism. These propositions could read: "The point in question is as true as that sticks float, and is therefore a direct lineal descendant not only from the experiments of Thales of Miletus but of primeval man."

You, yourself, seem to worship an idol of the tribe without knowing it: the Cartesian illusion of direct self-knowledge. Each of us seems to know "himself" to be something quite other than any part, or even the whole, of his body, of which "he" is the possessor. This sense is very vivid. But of course so are dreams, in which this entity, or identity, seems to leave the body (though taking a sense of it along). Thus E. B. Tyler argued years ago that dreams were the efficient cause of all superstition. We have discounted dreams; but the Cartesian illusion persists, perhaps because knowledge to the contrary is less dramatic and hence far less well known.

We know nothing by "direct," "inward" apprehension. All our supposed knowledge of ourselves we have in fact "read in books." I know that I was born in Lowell, Massachusetts on May 6, 1891, because the roster of the A.E.A says so, or because as my mother many times told me my birth was legally recorded at that time. (This proved not to have been the case, much to my embarrassment!) More significantly, each of us knows by all sorts of verifiable evidence that we are involved with all sorts of people in all sorts of various ways, beginning of course with our immediate families; and this (quite verifiable and floating-stick-pure) knowledge is what led G. H. Mead (following Dewey) to say that "selfhood" is awareness of "roles." But that it is "direct," "irrefutable" knowledge of "self" as "spirit" (or anything else non-floating-stick) is nonsense. (Freud, more than anyone else, brought home to us how utterly unreliable our "direct consciousness" of anything is.)

...The common expression, "You've got to believe something!" Why? Because the savages all do? A crutch is a fine thing for a cripple. But are we then all permanently crippled? I'm afraid my visual deterioration is permanent; but like Cato the Elder I don't regard myself as permanent. The human race is in trouble (as it has always been); but in large measure we know what must be done about it, and what we need is not more illusion but less.

To my mind the persistent flaw in logical positivism, operationalism, and "the sociology of knowledge" is its fatal commitment to superstition, implied in the prudential hedge that the world described by science may not be the "real" world and the prudential efforts to make things work may not be "really good." In each case, the implied alternative is superstition. In each case disavowing "ultimacy" means crediting the superstition which defined ultimacy.

In saying this I realize that I am contradicting what may be (I suppose it is) your central motive in examining "operationalism." But I am not "really" opposing you. I agree that confusion lurks at the center of operationalism, as it does at the center of logical positivism and the sociology of knowledge, and I agree that exposing this confusion and eliminating it is a real and important challenge.

Clarence

Chapel Hill, May 13, 1968
Dear Clarence:
   The paper arrived today. I had been waiting to get it before acknowledging both it and your letter, which came some time ago. Thanks very much for giving it such serious attention and for commenting on it so thoroughly. I don't know whether you realize how helpful I still find it to study your ideas and consider your positions. After you left, I re-read TOWARD A REASONABLE SOCIETY, with considerable profit and much interest. Of course your ideas have had a very strong formative influence on my own, which makes for a considerable intellectual resonance in the process of re-examination and helps me in a critical reappraisal of my own positions in addition. Actually, I'm convinced that you have added substantial and valuable increments to the instrumentalist tradition, which in turn has added fundamental depth to human understanding of human existence. On the other hand I have been brought back again and again, in the course of a lifetime of grappling with broader areas of study and reflection, to the conviction that it simply isn't enough, and my paper represents an attempt to grasp why, and to attempt to identify the missing elements without simply trotting back to the fleshpots of Egypt (superstitious error) or falling into the various other morasses and pitfalls of intellectual history. Doubtless I have not done very well, and doubtless I shall not achieve anything really significant. But the writing of this paper was one of the most satisfying things I have ever done.
   ...I was myself groping my way through it, and didn't myself know how it was going to come out when I started it....
   Meanwhile, I would like to respond more substantively to the comments in your letter....

Rip

Austin, May 16, 1968
Dear Rip:
   Your letter is so sweet tempered that I must reply at once. This is a curious experience I have been having. I believe I haven't told you before, but Bob Patten and I have been having an experience similar to ours. He is an old friend, now retired from the economics department of Ohio State. He asked me to read the manuscript of a book he has written. I found it utterly puzzling. It purports to be about "evolutionary economics," by which I thought he meant institutionalism. And I guess he does....

Bob seems to think that the biological process of evolution endowed mankind with some sort of what I can only call "spiritual" power or faculty that is qualitatively distinct from speech, speech-related ratiocination, etc. etc., but he never says, even as definitely as this, just what it is—all the time castigating "positivist[s]," who reduce everything to "mechanical" processes, etc., etc. Like you, he appeals every now and then to some sort of Cartesian "direct" self-knowledge. I have tried, without success of course, to urge him to be more explicit about it. I'm sure he realizes that the more explicit one is about man's spiritual powers the less defensible the position becomes.

I get the strong impression that there is some sort of emotional involvement in all this. It somehow outrages Bob (I think) to have it said (e.g., by me) that man is "nothing but" a talking ape. Not that I do say that sort of thing. On the contrary: "nothing but" is Dewey's bete noire "merely." What I would say is, of course, that the miracle of man consists precisely in the fact that he is geneologically an ape only very slightly different anatomically and physiologically from his ancestors, who (by virtue of those slight differences) can and does do things, carry on processes, etc., which are utterly beyond the powers of any other creature.

But the exercise of these powers is fraught with trouble. It is just as easy to conceptualize imaginary as real substances and entities—to imagine dark creatures lurking below the surface as to identity floating sticks as wood. Name it, and it's there. You of course are not indulging in any crude superstition. But you have a feeling that there is something more than stick-throwing and atom-splitting. And there is, of course. There is the human "heart" and all its complex concerns. Life isn't all stick-throwing and atom-splitting, and one is just as "real" as the other. They do not refute each other or cancel each other out. We can and do have both.

Bob Patten, most regretfully, brackets me with Dewey and the others who go right up to the threshold of the higher "evolutionary" truth but don't quite cross the threshold. I'm sorry that I disappoint him. But I view the matter differently—and after all, it's his book. He carries the burden of proof—or at least exposition. Just what is the insight evolution has brought within his grasp but not mine? After the exchange of several letters, the answer is still obscure.

I'm glad you are going to continue clarifying and perhaps concentrating your essay. I agree with you that the "positivists" have left the water muddy. Keep me posted on your progress.

Clarence

Chapel Hill, June 17, 1968
Dear Clarence:

I had supposed this letter would be written earlier; ... I've had not much time for reflective dialogue or correspondence.

I was very much interested in your exchange with Patten. His general thesis looks rather similar to some of the ideas of Teilhard de Chardin, and no doubt reflects some connection. Obviously all these people are groping for something, just as I am. Whether what we are groping for is substantial or illusory remains, I suppose, to be seen.

It seems to me that there is a perplexing lack of consistency in your exposition of your answer to the problem of truth. In your first letter you say, in effect, that an instrumental definition of truth (using the example, "sticks float") is "what we mean by truth," while "belly reaction," etc., tells us nothing. This I would suggest is a judgment identifying the technological or instrumental segment of human experience as somehow the locus of what we call true (as you have in other places identified it as the locus of what we call good). But then, in your second letter, you say, "there is [also] the human ["heart"] ["belly"] [the preceding three sets of square brackets are in Haisley's letter, added by hand, presumably by him] and all its complex concerns. Life isn't all stick-throwing and atom splitting, and one is just as 'real' as the other." Is truth, then, also to be identified, after all, with what our feelings tell us? In the one case you appear to show definite partiality to the instrumental and in the other you seem to maintain a careful neutrality. Surely you can't have it both ways on something so basic as this point is to your general system of ideas! Or perhaps you feel there isn't any partiality implied in your statement, "that is what we mean by truth [e.g., "sticks float"]". [Haisley's brackets] Isn't it also true that "red pepper burns," and how do we know it except by "experiencing the burning"? Isn't it also true that "Sirhan hated Kennedy," and does this statement hold its full meaningful content except through the projection of our own personal experiences of hatred?

Where I fell off the wagon of "pure" instrumentalism was in reflecting, many years ago, on the distinction we make in experimental science between alternative interpretations of certain effects (e.g., in the Geiger counter telescopic array I used in doing my Ph.D. research) as either "real" or "instrumental." This is a useful distinction, which scientists make whenever it's appropriate, and which they understand perfectly. But it's startling to the person with my own training (by Ayres) and belief (the whole matter of what's "real" is either defined instrumentally, or not at all). Perhaps what's at issue here is simply a distinction between two levels of instrumental complexity (if it's real it will affect many instruments similarly, not just my own individual equipment, etc.). However, the open-endedness was a little disturbing.

Another point of doubt and disturbance was the drift toward positivism in the self-interpretations of physicists, which I have tried to tackle in my paper. They end up by saying things which seem disgustingly nihilistic, and the upshot of this seems often to be the proliferation of random subspecialities which hardly, one may suspect, can be described as good and healthy science. Good science has always somehow managed to tie things together, but the contemporary scene is one of fragmentation. I suspect that epistemological nihilism and sociological disintegration may well have truly causal connections. Of course I can't prove this, and you may wish to dispute it. There is a great deal within contemporary physics which is healthy, of course, but I think this is partly due to the fact that "at heart" physicists aren't the operationalists they have officially claimed to be since Bridgman. That is, they are loyal to their quest for truth, and not merely to their technology.

With regard to the "Cartesian illusion of direct self-knowledge," this is an interesting notion with which I have not been directly familiar. Could you tell me more about it? When and by whom was actual scientific work done to produce knowledge making its illusory nature apparent? Or do I misinterpret your remarks in inferring such were the case?

I ask this question with sincerity (not in a spirit of forensic sarcasm) because I am frankly puzzled by the apparent implication that self-conscious awareness in human beings does not, after all, have perfectly well-defined foci which in some sense exclude each other. I would certainly agree with you that my knowledge of myself is based on a broad complex of learned material, and that the "self" which emerges from this is not isolated or private, but is in some sense part of the social continuum. But there is also surely a sense in which one person's experience is distinct from that of another.

I make use of this in the following way: A and B have different experiences (e.g., B's nose itches, while A's doesn't at the moment). A may (correctly) infer something about B's immediate experience by a combination of watching B's behavior and recalling his own past experience. Hence in a sense he projects his own feelings into some one else (namely, into B).

Such "social projection" or, in its more general forms, empathizing, give content and meaning to the question, asked by A, "does B's nose 'really' itch?" or "is my son 'really' sad?" By-passing questions about self-illusions, and the attendant lapses into meaninglessness of the question whether one's nose "really" itches or not, one notes that A can make the itch-observation directly on himself and conclude veridically that his nose is itching, with what I see as less necessary inference from the immediate than is required to conclude that B's nose is itching.

My point is simply, I suppose, that we can meaningfully talk about other people's experiences in terms of our own, whereas from a strict positivist point of view we would seem to be required to accept only our own personal testimony as legitimate empirical evidence. Bridgman carries this latter solipsistic trend to the point of denying emphatically the possibility of any public science, affirming instead a whole congeries of private sciences, and it is this kind of thing (and it's quite widespread nowadays) that I consider the unhealthy drift toward nihilism I spoke of earlier.

One can't "empathize" with electrons, sticks, or stones, of course, and so the "reality" query has to be answered in some different way. But since social empathy projections allow (or force) one to acknowledge the existence of experiences external to one's own, they go further and open up the existence of things external to one's own experiences and so weaken somewhat the positivist-operationalist claim that physically unobserved (or even unobservable) entities may not be meaningfully postulated except as part of an intralinguistic computing device. You may, of course, consider this an unwarranted extrapolation.

I have not got so far as I would like in developing this set of ideas (which go in a later part of the book), and perhaps they won't come through. I present them in their present muddled form to give you some clue as to why I consider the distinction important between those individual foci of self-awareness and "experience" which we sometimes call "selves." That this makes me a participant in the "Cartesian illusion of direct self-knowledge" I am inclined to doubt, in terms of my understanding of what this phrase means, but I am open to further clarification from you if you'd like to undertake it, as well as any arguments you may wish to advance that what I'm claiming veridically for in A's statement that "B's nose really itches" is "really" instrumentalist truth. Who knows—you might actually convince me (it wouldn't be the first time!).

Rip

Cloudcroft, July 6, 1968
Dear Rip:

With regard to inquiries such as ours the familiar maxim applies: In order to get right answers one must ask the right questions. It is equally important, I think, to ask: Who wants to know—and why? In the case of Teilhard de Chardin the answer is obvious—and significant. It's that old Jesuit who, despite his long preoccupation with zoology and archeology, is still a Jesuit. His master question is: Where does the human soul come in? He knows all the difficulties of a zoological hypothesis. So he anticipates all such difficulties by carrying his soul-stuff back to the fundamental stuff of the pre-planetary universe. But to the question, Why does he do this?, there is only one answer: Because he was a Jesuit before he was a paleozoologist.

Ceremonialism antedates all sophisticated intellectual inquiries. The beginning? I would argue that the "miracle" of articulate speech and the sense of the miraculous developed together: that for emotional creatures such as we, words (Platonic "ideas") seemed more real than the physical objects. Thus from the very outset mankind faced unanswerable questions: "What is a Snark? There must be one, since everybody is asking.["]

More historically, everybody is talking about ULTIMATE or ABSOLUTE reality. Is the universe of subatomic particles the REAL universe? Who wants to know.... what? Clearly the questioner is a cultural nursling of an ancient faith. What he means is: "Are the subatomic particles the ULTIMATE

REALITY? This might be called a nonsense-question, or (Dewey) a non-question, or (Ayres) a ceremonial question.

Thus it seems to follow that subatomic particles are as real as the cloudchambers by which scientists detect them; quasars are as real as telescopes, and all such are as real as sticks that float in water; and that any other question about realness is a ceremonial utterance and not a question at all, only a ceremonial utterance.

Is this disgustingly nihilistic? Towards the end of your paper you chide a scientist for saying (so it seems to me) that the entities revealed in his experimental work are just as real as sticks and stones. What's wrong with that? Is it not so? Or do you demur at this criterion? And what's wrong with the fragmentation you deplore? To an astonishing extent science seems to advance piecemeal, as technology (of which science is a manifestation) does. What's wrong with that? Do these scientists hypostasize piecemealness—make piecemealness an absolute, and not just a feature of the doing process?

I confess there is much about science as an institution that puzzles me. We have just finished reading the Watson book, Double Helix. It puzzles me. He speaks of DNA as being "up for grabs" and of himself and (and Crick) as being in a race with Linus Pauling for a Nobel prize. But if the molecular structure of DNA was as well known a goal as the finishing tape of a hundred-yard dash, why does it rate a Nobel prize? Much, it is presumed, will follow from it. But will it? Has it? Then I should think the prize should go to whoever first perceived that such is the case—that this peak would reveal a large landscape; not just the leg-man who climbed it first. Watson doesn't impress me. On the contrary, he appalls me!

As regards the evidentiality of direct self-knowledge: I suppose Freud is the most important name in the field. But isn't it notorious that physicians pay little attention to their patients' self-diagnoses—or rather give them quite a different interpretation from [what] the patients do. Your nose itch may be indicative of a neurosis, or of sunburn. I am subject to sensations of heat and of cold, as well as violent itching in my right leg, all of which, Dr. Jim Kreisle insists, is due to the pinching of the sciatic nerve where it leaves the spinal cord and gets pinched by enlarging vertebrae. These are trivial and common mistakes of supposed self-knowledge. But what about the psychoses investigated by Freud, and many others? Self-knowledge is of all supposed knowledge the most unreliable! It isn't your nose that itches, it's your ego!

What are the enormities into which operationalists have been led by what excesses of Bridgman? I wish you'd give me some idea. Perhaps I am barking up the wrong tree altogether. I know I ought to read these people. But it is so much more agreeable to ask you. I wish it could be face-to-face.

Clarence

Have you read Abe Fortas' little Signet "broadside": CONCERNING DISSENT AND CIVIL DISOBEDIENCE? If not, do. It's the real McCoy.

I have never met him, but have admired him ever since he defended Joe McCarthy's victims.

Chapel Hill, August 6, 1968
Dear Clarence:

In response to your question concerning the excesses of Bridgman, let me cite a passage from his THE INTELLIGENT INDIVIDUAL AND SOCIETY (1938, p. 158) which epitomizes his denial of "public science" and which I consider strongly solipsistic and even nihilistic in tone:

"The complete picture involves recognizing two operationally distinct things. My science is operationally an entirely different thing from your science, as much as my pain is different from your pain. This leads to the conclusion that there are as many sciences and arts and religions as there are individuals. It seems to me that this is indeed the case, and to recognize it is to get closer to what obviously can be seen, and is therefore better than to obscure what one sees by verbalisms, in spite of their convenience in many situations."

The more extended passage, which you might enjoy looking over—it is only a couple of pages in length— develops this idea. One might raise two questions: (1) is this conclusion inherent in the general operationalist position? and (2) has it really led to any harmful results? The first question would take a good deal of discussion and analysis; obviously, I suspect the tendency toward solipsism is indeed implicit in operationalist doctrine, but won't try to develop it or demonstrate that I'm correct. I think it is of a piece with the kind of fragmentation I'm concerned about.

As to the second question, I do detect a tendency among scientists of lesser breed, including colleagues, to deny that they are doing anything but playing a complicated game (with Nobel prizes "up for grabs"), whose import is irrelevant. In a recent conversation a few weeks ago, one of our bright younger people... affirmed frankly that his criterion of whether a new piece of research was worth doing was whether he could count on getting it published. Tactically, this may be good sense on occasion, but he didn't really seem interested in or concerned about anything more fundamental. Watson's book, which you cited and which has provoked a furor of discussion among scientists (mostly as to the propriety of making such relevations during the lifetime of the principals) is a fairly accurate presentation, I suspect (I haven't actually read it). I hope you would at least agree with me that the Bridgman citation represents something of a cul-de-sac (and I think you would), and that the prevalence of a state of mind within science where nobody cares any longer where it's going represents something of a drift toward potential sterility. Fortunately, the attitude of my colleagues is not an overriding one, it's too prevalent for comfort. Obviously, also, there are many forces at work. I do think, however, that the philosophical positions men hold make a significant difference in how they behave, in the long run, and also that operationalist doctrines have contributed to and intensified the fragmentation and loss of direction I've been claiming. I would be the last, however, to disagree with your comments to the effect that science/technology has and must operate from viewpoints of limited focus. All I would add in addition is that we are really all along hoping for grander and more accurately perceived vistas by virtue of this deployment, and that it is well not to lose sight altogether of this fact, or to deny it as a matter of principle.

Let me make one more point before cutting this off. In my paper I did not mean to "chide" scientists for saying their inferred or postulated entities were as "real as sticks and stones." What I said in fact was that this should be suspect to an operationalist like Bridgman (who only "believes" what he can directly observe and measure, if I understand them correctly), though it is certainly acceptable to me as it is, I gather, to you!

I would like to do some more thinking and writing about your identification of "reification" with ceremonialism, which I think was very cogently and clearly put in your letter. If I try to pose the question I have in mind it is whether what you and others have designated as ceremonial symbol behavior can lead to valid apprehension of "true" knowledge (technologically true knowledge, even). Certainly it can lead to meaningless hunts for snarks and phlogiston, as well as some god-awful bloopers in matters relating to contraception and the "reality" of the earth's motion (as many good Catholics would agree nowadays, and as indeed Chardin would doubtless have confessed). But I'll postpone that.

Rip

P.S. I'm including a copy of a letter I wrote recently to Bob Cohen, which I thought you might find interesting.

July 23, 1968
Robert S. Cohen
Department of Physics
Boston University
700 Commonwealth Avenue
Boston, MA 02215
Dear Bob:

The attached check for $12.50 is payment for my copy (I hope they are still available) of volume three of the Boston Studies in the Philosophy of Science.

I believe at our last meeting you invited me to write a "nine page letter" indicating why I thought Kuhn and Polanyi were intellectually significant rather than merely fashionable. It was a generous invitation, and if I thought you really had time to respond in symmetrical dialogue with a letter equally long I might be tempted to take you up. Since I suspect such a reply would indeed be overgenerous on your part, I'll try to put my reasons a little more concisely.

In Kuhn's case, I think his "paradigm" concept has usefulness and (limited) validity, even though (a) I do not accept the historical relativism to which he ties it, and (b) I recognize (as I know he does also) that his analysis is considerably in need of sharpening. As to the latter reservation, it is a matter of common knowledge that many basic notions (e.g., the idea of "force" in physics) have taken many generations of thoughtful analysis to clarify but have nonetheless served usefully during the interim, even though the end result of said analysis may be their elimination as ontologically basic (as would be true for the "force" concept in case general relativity holds up) or their relegation to subsidiary roles (such as being taught freshmen as intellectual scaffolding while they are building their knowledge of the subject).

How does one judge whether a new concept will prove thus fruitful instead of trivial and/or sterile? Here all I can invoke is heuristic intimation,—the instinctive, intuitive sense that there is "something there,["] and thus can only say that to me (in agreement with Hilary Putnam's remark in a Symposium discussion here) that Kuhn's paradigm analysis "smells right." Naturally I would concede that such testimony is incomplete without supporting analysis and critical scrutiny (such as that of Shapere), which may eventually force me to conclude that I have been having "olfactory" illusions (it has not yet done so!).

Science as practiced since Newton is relatively new, and we are continually in need of a better understanding of how it gets down in fact (as contrasted with the copybook cliches about "scientific method" and all that), so that it seems to me a person with the lucid expository talents of Kuhn does a service in pioneering fresh approaches, whether they "make it" or not. But to come more to the point, and give at least a plausibility argument for my claims of olfactory perceptiveness, it seems to me that in approaching the sociology of science (perhaps as a result of working among social scientists during some of his formative years) Kuhn has picked up something closely akin to Sumner's mores doctrines, and that his historical relativism reminds one of the cultural relativism which grew out of Sumner's work and related work in social anthropology. I happen not to accept either kind of relativism (as to the cultural variety, I have argued it—or rather against it—with considerable conviction in the face of prevailing dogmas of anthropologist friends), but it seems clear nonetheless that folkways-mores analysis has materially advanced and clarified our understanding of the way social groups come to accept and believe what they do about what is right and what is good. If scientists, considered as a social group generally, behave in somewhat the same way as people generally, this is hardly surprising. It seems outrageous only if one happens to be wedded to an outmoded form of "scientism," conceived as the one true road to salvation, so that there is something specially unique about the process of scientific discovery, advancement, and definitive analytical formulation. It would probably be unfair to tag my revered teacher and friend Clarence Ayres with anything so naive, but he is in that tradition nevertheless and was seriously disturbed by the implications, in a recent article by Stephen Brush in the GRADUATE JOURNAL ("Thermodynamics and History"), of Holton-type "thematic" elements in science. Perhaps Steve exaggerated the influence of realistic and romantic intellectual climates, and the like, on the formulations of nineteenth century science. But such thematic influences do persist and are clearly recognizable in our own day, and they play a key role as touchstones of scientific significance (e.g., "fundamental particles," which seems gradually being replaced as a basic theme by symmetries and the conservation laws). I think Holton is profoundly right in emphasizing the thematic, and while I suspect he might be uncomfortable in being thus linked with Thomas Kuhn it must nevertheless be apparent that there is a connection of sorts between the "thematic," which defines the current structures of scientific thinking, and the "paradigmatic," which focuses on the social mechanisms of their enforcement within the profession.

As to Polanyi, I cannot at the moment buy the idealistic implications of his "believing makes it so" doctrine, even when fortified with auxiliary codicils concerning "universal intent" or the like. Nevertheless he does emphasize in a novel and convincing way the indisputable fact that historically science hasn't been able, it would seem, to devise a system which is devoid of (technically) unprovable assumptions. This emphasis, combined with his scientifically buttressed analyses of "tacit knowing," seems to me to be very suggestive.

It seems fairly clear that we do indeed have to "accept on faith" new systems of ideas and world-views long before we can really develop their implications, test them, or even understand them fully, and in such acceptance there may (probably must) be elements of personal choice and commitment. We have to "guess" even though we hazard the chance of guessing wrong—this seems to be rather deeply embedded in [the] very nature of fundamental advances in knowledge both at the personal and cultural levels. Polanyi's "knowledge by fiat," as it were, seems too arbitrary for my bent; I would suspect that, since we are after all organisms interacting cognitively with our extended environments with more or less success, it would seem that the truth is forced upon us, though not without our active cooperation or even opposition. Somewhere along the line there come for each of us (as scientists and as people) moments where we have to believe things "whether we want to or not," and these are our "moments of truth," though the truth they testify to may be fragmentary or distorted. If this seems hopelessly revelatory, I should hasten to add that the process of finding truth is one to which empirical testing and critical analysis are both highly relevant, and to me one of Polanyi's attractions lies in his frank and honest attempt, after accepting his "tacit" elements, to seek by analysis for a better understanding of the manner in which the critical analysis of human beings has enhanced and integrated with the more intuitive forms of knowing which we share with the lower animals.

I certainly do not claim to understand all of Polanyi's analysis, nor do I find that I can agree with all he says. It is interesting to compare him with Kuhn, with whom he shares a good working knowledge of modern physical science as actively practiced as well as a certain iconoclasm which is rather inviting in a period seeming to call for radically new approaches. I think Polanyi is considerably the more profound of the two, and of course I like the fact that, unlike Kuhn, he moves away from rather than toward relativism. I have found the study of his work personally a liberating influence—partly, I think, because it has allowed me to put more trust in my own instinctual sense in intellectual matters, removing some of the tyranny of an iron-clad and prescriptive kind of rationalism without discarding the allegiance one nevertheless owes to rational consistency in intellectual matters even though one must temporarily suspend it in the press of practical conduct or in piecemeal empirical research.

I think I have said about all that is necessary to give you some clues to my own thinking on Kuhn and Polanyi. It would be very pleasant indeed to have a reply in kind, if you can spare the time for it.

Rip

Cloudcroft, August 11, 1968
Dear Rip:
I ought to be doing something else. But I can't until I have met the challenge contained in your letter to Cohen.

In trying to write for a collection of Ben Seligman's papers I remembered a letter Milton Friedman had written denouncing Ben for his concern about "the poor." (There are no such, he said; only those who have refused to take risks, or have taken risks and lost, which presumably served them right!) So I hunted up this curious letter, and found in it also Friedman's reference to "my revered teacher, Frank Knight"! As an object of reverence Frank Knight makes me laugh and Cohen might well be laughing at me, if he knew me at all. Shame on you, Rip Haisley! I know you wrote that with a twinkle in your eye. But does Cohen? Well, he does know you; so I guess the answer is Yes!

That Bridgman passage (which I don't remember, if I ever read it before) is certainly indicative of something.... but what? I suspect that Bridgman is squaring himself with "True believers." But qualifying scientific truth as the conviction of each scientist he is in effect putting it on a par with "revealed truth"—to which nobody can object—except Chardin's Jesuit superiors. You believe in God the father..., and I believe in the viscosity of liquids; and we repeat each other's beliefs.

It's amazing how reluctant scientists are to "dogmatize" about scientific truth. Isn't the whole "operational logic" a way of defining scientific truth in such a way as to avoid ever saying that any given proposition is "the real truth?" That is why I prefer to the technological criterion to operational [likely the first "to" should be deleted]. "Technological" suggests and emphasizes the continuity of atom-splitting with stick-throwing; whereas "operational" suggests the multiplicity of operations and might even be stretched to include ceremonial operations—which may be what Bridgman is suggesting.

The same, I think, is true of Kuhn. His "paradigms" emphasize the ideological aspect of the scientific "ideas": whereas what established the truth of those ideas and so defined their scientific meaning and validity is the technological (experimental) process which gave rise to them and defines (and limits) their meaning. By the same token, Michael Polanyi makes me uneasy. He too seems to be on the search for "higher truth." He's "deep." My impulse is to button my pockets.

I am not surprised that the Watson book has fluttered the doves. What surprised me most about the book was Bragg's introduction. But of course as Bishop of Cavendish he had a finger in the pie. I judge that Perutz (sp.?) is much more of a scientist than either Watson or Crick. but 'tis always thus. The 1929 edition of the Encyclopedia Britannica contains an excellent article on American music by Deems Taylor which makes no mention of Charles Ives!

Clarence

Chapel Hill, August 18, 1968
Dear Clarence:

Got back from a trip to Oak Ridge to find your letter waiting. The reactions to Kuhn and Polanyi were consistent with your general position, of course; I confess I was a bit slack-jawed at the ease with which you got Percy Bridgman off the hook—ostensibly, at least! I'd be careful, though, in attributing to him a reluctance to "dogmatize." He's one of the most dogmatically antidogmatic guys I know; I still remember vividly an evening colloquium at Brown when he startled me by publicly affirming his conviction that statistical mechanics was all a bunch of nonsense—this, I suspect was a heritage from the influence on him of Mach, who apparently never brought himself to believe in atoms. Reread the first section ("Broad Points of View") in THE LOGIC OF MODERN PHYSICS, Ch. I, and see if you won't admit that PWB was engaged to the hilt in "the quest for certainty," just like the rest of us. I cite particularly the passage "We should now make it our business to understand so thoroughly the character of our permanent mental relations to nature that another change in our attitude, such as that due to Einstein, shall be forever impossible." And if you regard Bridgman's early passage I cited before as merely "squaring himself with true believers," then is public demonstrability a mere fiction, and if it is must I also grant the "Jones who prefers pipe wrenches" a similar immunity for his private opinions and if so what happens to a technological theory of value????

Probably we've reached the stage of merely reiterating our position statements....

One last word about the phrase you were twitting me about in the Cohen letter; namely, my reference to you as a "revered teacher and friend." The phrase was of course intended to convey something like this: "I respect this guy and am rather reluctant to cite him publicly as someone with whom I have to take issue, but nevertheless he is an example that comes to mind which I can't resist using." In matter of fact, I do have an attitude toward you and your work which is in fact describable by the word "reverence", which in my own vocabulary connotes respect plus a certain gratitude for the impetus and substance you have provided for the development of my own ideas—of course you know all this and of course you have had similar attitudes toward your own intellectual ancestors (e.g., Meiklejohn, Dewey, Hamilton). If the phrase was nevertheless on the pretentious side or put me in bad company (namely, Friedman's), I can't honestly claim the mitigating irony you were kind enough to attribute to me, though I can insist that the tribute was sincere as well as that you deserve the reverence you have inspired in your students, which I share with a lot of others. Sorry about that! But I doubt that Cohen will find it laughable that a good teacher is remembered with fondness and respect by the students he helped to launch—he's a very good teacher, himself.

Rip

Austin, February 18, 1969
Dear Rip:

I am shocked by the date on your letter. I knew that I should have written you early last fall....

So now...should I resume the discussion of Percy Bridgman's probable meanings and intentions? If I were to undertake that, I really ought to go and read some Bridgman, and that I am too lazy to do. It would be easier to concede that I must have been wrong in supposing that he might have any wish to assuage any critics. But when you quote him as saying "that we should now make it our business to understand so thoroughly the character of our permanent mental relations to nature so that another change in our attitude, such as that due to Einstein, shall be forever impossible," I am tempted. This, you seem to be saying, convicts Bridgman of questing for certainty "just like the rest of us." Maybe so. Certainly it is profitless for me to try to guess what Percy Bridgman was up to. But I do have the feeling (it can't be more than that) that the <u>Weltanschauung</u> of present-day physics (and related sciences) is decisively different from that of Newtonian physics.

I get the impression that Newtonian physics was Euclidian, in the sense that a straight line was a straight line "such that if any part of it be cut off and laid upon any other part or that the end of one coincided with the other, the two would coincide throughout and be one and the same straight line." In short, carpentry. A mathematician once called my attention to the fact that a straight line thus implies sighting, which is to say the (supposed) path of light. But suppose that the path of light isn't like the path which is "the shortest distance between two points." As I gather, modern physics is built on all sorts of presumptions such as those of non-Euclidian geometry, Riemann manifolds, and all that sort of thing. I have read statements of modern physicists to the effect that they can't translate their ideas into the ordinary language of my stick-throwers. Their concepts themselves can be articulated only in the language of mathematical physics. <u>In this sense</u>, the simplicities of Newtonian physics are gone forever.

Such being the case what has become of my stick throwers? I would say, Nothing. Carpenters still sight along the edge of their board to <u>see</u> if they are "straight," and they know quite well and truly what they mean by straight, and Einstein runneth not to the contrary. I would argue that Einstein's equations are something you do with chalk on a blackboard, and the are as true and real as the chalk, but a little more complicated.

You speak of Mach never bringing himself to believe in atoms. Such a statement, it seems to me, turns more on the meaning of belief than on the concept of atoms. I try to confine the concept of "belief" to the emotional commitment to institutional matter (the Eucharist, etc.), identifying recognition of such matters as atoms by the word "conviction." Thus one might say the Heisenberg conception of atoms is convincing (and just as convincing as the buoyancy of sticks, to those who can follow his mathematics). I wonder if Mach isn't an exemplar of the way of thinking which Bridgman says we can never return to. If so, I would agree. It is thus in the conviction sense that I would agree with the scientist you chided, late in your paper, for saying that something (say the Heisenberg atom) is just as real as hot cross buns, or what have you. I have always said that the moons of Jupiter are just as real as Galileo's telescope; and in the same sense it seems to me that Heisenberg's atom is just as real his equations. The stick you throw in the river is just as real as the river (in which you swim), and no realer. But if we are such things as dreams are made of—then nothing physical, whether Newtonian or Heisenbergian, is as "real" as that. Thus it seems to me that Bridgman <u>may</u> be saying that Newtonian physics was naive in a sense that is now forever impossible. Which I would go along with.

Clarence

Chapel Hill, March 30, 1969
Dear Clarence:

I want to get this letter off in tonight's mail, so will defer comment on your latest remarks except in relation to the fact that Mach did not "believe" in atoms. Perhaps my own concept of physical reality can be exemplified by referring to the perennial discussion we have with the kids over which way current "really" flows. We usually tell them that current may be considered conventionally to flow from plus to minus in a resistor, even though the electrons "really" go from minus to plus. (In an accelerator, on the other hand, a proton beam contains positive protons, which "really do" go in the same direction as the conventional current.) To my mind the conventional current concept represents the technological efficacious device which is useful and may be employed when considerations of "reality" are irrelevant; the latter are nevertheless truly distinguishable, when one wishes to do so.

Rip

Austin, May 20, 1969
Dear Rip:

Your paper is greatly improved. I read it with fascination, though (or perhaps because!) I am still a little puzzled as to just what you find offensive in the operationalists and positivists. Is it only their rigid dogmatism, or is it what they are dogmatic about? Thus I puzzle over the passage cited on page 70. I suppose the enigma of "waves" stems from the fact that we conceive waves as what happens when a stone is thrown into a pond. This involves the supposition that water is a sort of solid substance (though, paradoxically, not as solid as ice—which, however, floats like the stick).

Some years ago a German philosopher named Hans Vaihinger published a book named (in translation) "The Philosophy of As If" (Die Philosophie des Als Ob). He has a point. Wouldn't you and Leighton be satisfied to say that all particles behave *as if* they were atmospheric, or Hetzian, waves with measurable frequencies, etc.? After all, that's all that anything does. When you jump in the water you do behave as if you were a stick, though with measurable differences, etc., etc., etc. What is now being said that shouldn't?

Or what do you want said (or implied) that isn't? You quote Michael Polanyi as saying in effect that "believing" is a precondition to "knowing." Well...I make a distinction between "belief" and "conviction," defining conviction as a phase of knowing (or of what Dewey calls "inquiry": an incomplete inquiry), and then would say of it what Polanyi says of belief. But I define belief as a supposition which arises not from inquiry but from community tradition, emotion-tinged, etc.; and I would deny that it leads to knowledge accept by contraries. Beliefs often do lead to inquiries, the result of which is the conviction that the belief "ain't so." I haven't read Michael Polanyi much for precisely this reason. I distrust him. He is very learned and very adroit, and I feel that he is trying to trick me into believing what ain't so, for reasons which he is very skillful at concealing. Why is it that he persistently uses words that put my back up? I distrust connoisseurship. Characteristically it pretends to knowledge I don't have and uses it to hip [sic?] me. I respect amateurism. It frankly admits to being in love, so that all its declarations may be subjected to discount. Once I was invited to be one of a small group privileged to hear Michael Polanyi talk. Flattered by the invitation (and because I admire his brother) I went. He convinces me that he is a connoisseur, whom I distrust. No sale!

Clarence

Chapel Hill, June 9, 1969
Dear Clarence:
...I have come to the conclusion that we are really not so far apart as it might appear, even though there are some things which we view in a somewhat different perspective. I am anxious to keep whittling on the subject....

Rip

Austin, (ca. July 1, 1969) [by hand at top of page]
Dear Rip:
Recently I have received quite a shock, which I think will amuse you. This came from a letter I received from a chap on the staff of the Ford Foundation. He had been in Mexico City where had run into Pat Blair, one of our young professors now on leave and working for the F.F. there. Somehow I came into the conversation and the Ford chap recalled me as (he thought) the author of a book entitled "Theses to be nailed on the Laboratory Door." It seems he had read this book about 1940, recalled it fondly, had lost his copy and been unable to get another, and so was writing me, at Pat's suggestion, for help.

I recalled that "Theses" bit at once. It headed the conclusion of a book I wrote in 1925-6, before I came here, and when I still thought of my field as philosophy. I still have a copy, but I haven't dared to look inside it for many years—not since we came here, I think. However, since the "Theses"-conclusion is only 2 1/2 pages long, I thought I would send the guy a photo-copy; and that is how I came to read the first "thesis," which is:

That the truth of science is established only by belief, after the manner of all folk-lore.

What can I say? What in the world do you suppose was eating me? I suppose the way to find out is to look in the book. But don't dare! I would be in sackcloth and ashes except for another recent event: a recent letter from Van Meter Ames telling me of a recent book on "The Chicago Pragmatists," in which he says I am mentioned. This leads him to say that he heard me lecture (at Chicago, where had just taken his Ph.D.) in the summer of 1923. I have a vivid memory of that lecture and the sense of temerity with which I dared to argued that all scientific discoveries resulted from prior (or concomitant) invention of instruments. If I was arguing to this effect in 1923, I couldn't have been an utter ass in 1926. But what in the world I could have meant by that "thesis" I can't imagine. I'm afraid I shall have to risk reading that book!

Clarence

Chapel Hill, August 14, 1969
Dear Clarence:
    Your rediscovery of your own 1925-6 "thesis" about scientific truth would be amusing did I not also sympathize with your dismay at having once said something in print which you now find embarrassing....
    I got out my own copy of SCIENCE THE FALSE MESSIAH and looked it over without the hampering anxieties of personal commitment. The thesis, as you no doubt discovered if you carried out your resolution to "risk reading that book," was the central idea of the its first chapter. Of course it seems badly stated now, from the perspective of your later and more mature conclusions, but the substance of that chapter can hardly be said to be discontinuous with your later position regarding the validity of science. Thus you would still not deny today that many popular beliefs today about the findings and origins of modern science partake of the nature of folk-lore, nor that, as you cited from the essay by Charles Cobb, "folk-lore, like science, is founded upon axioms." At the time you wrote the book you were still, I would presume, in the grip of Sumner's <u>mores</u> principle, before you went over to the technological principle as the touchstone both of truth and value.
    I remember your leading a discussion in the first course I ever took from you (BACKGROUND OF ECONOMIC THOUGHT, in the fall of 1934) on the question (relative to the nature of classical economic theory) of what distinguishes science from theology. Your answer, of course, was "the use of instruments of precision." You remarked further that, in their official pronouncements, you found a striking similarity between scientists and theologians—a statement which, as I remember, puzzled me profoundly and, as you see, stuck with me. You felt that scientists and modern physical science generally had succeeded in liberating themselves significantly from theological pronouncements—to a greater extent than was the case currently in the social sciences. But not, I suppose, completely. In 1925-6 you had not yet read Bridgman, and you were incensed, moreover, with the role played by leading scientific figures of the day in the contemporary flaps over evolution and the

impact of scientific discovery on traditional Christian belief. In SFS you make specific reference to the "scientific Credo" of 1923, publicly issued by 40 leading scientists & university presidents from Washington, D.C., as well as to the Tennessee evolution trial. Personally I think the book was excellent and spirited writing and still makes provocative and helpful reading.

The position you took (implicitly, at least) in the earlier book is that the essential truth of science is limited to its instrumental activity, and that the larger significance imputed by scientists and others to their work (what I have called "overclaims") is relevant only to the context of the "true believer." So I don't believe the later Ayres really contradicts the earlier Ayres so very seriously, and with a little doctoring the offending "thesis" could be fixed up into something you could still wholeheartedly endorse.

Rip

Cloudcroft, September 22, 1969
Dear Rip:

On the basis of your favorable report I have signed a contract with Augustus Kelley to resuscitate <u>Messiah</u> and <u>Holier</u>. I made it a condition that I be allowed to write a short introduction to each, and somewhat to my surprise the chap who was handling the deal (Frederic Cheesman) not only acquiesced but made it a condition of the contract. So if I am indicted for grave-robbing, I shall plead that it's all your fault.

...Leonard Loeb...is the son of Jacques Loeb of tropism fame, who was a friend of Veblen's Chicago days, from whom Veblen got his vague references to tropism, and also some of the stories in <u>The Higher Learning</u>....

However tardily I must thank you for sending me the off-print of Stephen Brush's piece....It is an extraordinary essay, especially in the breadth of its coverage—extending to the Adamses and Clarence King. The treatment of Lord Kelvin and Huxley especially interested me, of course. What is there about The Second Law of Thermodynamics that paralyzes the mind and terminates all further discussion? Even Oppenheimer genuflects to it. What amazes me most about Kelvin's demolition of Darwinism is not the brevity of the earth's timespan but the dogmatism of his calculation of the cooling of the sun—when he hadn't the faintest notion of the processes which generated the sun's heat. It makes me wonder what other "certainties" about which the present generation of scientists are unanimously positive just aren't true at all.

Clarence

Chapel Hill, April 25, 1970
Dear Clarence:

Before writing this I was...reflecting over your comments on Steve Brush's piece....It is timely, since later today I am supposed to sit in on a discussion between two of our local "pro" historians of science and a young man who has been doing his thesis on Kelvin, and I spent some time yesterday afternoon chatting with him about his work, which has been going on now for several years. He says the central theme of his interest now is not "Why couldn't Kelvin accept Clerk Maxwell?" but "Why was Kelvin a failure?" He has come to the conclusion that K was essentially a very conservative and rather arrogant person, and that perhaps his worldly success contributed substantially to his failure to live up to his real potential as a creative scientist able to identify the significant innovations of his generation. Apparently he never really gave official assent to the relevance of new discoveries in radioactivity to the age of the sun, and was equally dogmatic in his rejection of other significant advances.

Rip

Austin, April 29, 1970
Dear Rip:
Thanks for making that copy of Frank Oppenheimer's review of the Davis book. [*Lawrence and Oppenheimer* is discussed in Haisley to Ayres, September 22, 1969 and Ayres to Haisley, January 1, 1970. Most of the discussion concerns their work and careers as physicists.] It is in very poor taste—calamitously poor....

What does matter is Robert's character and temperament. Davis draws a picture of Robert as painfully naive—as I had supposed he was. For example, his behavior under questioning by the Hickenlooper committee seems to me to have been childish. For example: after Robert under questioning had infuriated the committee, he paused on the way out to ask one of his associates, "Did I do well?" The associated replied, "Too well." Robert had flapped the banner of his idealism in the faces of Hickenlooper and his committee—but to what end? Was he doing his best to infuriate the Senate Committee? Did he want to goad them into getting him fired? Why? Judged in terms of his own ideals, what was gained by his removal and Teller's being put in command? If Robert wanted to stop the arms race between the USA and the USSR— well, he should have been an entirely different person. Was he really not so naive as he was represented by Davis? Frank doesn't say so. He says he had a grand piano—or didn't have.

Human egotism is limitless. I suspect that it plays a key part in all ceremonialism. For some time now I have been cherishing an idea with regard to the aboriginal origin of tool-using, and even articulate speech: viz., that the physical materials by which man is surrounded (including, of course, physical processes such as fire, sound production, etc., etc.) are an essential and genuinely creative factor in the incipience of tool-using, articulate speech and so technology-knowledge. Could a creature with the species-endowment

of mankind <u>fail</u> to develop articulate speech and primitive tools? A baby emits
cries. So do the young of many species. But the baby notices the effect of
his cries on other people. and so <u>learns</u> to cry <u>on purpose</u>. The next step
is differentiating the vocalizations—and speech is on the way. So also with
sticks and stones—and technology-science is on the way. The relation
between empirical observation and theory at the highest levels of scientific
discovery is just the same. The fact that atomic particles travel
perpendicularly to a magnetic field seems to me to bear the same relation
to the scientific discoveries of Lawrence and such-like scientists that primeval
invention-discoveries bear to the actual properties of wood and stone. It's
all one process.

I would like to try to work out a general theory of discovery and invention
along these lines. Do you think I could bring it off?

Clarence

Chapel Hill, May 2, 1971
Dear Clarence:

Next Thursday, I believe, is your 80th birthday, and so perhaps the enclosed
paper is in the nature of a birthday present, since it is one I think you may
especially enjoy. The title ("The Pernicious Influence of Mathematics") drew
me irresistibly to it when it was recommended by a colleague this spring, and
since it speaks from the hallowed depths of professional competence in
mathematics I find the "academic clout" of the author's conclusion (i.e., that
all too often "mathematical formalism may be hiding as much as it reveals")
particularly appealing even though his thesis may hardly be said to be new.
You'll find all of it highly intelligible except that bit about Birkhoff's ergodic
theorem, which I don't really understand either except in a very general way
and whose details are irrelevant to the main thrust. The point is that there
are a lot of people in this world of Academe who are dazzled by mathematical
virtuosity to the extent of being impervious to the import of the argument (e.g.,
in relation to mathematical economics) except by virtue of such a concrete
example presented in full logical detail. My colleague Wayne Bowers
(theoretical physics) is such a person, and the fact that he found the article
cogent is as significant to me as the fact that it says so succinctly what I first
learned from your course in "The Background of Economic Thought" more
than thirty-five years ago.

Anyhow, perhaps you'll get some satisfaction from the Schwartz piece—
I certainly hope so. The J. Schwartz who wrote it is apparently Jacob Theodore
Schwartz, a mathematics professor at NYU.

Eighty years is indeed a venerable age, and I find myself wanting to bow
down in some ceremonial act of reverence. Since I'm not sure how you would
feel about such obeisance I'll refrain from pursuing the impulse. I wish, though,

that I could really put into succinct expression the sense I have of intellectual debt to your teaching and encouragement over the past 3.7+ decades. And there are many more such as myself who bear witness in their lives to the effectiveness of your teaching. Whether we do full justice to the vision you were trying to pass on to us is (I hope!) beside the point. The essential fact is the profound difference it has made in all our lives to have come into contact with your words and personal intellectual forcefulness. In my own case, I can say with vehement sincerity that there are few people who have made a more important difference in my life than you.

W.E.H.

Austin, June 30, 1971

Dear Rip:

...My resistance to the mathematization of economics has nothing to do with mathematics as such. In economics it means obsession with the operation of "the market"; which means taking private property for granted as "given" which I regard as Adam Smith's basic mistake. We can do much better than the market if we can rid ourselves of the supposition that mathematics proves that the market does best.

I am more and more obsessed with the creative role of technology. We owe everything, including what we think of as human brain power, to tools— including the noises we make and call articulate speech. I am more and more obsessed with the idea of trying to show this. I would start with the industrial revolution "of the eighteenth century in England," in which I would try to show the machinery itself plays the leading part. The inventors can devise only the gimmicks which the spindles and looms have showed themselves capable of doing and being; and I would work back through the agricultural revolution to the dawn of mankind.

I will have to confess that it is that Oklahoma agriculture chap who started me by showing domestic animals sought man out, so did the crop plants. Man does have the faculty of putting things together. He puts together the noises the air is full of and the result is language. He puts fire and wood together (since both abound in his world) and the result is cooked food—and everything else. But always the things man puts together are there, just waiting, so to speak, to be put together.

I don't know whether all this is economics or philosophy, and I don't care. Should I? ...

Clarence

Chapel Hill, December 31, 1971
Dear Clarence:

I was a little disappointed in your response to the Schwartz article on "The Pernicious Influence of Mathematics on Science." I think his central point can be translated into technology-institutions language by saying that the use of abstract material (in this case, mathematical physics), which is of vital value when used correctly (i.e., technologically), can be pernicious if used ceremonially and in the wrong way. The ceremonial misuses (misuses from a technological point of view, that is) may be to obscure the real issues at stake (as in your comment regarding the mathematics of the "market" and private property); they may also be to divert people's attention away from those areas where investigation of a more concrete and immediate nature is the most promising in fruitfulness, simply because academic prestige decrees that the more abstruse a subject is in treatment the more profound and cogent it must be, and/or because of the widespread prevalence of the impression that the more mathematically a subject is treated the more "scientific" it is bound to be. Schwartz's illustration from mathematical physics was an attempt to present as illustrated a case where a mathematical theory (the "Birkhoff ergodic theorem") had served the function, not of "proving" rigorously that the fluctuations in such things as the pressure of a gas, and the like, must be small, but of obscuring the fact that theoretical grounding for such expectations rests on a relatively simple hypothesis, which though plausible is nevertheless an assumption. Mathematics in this case obscures an assumption, which it would seem is equally true of much mathematical economics, as you yourself suggest when you note that it was really Adam Smith's taking private property for granted that should have been more closely scrutinized—an assumption which is pretty hard to see clearly beneath a luxuriant proliferation of TUC curves and the like. N'est-ce pas?

                                                                    Rip

Austin, January 9, 1972
Dear Rip:

I'm sorry to have disappointed you by my apparent lack of enthusiasm for the Schwartz article. Partly that was due to my ignorance of physics. Evidently I failed to appreciate how daring he was. But more important is the difference in the social science context. As you know, I am vigorously opposed to the mathematization of economics. But there the reason is that the mathematics all turns on price calculations, which turn on the acceptance of "the market" as the guiding mechanism of the economy, which in turn assumes the institution of property and the prevailing distribution of property.

Of course, if you don't make those assumptions, your basic problem is how all the good and useful things (which stem from the prevailing technology) should be distributed. That is a very great problem indeed. Hence it is very tempting indeed to leave things as they are, especially in view of the mathematical intricacy of the operation of the price system, the up-shot of which is the very great likelihood of things remaining substantially as they are.

Your philosophy of the "hippy" movement is interesting, and perhaps true: the music is what is most real and perhaps enduring. The "Hallelujah Chorus" (which is one of the greatest pieces of music ever written) may well survive Christian theology, if it hasn't already done so. I don't understand "rock" music. But it may be impregnated with eternity.

Clarence

Chapel Hill, April 12, 1972
Dear Clarence:
...we can have another go at the Schwartz article. I thought your remarks in your last letter were very much to the point, and I see why you make the distinction you do between mathematical economics and the mathematical obscurantism in the sciences which Schwartz was getting at.

I guess my reply would be directed to the fact that the higher learning of every era is infected with a fairly impressive quantity of mumbo-jumbo, much of which goes undetected in academe, largely because it is recondite and therefore presumably profound—economics is no exception in this regard, although as you say the motivation for obscurity is more exceptionally clear cut and notably pernicious. But it is true in both economics and physics that the immediate motivation of those who lose themselves in playing games with abstractions is complicated, interesting, problematic, and relevant to the problem of how to make the marriage of highbrow knowledge and daily living a fruitful one. In particular, both mathematical economists and mathematical physicists spin their fabrics in the firm belief that this is the way to be "scientific," and this presumption aids in the collective self-deception of market-minded economists who participate in the process. Hence the importance, methodologically, of drawing a distinction between the ceremonial and technological uses of mathematics even in the presumably purified areas of mathematical physics....Of course, you also presume that the epistemological problems of physical science are basically solved (i.e., by the instrumental principle), where I don't have the comfort of this faith, and so I have a harder problem than you!

Rip

Austin, April 17, 1972
Dear Rip:
As regards our common affliction, it seems to me that in the case of economics something more is involved than intellectual fascination. The basic

axiom of all price theory is the proposition that given the prevailing distribution of wealth and power the allocation of resources will be optimal. This is what the mathematics "proves," in an infinite variety of market patterns, and the procedures by which it is proved are so infinitely various and subtle—so completely intellectual and satisfying—that attention is effectively diverted from what everybody knows to be the qualifying assumption: the prevailing distribution of wealth and power.

Wealth is power, of course; and I duplicate the power aspect of wealth only because the state of mind induced by the whole rationale is one of disregard of that aspect of the situation. It is the opiate of the intellectuals. (Mathematics as the opiate of the intellectuals!) Consider what has been happening to the income tax. Originally decried as revolutionary (which it is, of course): it was finally adopted as a Constitutional Amendment. The central idea was a redistribution of wealth by employment of the progressive principle. But then as the country gets richer, millionaires become commonplace and billionaires begin to appear, a spirit of pity for millionaires begins to replace the earlier "populism." Since things have worked out so that nobody actually pays the higher rates in the income tax law, the whole thing begins to be recognized as a mistake.

But hold on! Why am I lecturing you? But perhaps I have made my point, that in economics addiction to mathematical analysis is in effect an endorsement of the capitalist status quo.

Clarence

NOTE

1. "I had two courses under Ayres, one in the fall semester of 1934 (called "Background of Economic Thought") and the other in the fall of 1935 (called "Economic Motives"). The first of these traced the origins of Adam Smith's assumptions in the work of the seventeenth and eighteenth century philosophers, and the second presented Ayres's theories of technology and institutions as they stood at that time. They were taught as seminars rather than as courses, and the format was Socratic, so that note-taking was discouraged (he did so explicitly, in fact). I find no notes at all in my records, although there is a list of the bulk of the books and articles which he read out to us at the beginning of the second course..." W. E. Haisley to Warren J. Samuels, August 26, 1973.

ROSWELL CHENEY MCCREA'S COURSE ON ECONOMIC DOCTRINES AND SOCIAL REFORM, COLUMBIA UNIVERSITY, 1927-1928

Warren J. Samuels

Economics b 101 and 102 was a two-semester course entitled "Economic Doctrines and Social Reform" offered in 1927-1928 by Professor Roswell Cheney McCrea in the Business School of Columbia University. In early November 1993 Professor James F. Becker of New York University kindly provided me with the set of notes from that course taken by Arthur Zapolsky Arnold. The notes are contained, except for some loose pages, in a bound notebook with "Economic Doctrines," "A.Z. Arnold," and "Columbia University 27" on three lines on the outside front cover. The original materials will eventually be deposited in the Rare Book and Manuscript Library of Columbia University's Butler Library.

The notes run to slightly over one hundred pages (in three groups, numbered in red), for the most part in small cursive writing, typically two lines between

Reasearch in the History of Economic Thought and Methodology,
Archival Supplement 5, pages 221-242.
Copyright © 1996 by JAI Press Inc.
All rights of reproduction in any form reserved.
ISBN: 1-55938-094-2

ruled lines. Most of the pages are, or seem to be, Arnold's notes on various readings. Some appear to present notes on McCrea's lectures which summarize or comment on the readings. Internal evidence suggests the possibility that McCrea dictated at least some of the summaries of readings. In addition, the volume of notes is clearly small relative to what one would expect in a year course—even a one-semester course; just why this is the case is, however, unclear. (Compare the notes from courses by John Dewey and E.R.A. Seligman in earlier volumes of this archival series.) The lecture notes are summary and not an attempt at a verbatim record. To this reader the fact that McCrea was a professor in the business college does not seem to have significantly if at all influenced what he is recorded to have covered and said— although the course had much more to do with economic doctrines than social reform, both terms comprising the title of the course.

Roswell Cheney McCrea was born in Norristown, Pennsylvania, July 30, 1876. He received an A.B. from Haverford in 1897, an A.M. from Cornell in 1900, a Ph.D. from Pennsylvania in 1901, and an LL.D. from Columbia in 1929. He taught at Trinity College, Bowdoin College, the University of Pennsylvania, and Columbia University. He was Dean of the Wharton School, 1912-1916, after which he went to Columbia, where he served as Dean of the School of Business during 1932-1941, retiring in 1942. He was the author or co-author of books, articles, and reports on public finance (*Essays in Taxation*, 1905), international trade (*International Competition in the Trade of Argentina*, New York: Carnegie Endowment for International Peace, 1931), and transportation (*The Taxation of Transportation Companies*, Washington, DC: Government Printing Office, 1901; *Report of the Industrial Commission on Transportation*, idem), and other subjects (*Legislation for the Protection of Animals and Children*, Columbia University, 1914; *The Humane Movement*, Columbia University Press, 1910). In 1915 an essay entitled "The New Optimism in the Viewpoint of Economists" was published in the University of Pennsylvania, *University Lectures* (vol. 2, pp. 349-362). He published a number of articles in the *Journal of Political Economy* and *Quarterly Journal of Economics*, principally on taxation and business education, including a 1909 review article (QJE) on recent textbooks in economics. Among other professional activities, he was President of the American Association of Collegiate Schools of Business, 1924-1925. He died on July 2, 1951.

Arthur Zapolsky Arnold was born in Armavir, Georgia, Russia, March 1, 1898. He came to this country in 1914 and became a naturalized citizen in 1925. He received an LL.B. from Hamilton College in 1922, though he never practiced law. He received an M.A. from Washington University in 1928 and an MS. and Ph.D. from Columbia University in 1928 and 1937, respectively. He taught economics at City College of New York from 1928 to 1938 and at New York University from 1936 until his death, December 28, 1965. He authored *Banks, Credit and Money in Soviet Russia* (Columbia University Press, 1937; translated into Japanese in 1941). No citations in his name are given in the *Index of Economic Journals,* although he published in outlets not included therein, including the *Annals.* An obituary article appeared in *The New York Times* on December 30, 1965, in which it is reported that at the time of his death Arnold was working on a manuscript for a book on the history of economic theory.

The following is an account of the contents of the notes. Recorded are the initial bibliographical materials; the *identity* of notes on readings and the *content* of what appears to be lecture notes. I am indebted to Hollee Haswell of Columbia University and Michael Unsworth of Michigan State University for assistance. Only minor editorial changes have been made in the materials; these include the completion of the spelling of abbreviated words; uncertain completions are placed in square brackets. All underlining is in the original. (Only the original ink underlining is presented here; red underlining, perhaps added while studying, is omitted. However, some of Arthur's editorial changes in red, such as inserting a word, are reproduced here.) Occasionally Arthur used square brackets instead of the usual parentheses, for no apparent purpose; these have been changed to parentheses so that square brackets signify only my insertions. The reader is reminded that the notes on lectures are not necessarily informative of what McCrea said, only of what Arnold heard and recorded. I intentionally restrict my comments to very few.

Overall, the notes are suggestive as to what was and was not covered and how the history of economic thought was presented, especially nuances of ideas and other twists different from those more or less common today. The course, at least as recorded in these notes, covered the classical school with some attention to the marginal utility school, especially Bohm-Bawerk, with very little attention to individual later writers, such as J. B. Clark, Fisher, and F. W. Taussig, who were typically mentioned only for comparison. Marx makes a brief appearance; Marshall is mentioned without an indication of his importance. Given the principle that the historian is too close to contemporary economic writers to have perspective, the lack of coverage of twentieth-century neoclassical and institutional economics is understandable, if not laudable, in lectures given in 1927-1928.

The reader is encouraged to read the materials not for what is or is not true by present-day accounts, but with regard to the particular story presented, and that story as a discursive, or rhetorical, product, not a matter of truth or falsity; and also to look for subtle differences of nuance and interpretation. McCrea was no Wesley Mitchell or Edwin Seligman—contemporary master expositors of the history of economic thought, both also at Columbia—but what is recorded here is suggestive of his view of the subject. This view was not a specialist view but also not one that was uninformed. Perhaps the notes serve as an indicator of nonspecialist history of economic thought. What is important for present purposes is not what the history of economic thought "really is," but what it is made out to be. And clearly at various points the notes suggest that simple reductionist summaries of what was then believed are likely to misrepresent the complexity of what was in fact believed—at least as suggested by what was recorded by this combination of lecturer and student.

One characteristic of McCrea's interpretation of the development of economic ideas and theories is his quiet relating of ideas to changing contemporary economic development. Although he may think of economic progress in everyday affairs (from feudalism through mercantilism through industrial revolution), this does not seem to mean that he believes that economic thought progressed *independent* of economic change.

On the inside front cover the following are listed in now-faded light red ink as books to read: J.K. Ingram's *A History of Political Economy*; W. Ashley's *An Introduction to English Economic History and Theory* (with *Economic History* noted just below in pencil); E. Cannan's *History of the Theories of Production and Distribution*; G. Cassell's *Theory of Social Economy*; L. Edie's *Principles of New Economics*; A. Marshall's *Principles of Economics*; H. R. Seager's *Principles of Economics*; and H. George's *Progress and Poverty*. At the top of the page in red ink is a reference to C. E. Griffin, *Principles of Foreign Trade*, with the comment "very good"; and in black ink a reference to W. D. Moriarty, *The Economics of Marketing and Advertising*, with the comment "good summaries of Mercantilism, Physiocrats, etc." The word "read" is given first alongside these two references and before the long list in red.

On the next page is a mimeographed list (to which some page numbers are added in pencil), glued to a page of the notebook, entitled "readings in Economics b 101," which reads in the original as follows:

References are made to the following works:
John Stuart Mill: Principles of Political Economy
Gide and Rist: History of Economic Doctrines
Adam Smith: Wealth of Nations
Wicksteed: The Common Sense of Political Economy
Hobson: The Industrial System
Ricardo: Political Economy
Tugwell (Editor): The Trend of Economics

I
Mill: Preliminary Remarks, and Book I, chs I-IV
Gide and Rist: Book I ch. I

II
Mill: Book I, chs V-IX
Gide and Rist: Book I ch. II
Smith: Book I Introduction and chs I-IV. Book II chs I, III, IV
Hobson: ch III

III

Mill: Book I, chs. X-XIII
Gide and Rist: Book I ch III
Wicksteed: pp. 346-367

IV

Mill: Book II chs I-IV
Gide and Rist: Book III

V

Mill: Book II chs XI-XVI
Smith: Book I chs. VIII-XI (in ch XI covering only parts I, II, III to the digression on silver)

VI

Mill: Book III chs. I-IV
Ricardo: ch. I
Tugwell: pp. 3-34
Also read in the course of the semester
John Stuart Mill's Autobiography

On the page facing the first page of notes is a large (4" x 5") clipping of a newspaper photograph of the statue by Daniel Chester French in front of the library of Columbia University, with the caption, "Alma Mater." Above it are references to Gide and Rist's *History of Economic Doctrines*, J. D. Brannan's *Negotiable Instruments Law Annotated*; the Everyman Edition of Smith's *Wealth of Nations*; and Leon Carroll Marshall's *Business Administration*, with "very good" in parentheses alongside; and Percival White's *Market Analysis*, noted to be "very good" and "buy."

Altogether the foregoing comprise an interesting combination of original early sources (Smith, Ricardo, Mill), then-standard history of economic thought texts (Ingram, Cannan, Gide and Rist); several relatively recent and contemporary works (Marshall, Wicksteed, Cassell, Tugwell), and a variety of other books selectively pertinent to the interpretation of the history of economics. Especially interesting is the inclusion of works by Hobson and George.

At this point is a folded page with some notes on T. R. Malthus's *Essay on the Principle of Population*.

The first notes are lecture notes somewhat corresponding to Ingram's *History of Political Economy* on pre-Smithian economic thought (3 1/3 pages). Arnold wrote as follows:

Up to about 50 years ago a body of deductive principles was accepted. Much more recently two sets of [word undecipherable]: growing of vocational psychology and induction— preceded by:

1. Growing importance of historical studies; historical approach with <u>evolutionary</u> ideas—these results were summed up by W. Ashley: 1. Political Economy is not

a body of true doctrines but a number of valuable theories. he attempts to inject a note of relativity into theorizing.

There was no well-rounded theory until Adam Smith [undecipherable word] the field. But of course there was theorizing before, as Ashley points out. The economic side of those people wasn't developed. Geographic knowledge, transportation—little developed. War—spirit of life.

Middle Ages: Thought influenced by Christian doctrines antagonistic to wealth. Poor and hungry—the blessed. No justification for wealth. This was strengthened by the idea of Law of Nature. 1. The character of nature [undecipherable word], similarly. 2. All people were by nature equal. Christ[ianity] purified domestic life. Made labor a dignified occupation. The crusades broke up feudalism; contributed to growing independence of towns; increased use of money. The canonists recognized private property (while the church was friendly to communism).

Slaves, serfs, freemen—from whom sprang the bourgeois.

Early modern times—from middle ages—difficult to distinguish.

Second Phase

Middle Ages: 1. 14-15 century—epoch-making development—breakup of feudal system. King aligns birth [undecipherable word].—Discovery of America, [undecipherable word] Protestant Reformation; increase of use of money, influx from America, beginning of international trade.

Beginning 16th century: Two phases—1. Growth of strong central authority as ag[rarian] feudalism. 2. Growth of industry and trade accomp[lished] by government promotion. Government regulated every phase of economic life—monopolies encouraged. Applied internally and externally. Mercantilism is associated with this phase.

Cunningham book (on Trade and Industry) shows how the government regulated every phase of economic life—to make it subserve political ends to build up a central authority.

Mercantilism—balance of trade, colonies, etc., best treatment in Sir Thomas Mun, English [sic] Treasure by Foreign Trade

Theoretic tendencies of mercantilists:

1. overestimate of importance of possessing a large supply of precious metals. At that time they had no credit arrangements and they tried to store up for wars—only justification.

2. Undue excitation of foreign over domestic trade and of industries that work up mater[ials] as against those which provide them.

3. Undue emphasis on dense population—a nationalist point of view

4. Undue reliance on action of state to gain large surplus of metal, manufacturing industry, large population

Ingram in his History of Political Economy says: religious wars, court expenses heavy; statesmen saw that industry must flourish in order to support it. They have outlived their usefulness. Adam Smith pointed out the insufficiency. As war was a frequent occurrence—carryover of gold was justifiable. Mercantilism persisted through 18th century.

Third modern phase—"Natural Liberty"—which found its way in the writing of Physiocrats in France and Adam Smith in England.

There grew up a use of machinery—Mercantilism promoted the dignity of workers and widened the gulf between employers and employees. During mercantile system national system was supreme as against industry. Now, under ["Physiocrats" lined out] industrial[ist]s and commercialists were in saddle. There was a reaction in France and England at the end of 19th century to these new tendencies—in France they culminated in Revolution. Exaggerated mercantilism.—Unsound public fiances, overtaxation.

The rest of the page may be reading or lecture notes; in either case, it more or less closely follows Ingram on the two subjects:

Pierre Boisguillebert 1700—antagonist of mercantilist school ideas: wealth is not merely gold and silver. Condemns arbitrary regulation. Government regulation to be done away with. An early international solidarity among nations—unfettered intercourses. Two classes of people, 1. those who don't do anything and 2. workers. In matters of taxation, he'd make it an income tax so as to secure equality of burden (wherein he differed from Physiocrats). His ideas of rent anticipated Ricardian. Also Montesquieu.

Physiocrats 1750-1775. Quesnay, Gournay, DuPont de Nemours, Turgot. Their notions— political theories of the day.

All people have same natural rights and each can follow his own natural inclination— which should be limited only as it interferes with the rest. Government is a necessary evil, and should be limited to extend where absolutely necessary. Property—sacred. (It is said that Jefferson was influenced by Physiocrats.) Freedom of exchange. Competition—no monopolies. Only those laborers are productive which add to raw materials. The excess of raw material (agriculture and mines) over expenses—net wealth—"produit net" (Total farm product minus upkeep of farmer etc). Upon this produit net depends the welfare of society. Agriculture main line of activity. In terms of net product that the wealth could be measured (gross minus clothing, shelter, food, etc. for population). Commerce transfers the wealth as defined—already created—let it be small. Encourage commerce and manufacturing and you diminish produit net. Laissez faire, laissez passer.

Revenue of state in a direct tax—land tax, impot unique (original single taxers),

Pursuit of wealth condemned in earlier ages. Then concessions were made. Last stage, wealth could be pursued for its own sake.

The first reading notes cover Gide and Rist's chapters on the Physiocrats (5 pages). In the midst thereof are two pages of lecture notes. At the top of the first page is the sentence, "Thomas Jefferson influenced by John Locke and not Frenchmen." The notes as follows:

Adam Smith—the English "Physiocrat"—he was not a single taxer—but because of his opposition to Mercantilism and government control. He was not influenced by

Physiocrats. His Wealth of Nations, 1776, more of a sociology. General philosophic approach. He was influenced by Locke and Hutcheson.

1: Laissez-faire. 2. Mercantilists restrict, too burdensome. In England economic development went further than in France by that time. Though Smith never was an industrialist, he was a countryman. He was impressed with the damage done by mercantilist interference. Interested in working out a theory of prosperity. The national prosperity depends on nat. [uncertain completion: natural or national, probably the latter] division of goods.

Division of Labor. From 1776-1800 increasing emphasis on laissez-faire. Up to Industrial Revolution the south of England was the seat of power, there because of location of mines etc. It shifted to the north following development of water power. The whole philosophic interest of the time—to let nature take its course—not to interfere with the trend. In politics, religion, social relations—same. Godwin's "Political Justice": Godwin stressed the interference with God's plan. He condemned legalized marriage institutions. Wordsworth in his poetry emphasizes "nature" order. Locke. Hutcheson.

Smith—no recognition of class divisions. No problems of distribution (industrial revolution did not go far enough yet)

Distribution—wages of workers; profit of capitalists; rent of landowning class. In writings of Ricardo after 1800, it does appear.

His emphasis on laissez-faire most important. After 1800 ideas of Smith, Godwin—thinkers optimistic, the world a good place, but you have to get rid of mercantilist ideas. England was prosperous, industrial revolution. England clothing the continent— Napoleonic armies—but there was also a lot of poverty, exploitation, evil conditions. In the midst of these conditions Godwin advocated a complete policy of hands off. It was in connection with discussing Godwin's points, Thomas Malthus and his son clergyman—criticized it (one taking the optimistic view). After discussing these views the son set out his opinions in his Essay on Population. (Population multiplies at a geometric ratio of speed.) The Malthusians said it is not a great world but let us leave it alone just the same. Around 1800—Population Laws—Malthus. By 1850 a body of economic doctrine brought together by Mill ["Ricardo" written between lines], absolute (natural law) rigid, rigid class divisions, rigid income divisions. Mill welded in Ricardo, Malthus, Senior into Smith.

After the notes on Gide and Rist on the Physiocrats come the following lecture notes:

Mill's Work

His book is divided into: production, distribution, exchange, etc. The subdivision should be: production, distribution, consumption. Mill omits consumption—they didn't regard this as a problem. Professor Patten was the first to speak of consumption. Clark said that this is a personal matter.
#Mill: Production, Distribution and Exchange.

Production—creation of utilities. In Exchange Mill cosiders Price and Value. Value in those days a secondary phenomenon built up of other elements. The present view—value a primary phenomenon, rises out of attitude of individual towards goods—we make estimates. You start with evaluation. The distributive question [uncertain] comes later.

Production—definition, factors—labor, land, ["material" lined out] capital (and business organization as a fourth factor)

Adam Smith was interested in <u>per capita</u> goods abundance. How to make goods. How the subject should be treated:

1. Economics <u>Statics</u>: cut a cross-section of economic structure, process and function

2. Economics <u>Dynamics</u>: two parts: a. Principles of change and b. What principles govern the changes e.g., in production.

3. <u>Art phase</u> (as distinguished from science)—methods and decrees for improving of conditions, public policy. Betterment. (Professor <u>Clark</u> approaches this classification)

Mill and most economists don't differentiate these points of view. He shifts from one consideration to another. The attempt to subdivide as above (Clark tried it) may result in a difficulty of finding a practical application of what the authors did (one fact too abstract etc).

<u>Mill</u>

Productive factors according to Mill: <u>labor, land and capital</u>. How did he happen to get this classification?

England in his day: in industrial revolution and came out with a line-up of landlords, wage-earners, capitalists—distinct classes.

Professor McCrea says that there is more conflict between various enterprises than between capital and labor. There are enterprises which are less controllable than others e.g. take an agricultural enterprise and commercial. Agricultural—you did with more uncertain factors: you make financial commitment that you can see far ahead—you don't know what'll happen. The trader makes short time commitment, can make the shifts much quicker. Trader wants no interference—agriculture longs for government intervention—he needs all help. The attitude of trader—laissez-faire, "let us alone." Farming group says "we are at a disadvantage as compared with trader."

<u>Sugg[estion]</u>: <u>Extractive, elaborative, distributive</u> industries as a division as against land, labor and capital.

Next comes notes on John Stuart Mill's *Principles of Political Economy*, Book I, on production (5 pages).

The next lecture notes deal, briefly, with Mill on the labor theory of value. The notes have Mill analyzing a commodity such as bread into labor and flour and equipment, the flour itself reduced to labor and wheat and equipment; the wheat reduced to labor and seed and equipment and land; so too with the seed; and the equipment likewise plus materials. The notes then record the statement, "No justification for this analysis" and the question is raised, "Is <u>labor</u> the only thing that enters into [the] value [of] a commodity?" The notes continue as follows:

Malthusian possibilities a nightmare then—that's why Mill takes up labor as [?] subsistence. Another reason—the world he was living in—His picture of the economic world was local self-sufficiency and epochal (crop-prices [?])—a picture of different pieces of the world—pieces self-sufficing in time of crop-periods (he speaks of wheat) in North Temperate zone.

We reason in terms of a perennial world economy, north, south, etc. zones. We think of the flows of many commodities. His epochal, local view (carry-over) is also responsible for his picture of the remuneration of workers immediately engaged in production.

At this point is a line of terms connected with arrows, below which are further arrows indicating that the latter terms have influence on the earlier terms: Extract—Labor—Distribution—Goods (capital goods)—Consumption goods; after which comes the statement, "all of them get goods as compensation." The text continues:

A continuous process of production. Mill wants to build the remuneration around the extractive because that provides food and we need it.

At the top of the next page is written:

Clark—"Philosophy of Wealth"

followed on the next line by

Productive and unproductive labor

and then the notes continue:

Labor spent on maintaining human capacity—is it capital? Depends upon definition of capital. Arbitrary depending upon that definition. (Fisher regards capital as wealth and human beings.) Prof. McCrea says, it is not capital; it is merged with individual and that will come under "labor."

Assuming the accuracy of the notes, McCrea's discussion of human capital is obvious but seems to have been more taxonomic than analytical in content, or at least that is the way it impressed Arnold.

Productive labor (Mill)—labor creating material wealth or object. 1. "Possible shortage" was what Mill had in his mind—be sure that you have food before you have singers etc. 2. And besides it was a traditional topic for discussion. He accepted the distinction as laid down by others and injected his other questions—which makes us question the distinction. (Taussig calls "unproductive"—predatory, parasites) Army, Policemen. "Dismal" philosophy was applied to this pessimistic view—supply the people with food foremost.
Distinction between productive and non-productive—artificial and its usefulness limited.

At top of next page is written:

Mill - p. 90
Gide and Rist

And the notes continue:

Capital
Differentiate between capital and capital goods.
Capital goods: wheat, flour, ploughs, harnesses. Concrete productive instrument
Capital—in terms of dollars—aggregate values, invested values
When we speak of capital we mean money or machines; Mill: food, subsistence
    Paper money is capital as far as the paper end goes, but gold, silver is

    Goods divided into: producers' and consumers'
    Production—creation of utilities (from time etc.)
    Consumers' goods could be thrown into capital goods
    Consumers goods—only those goods which had all utilities added to them

With Mill the capital ["goods" lined out] could include the sense of all values destined
    for production (mind of capitalist important—depends upon what he intends to
    do with it)

Mill says "tax on production in one of its early stages—as raw materials—is a tax on
    capital." Implication being that if it is in the latter stages then it is not. Why isn't
    any tax a tax on capital? It is.

        In case of sales tax, tickets, etc.—the theatre owner has yet use of the tax collected
        until tax is paid.

The vast bulk of taxes—if viewed from community point of view is a tax on capital. From
    the individual point of view it makes difference as to stage—although in case of
    going concern it hurts other producer if it is brought in [at] an early stage.

It depends upon what government is going to do with the tax - what should one do with,
    say, $1000?

        Mill says, add goods—production—build a factory. But it might be better to use
        it for a painting or a playground.

The next page carries the heading, "Fundamental Propositions Concerning
Capital" and the words "Prof. Mitchell" are written at the top of the page,
with "Prof." apparently written first and "Mitchell" added later (the first word
is horizontal and the second, on a slant). The notes *may* have been from a
lecture by Wesley C. Mitchell but the name at the top of the page is more
likely only a reference to him (conceivably the reference is to some other
Mitchell, though this is unlikely). The content seems likely to be McCrea's
summary of the content of Book I, chapter V of Mill's *Principles*. The notes
read as follows:

Fundamental Propositions Concerning Capital

1. Industry is limited by capital—obvious but he had something else in mind. That was a crack at the Protectionists—Mercantilist theory—Legislative acts, government, are not the ones who create industry.

   (Function of protective tariff—to direct capital and labor into certain channels; but ordinarily capital and labor flows into productive channels—hence, Mill says, this diverts it from productive uses)

   There are ways in which government can cause such increase of human efficiency and through it increase of capital. (social laws—education, sanitary laws, etc)

   Corollary:

   Mill: Every increase of capital will give employment—no over-expansion possible according to him.

   Practically consumption could be expanded infinitely—is there any reason there why capital could be used likewise? The classical economists say that capital can expand, we can consume more.

2. Growth of capital caused by the uneven distribution of incomes. Two factors: growth of invention—improvements—production; institutions which permit the investment. Not the savings by the common people. No thrift involved. [In margin: by corporate investment however]
   The old economists put too much stress on individual choice—saving.

Mill's Third Proposition. Capital goods are consumed but capital values are replenished. He was reasoning in terms of shortage. Produce enough for everybody. As a general proposition it is true that the less you spend the better.

Effect of borrowing for war purposes. Loans. We fight a war with capital goods that were already produced. No amount of borrowing can create capital goods. You draw on the same goods whether [sic] the form be: borrowing, or taxation. A borrowing policy—government gets funds and bids for goods. Prices going up and government is enabled.

Next comes one and one-third pages of notes on chapter 3 of J. A. Hobson's *The Industrial System*, "Spending and Saving." This is followed by the following lines:

Continued (Lecture)
If you tax instead of borrowing—individual would have nothing left to fight for purchase of goods—result the same. Insofar as income goes: if we tax, we should take from those who have; if we borrow [blank]
Demand for Commodities is Not Demand for Labor. What Mill means is that a shift in demand for commodity is a shift in demand for labor. He recognizes two possibilities: it may be beneficial if there was a slack before.

The next five and one-third pages comprise summaries of Book I, chapters VI through XIII of Mill's *Principles*, with some comparative comments by McCrea, in part on the ideas of other economists.

Apropos of the idea from Mill that "Labor has been gradually displaced but it has come to be employed in other lines," Hobson is noted to have written that "this labor went into 3 directions: 1. Inventions, making the new machines. 2. Distribution—that is, trade. 3. Supply of new forms of wealth—artistic, intellectual; tremendous increases of local services (as in connection with autos); learned professions. If the consumption is increased and variable [Arnold seems to have written "invariable" and blacked out the "in"], there is no diminution in demand for labor—though it tends to diminish employment in manufacturing (they turn to trade)—but it is (employment) unstable and precarious of tenure."

Some lines, which appear to be lecture notes, identify "modern occupations" as machine work, trade, and transportation for which the necessary qualifications are "balance, self-control, stability, punctuality, quick to perceive. In machine work, quick to learn, dexterity, punctuality. The big thing here is standardization—be able to adapt himself—." The notes then read: "Cooperation: simple, complex, compound" and divide cooperation into (1) territorial—utilize production of various areas; and (2) personal, which in turn is divided into homogeneous ("both do the same things") and heterogeneous, and this into occupational (different occupations) and functional ("you have division of labor"). Then one reads, "Manufacturing gets a start—farmers become supplied with more goods, better tools etc.—standard becomes higher. History shows that this was the way countries were built up—hence this may be used as an argument for protective tariff."

The notes summarizing Mill on large scale production seem to be a combination of notes on the text and on lecture, but largely the former. Of interest is the following from lecture:

> Points most interesting—disadvantages: Mill lays down this generalization…the organization will depend upon interest, zeal and fidelity. Fidelity can be expected from hired servants. But zeal not be expected. Criticism—just the reverse—zealous service can be expected (incentive—profit sharing)—his own interest is involved but not fidelity.
>
> Economy of small things—just the reverse—in a large organization they accumulate so as to constitute something important. They use by-product.
>
> Modern large scale production turns on delegation of authority (Mill didn't speak about it).
>
> Large Scale Production—Unified control—[word undecipherable] etc. waste if several companies are admitted to the field. Wherever you have the requirement of heavy fixed expenses it might be advisable to eliminate competition.
>
> Agriculture—small scale. 1. Malthusian fear. 2. Smith's view.
>
> Law of Increase of Labor in Mill synonymous with growth of population theory. But supply of labor does not vary directly with growth of population—you would have to allow for women, children, old men.

> Malthusian theory. There is a tendency for population to increase faster than means of sustenance. Newtonian logic the basis—the ball is thrown in a straight line—being deflected by a [word undecipherable] function of air and gravitation. In social sciences induction with statistical data should to be used.

There follows two sets of lines. In one population grows at an increasing rate and food/subsistance at a decreasing rate. The other is not decipherable. These are followed by the parenthetic remark, "Remember the fallacy 'of the rising curve.'"

Apropos of the doctrine that the increase of capital, according to Mill, is due to saving, and following the statement that "But we say that a variety of institutions arousing such investments. Of course, thrift too counts," the notes read:

> Bohm-Bawerk - average person prefers present instead of future goods. Why? 1. Uncertainty of life. 2. Defects of imagination—we can see the present, future indefinite. 3. Defects of will. 4. Differences in wants and provision for wants (he thinks he'll be in a better shape to take care of himself in the future). To overcome this a premium has to be offered.

> Another point in Bohm-Bawerk that was not logical is "technical superiority" of present goods—a greater use from foreseen possession of goods.

The notes then say that "Rae anticipated some of these points." Thereafter the notes read:

> Saving—three types: 1. Without inducement of interest.
> 2. Annuities—savings vary inversely with interest.
> 3. Directly.

Immediately afterward one reads, "Exam."

The notes from Spring Semester, Economics b 102, commence on page 31, with notes on the first chapter (property) of Mill's Book II, "Distribution," and run through chapter 5 (rent in relation to value) of Book III, "Exchange." They conclude on page 51, interspersed with notes on lectures, some designated as such and some evident from their neater and less compact handwriting. Some of this material consists of two lines of writing between two ruled lines, but some, in the manner of lecture notes, consist of one line between two ruled lines. Comparison of the content with Mill's text indicates rather straightforward summary in both cases—and the possibility (how likely one does not know) that some of this was dictated by McCrea—suggested by the use of expressions like "says Mill" which most of the notes on readings do not use.

The first set of lecture notes, labeled by Arthur as such, one page, reads as follows:

Production and Distribution

There really is no such difference between production and distribution. Both are phases of the same economic process. Meanwhile he went to Europe—influence of communists, Mrs. Taylor. As for Distribution—there, too, are limits: Malthusian theory; you can't distribute more than you have. Of course the limitations of production were led up to by his previous fundamental truths as to land, labor, capital.

Private Property—could be discussed either under production or distribution. Very few economic writers touch upon this subject. Mill discusses it in connection with [?] Communism,—Mrs. Taylor's influence, French philosophers and propagandists. Times were very bad at that time.

Communism: 1. Incentive to activity. At present, fear, promotion, bonus, premiums, profit-sharing

Not much incentive as far as the greatest majority of workers are at present concerned.

But we get the push at present from above: inventors, leaders, innovators, etc.

The next notes which appear to come from lectures as follows:

Present day evils:
1. Unemployment.
   Shouldn't we test it by human liberty and spontaneity—criteria as used by Mill in other cases.
2. "Interest" objections:
   1. Capitalists were charging 20% etc. If only pure interest were charged the socialists wouldn't have objection.

   2. [Undecipherable word] time.

Interest is paid as an inducement to save.

Suppose a check is put on inheritances, say, you can't transfer more than 100,000, would that operate as a check?

   1. Incentives not necessarily diminishing—he is now (after making 100,000) interested in the business.
   2. Limitations to bequests:—1. In perpetuity. 2. Dower rights. Child ought to be given every opportunity to then be able to make a living by his own exertions.

   As to England, Tenant-farming an evil (no improvements).

After notes on Mill's chapter II.IV, "Of Competition and Custom," the notes on lectures read as follows, immediately following the sentence, "Professional remuneration is regulated by custom":

Not under dynamic conditions.

We distinguish between competition and monopoly.

Nor does a technician get more than an untrained worker because he spent more money in obtaining a training etc; there are fewer of them.

Competition within certain groups and among certain groups depends upon numbers, organization of workers, standard of living, etc. Labor organization, standard of living, etc. all exercise an influence.

> Wages Fund (short run)—a definite amount of goods. A local, epochal view, north temperate zone interpretation. From a world point of view the goods are not rigid. Malthus originated it (long run); Mill states combinations of laborers could force it up (wages) in one industry at the expense of another. Trade unions not needed.
>
> How did the theory grow up:
>
> When Malthus wrote his essay there were a few years of bad harvests. Population was growing faster than subsistence. It applied only to that period (up to 1815).
>
> Taussig takes old concepts and gives them new meaning. He says there is a wages fund— if "add up all the salaries and wages and there is your fund."
> Iron law of wages an offshoot of Malthusianism.
>
> Discount Theory of Wages—advanced by Stuart Wood (offshoot from Bohm-Bawerk's theory). A general theory. Worker gets out so much iron ore; he can't eat it; the employer discounts his claim. There is no acceptable wage theory.
>
> Clark's Theory—Marginal Productivity Theory. Each gets the value of what he's produced (capital, of course, too produces).
>
> First one worker works with a sledge-hammer, then second added—they produce more, and third—still more (4th in the way). [In a diagram of descending blocks] the pencil line shows what each is to be paid—determined by marginal worker.

The foregoing is striking in its recording of the statement that "There is no acceptable wage theory." It is noteworthy for its reference to Stuart Wood, whose work is now largely forgotten.

After a one-third page summary of Mill's chapter II.XI, "Of Wages," which concentrates on the Malthusian view that workers cannot improve their condition unless by changing the proportion of their number to the capital and other funds devoted to the purchase of labor (the wages fund theory), the reading notes blend with apparent lecture notes. A pyramid is presented with executives at the top, followed downward by minor administrators, various technical occupations, such as technicians and mechanics, then clerks, and finally the untrained. Referring to Mill the notes say that "wages, like other things, are regulated either by competition or by custom." Referring to casual and untrained workers, the former are said to be very mobile. "We are dealing with non-competing groups. The theories of wages that we have are all based upon the first group (untrained). Danger and smell has nothing to do with competition."

After notes on chapters II.XII and II.XIII (including a passage likely from lecture referring to a change in the text introduced in 1865), both on popular remedies for low wages, are the lines:

> His principles of education, doing away with competition, etc. ok.
> Large families in the U.S. only among immigrants, but not among the first generation.

The single sentence not a part of the notes on chapter II.XIV, on differences of wages in different employments, reads: "In this country minimum wage laws are applied only to women and children."

The lecture (designated as such) on profits, following notes on II.XV, is as follows:

Profits

A fairly natural outcome of the thinker's picture of business of that day (sole proprietorship);
    the use of difference between wages and interest when the owner is himself working.
He does say that labor produces a surplus. But the profit-taker is most important—Mill.
Malthus took a country (village) view; Ricardo, city man—hence profit. Same about Mill.
We tend to break up profits into many lines: wages, interest, profits (as something else).
Capital, locationally, is not as mobile as some people think; so risk as a part of interest
    is not very important—other items influence it.
Ricardian idea of wages—to profit
No clear-cut theory of interest or profit by Mill.

Recent Theory

1. Considerations of Time Preference (Bohm-Bawerk)
2. Marginal Productivity of Interest (Clark)—typical place reference

Why is interest paid: Bohm-Bawerk—a bird in hand in worth two in the bush. Stimulates saving. Time preference of present over future goods (Fisher, Fetter, etc. essence the same). Bohm-Bawerk, too, speaks of technical superiority of present goods over future goods.

Senior asks: why do those who borrow pay interest? Then he presents marginal productivity theory (Clark)—in this case Clark illustrates it by starting with labor and then adding necessary units of capital. (When illustrating the marginal theory remember Prof. McCrea's example of blackberries [undecipherable words]—satisfaction and cost— blazing sun, etc.)

In a normal society (Clark says) there is no profit—competition will reduce price to such level that it will cover only cost. That's why it is said that there is a normal tendency for profit to disappear.

Next comes notes on Mill's chapter on rent, followed by these notes on lectures:

As to decreasing of profits. Competition is no regulator of costs and is not the way to a profitless [undecipherable word] because

(1) competition does not take place where capital is too large
(2) instead of competing, concerns very often combine when it comes to cut-throat competition

Walker says: profit is a differential return which goes to most able organizer or producer (fashioned after Ricardo's rent theory)
Mill: "profits" include a good many things

The next notes appear to have been copied from another student and relate to Gide and Rist's treatment of Bohm-Bawerk's theory of interest. The lecture notes continue:

> Rent - for the use of land
> 1. Contract sense - a payment. Rent in a still narrower sense. A yield underlying the payment.
> 2. In the economic sense rent is a yield over and above production cost (cost of production in the sense of expense: interest, your own wages included)
>
> According to Ricardian economics the difference in yield between the poorest land in use and better is the rent.
>
> Clark eliminates rent as a yield and says this: If your land bring in a certain you tend to capitalize the return and thus it becomes interest and not rent.

A numerical example is recorded, albeit with erroneous numbers; the conclusion, however, is unaltered: after capitalization, "now you get interest and not rent."

> Ricardo's method measures land extensively; it can be also measured intensively.
> Ricardian theory—rent is price determined, not determined by price (cost theory) [sic].
> Equally good fertility and situation—as soon as all land is taken up, there'd be rent.

Next follows notes on Mill's Book III, chapters 1-5, followed by these notes on lectures:

> Ricardo and Mill—labor theory of value. Then Marx. Mill—cost of production theory.
> Labor theory to subjective—consumer's mind theory
> Welfare depends upon variety of goods present
> "Value in use" as used by Smith means "utility" and not as used by subjective writers.
> Value in subjective sense—importance attaching to goods units by consumers. The measure of that importance is marginal utility.
> Value: cause and measure: Ricardo and socialists: labor cause and measure. Subjective theorists: mind of consumer—that's where value is originated—a naive psychology.
> Value from subjective theorists' point of view. They start with utility idea. Classical theorists were satisfied with the objective exchange phenomena. Subjective: goods—bundles of utility. The more units you have the less the utility of each unit.

Then follows a simple diagram of three boxes representing, respectively, the utility of three, two, and one apples, the declining height of each representing "diminishing utility trend."

> Marginal utility—utility of last unit—how can you find the value of that unit—why take one unit away and see what you lose.
> Demand determines supply and not reverse.
> Demand price curve very important.

Then follows a diagram with a Marshallian DD-labeled demand curve but with an unlabeled line commencing at the origin and more or less bisecting the quadrant. The intersection is marked "marginal utility."

> Inadequacy of cost explanation of value:
> 1. Uniqueness (work of art).
> [2.] Goods must be sold
> In case of reproducible goods, cost of production determines the <u>marginal cost</u>.
> "The genesis of value is to be looked for in mind of consumer instead of labor."

Next follows almost a page of notes on George's *Progress and Poverty*, Book I, on wages and capital, followed by these lecture notes, with an interesting, even fascinating, juxtaposition of the wages fund and productivity theories of wages:

> Malthusian theory [and] diminishing returns: two outstanding characteristics of classical economists.
> George said the trouble was with <u>distribution</u>. He said that Malthus, and wages fund theory, wrong with capital. econom. [unclear how to edit] (Should have said as above: Malthus and diminishing returns)
> Wages don't come out of capital.
> <u>Interest rates</u>, short term and long term. There is a short period of divergence right after a prosperity.
> From a <u>long point</u> of view, wages have been rising and interest rates falling, so George is wrong. His reasoning due to the fact that he lived in a <u>new</u> country, California, where both capital and labor were scarce.
> The big phase of his argument: <u>source of wages</u>: wages, says George, are not advanced by capital—worker creates it
> "Capital—wealth in course of exchange"
> Wages, he could have said, don't come out of a <u>fixed</u> fund.
> (Clark took much from George and Clark says that virtually and essentially laborer produces his own wages)
> Ch. III. <u>Sources of wages</u>: simple and complex. Labor always precedes wages, he says, but that does not say whether it comes out of capital.
> He is right in emphasizing importance of <u>present labor</u>.
> Book 2. Malthusian Theory
> Analogies from animal and vegetable kingdoms
> Darwinism. Rapid growth in new countries, retarded in older. Vice, poverty, misery to be found in densely populated countries. It serves as a powerful weapon in the hands of a ruling class—which says it is not our fault.
> George's attack: 1. Facts don't prove that theory. 2. Analogies are defective. 3. Facts <u>disprove</u> the theory.
> As regards the facts: 1:
>> Malthusians say that overpopulation causes bad government etc. George says that overpopulation is caused by bad government etc.
> Religious leaders etc. emphasize importance of growth of population because of <u>power</u>.
>
> (India, China, Ireland)
>
> Malthus does speak of effect of government.

Second phase of attack: inferences from analogies (vegetable and animal kingdom): Jay-hawks eat chickens and men eat chickens—but more men more chickens. George. If scientifically managed and then—increased, diminishing, or constant cost.

Law of diminishing returns: "Niggardliness of nature"—George denies it and says that the reverse is true. That a larger population can exist more easily than a small. People bring hands with mouths.

George does not differentiate between producing more goods and producing more value—whereas you may have less goods and higher value.

When he says that a large population can get along better, he has in mind division of labor.

Just below this is: "See A"—meaning unknown.

The foregoing is followed by notes on George's Book 2 on the Malthusian theory, through chapter IV. Then follows several pages of notes on lectures:

Increase of population causes rent to rise: (1) By lowering the margin of cultivation, calling into use poorer lands. (2) By bringing out in land special capabilities otherwise latent (George means for industrial etc. purposes).

Improvement in the Arts: saves labor—increases the production of wealth (and for this land and labor are requisite) hence rent will go up

Law of Diminishing Returns: ok—when applied to agriculture "under existing state of arts"

Distribution

George criticized Mill. [Adjacent is a pie diagram, half labelled rent and the two quarters labelled wages and interest.

Objections: 1. As to terminology.   2. As to relation between the three factors.

As to terminology: George suspects Mill of purposely having used interest, wages of superintendence etc. in order to conceive [?] wages of management in profits. Mill did it, probably because in his day he could observe a single entrepreneur. George accepts the theory of rent and denies (1) the law of diminishing returns. George says labor comes first and capitalist second. It is true that labor came first, but a criticism of this is not vital.

Rent

Produce = Rent + Wages + Interest (A close correlation). Therefore, says, George, if rent goes up, wages and interest must go down.

Land being the most slowly increasing factor, the landlord will be the one to be in a better position.

Interest

He does not accept the "productiveness theory" that is that when labor and capital are productive, he says, interest is lower. George does not differentiate between goods productiveness and value productiveness.

He says—abstinence does not account for interest—because abstinence (!) does not produce anything. But he justifies interest (you take advantage of the vital and reproductive forces of nature). And he does not accept "productivity" as "abstinence." If it is in terms of "natural surplus" why not regard it as rent instead of interest

Relation of Wages to Interest. Capital, says he, is a form of labor (accumulated). Speaks of a "substitution": if return to labor high, there'll be a flow to capital and vice versa.

His theory of Wages: Labor can get what one could get on <u>free</u> fertile land. If only poor
land (free) is still available, then this standard —(Marginal of employable
opportunity) (Taussig) [Red check mark alongside in margin]

"Non-competing groups" idea (as among groups of workers, almost original with him)

(His rent theory almost same as that of classical theorists except that he rejects "law of
diminishing returns" [Red check mark alongside in margin]

<u>Statics and Dynamics</u> (genetics of situation, changes)—original with George. Clark,
probably, borrowed from him.

1. Population grows.   2. Improvement in arts.   3. Institutional changes.

Again his (as to (1)) confusion of capital goods with capital values.

But why go to poorer lands if there <u>is no diminishing return</u>? 1. Increased division
of labor, indefinitely (says George). "Wealth is greater" in a populous country.
Yes, <u>values</u> go up. [Double underlining]

The topic now changes:

<u>Socialism</u>

1. An indictment of private property.   2. An analysis.   3. A substitute form.   4. A
campaign—a political movement—tactics.

<u>Scientific aspect—Marxian analysis</u>:

1.   Marxian theory of value
2.   Materialist (Economic) conception of history
       Law of capitalist development—industrial army—crises

<u>Economic conception of history</u> (Seligman)
(1)   Hegelian philosophy—used by Marx
       Two readings—right and left of the Hegelian school. Hegelians of the left were driven
       to the French thinkers. They placed the stress on <u>economic</u> conditions.

[No (2)]

(3)   <u>The Communist Manifesto states it</u>
       1. Economic factor.   2. Economic factor and class struggle: Marx (1): Exploitation
       of the masses is the keynote.

Economic factors—not ultimate forces in human life. Where operative they don't necessary
       imply a conflict of interest. And men are not necessarily guided by interest. Groups
       not well-defined—opponents of yesterday, friends today. If class struggle is the
       motive for progress, where will progress come after the struggle is accomplished?
       [sic]

Marx put Hegel's dialectic upon a materialistic basis and made social evolution a matter
       of material and economic forces

"Economic factors dominate all history and determine social organization, classes and class
       interests."

After four leaves of blank pages, next comes about five pages of notes on
the first five chapters of Book I of Smith's *Wealth of Nations*. After seven
additional leaves of blank pages come thirteen pages of notes on Gide and
Rist, starting with Book I, chapters II and III, on Smith, Malthus, and Ricardo;

going on to Book III, Liberalism, chapter I, the optimists. Beyond this are several dozen blank pages. Inserted inside the rear cover are five sheets paper with highly summarized notes on Mill's *Principles*.